REALITY AND COMIC CONFIDENCE IN
CHARLES DICKENS

Reality and Comic Confidence in Charles Dickens

P. J. M. SCOTT

First published 1979 by
THE MACMILLAN PRESS LTD
London and Basingstoke
Associated companies in Delhi
Dublin Hong Kong Johannesburg Lagos
Melbourne New York Singapore Tokyo

Printed in Great Britain by offset lithography by
Billing & Sons Ltd, Guildford, London and Worcester

British Library Cataloguing in Publication Data

Scott, P J M
    Reality and comic confidence in Charles
Dickens
    1. Dickens, Charles. Bleak House   2. Dickens,
    Charles. Little Dorrit   3. Dickens, Charles.
    Our mutual friend
    I. Title
    823 . 8   PR4588

ISBN 0-333-23383-2

To my Father and Mother

Contents

Acknowledgements

I wish gratefully to acknowledge the help of Dr Tony Ward and Dr Alan Charity, of York University, in my work upon this study.

Also the author and publishers are grateful to the following for permission to quote copyright passages from the books named:

American Imago, for extracts from an article by John Bayley published in their *Journal*, vol. 12, 1955

Edward Arnold Ltd., for extracts from J. C. Reid's 'Dickens' *Little Dorrit'*, from *Studies in English Literature*, series no. 29, edited by David Daiches

The Cambridge Quarterly and Dr. John Harvey, for an extract from his article in vol. 6, no. 1

Chatto and Windus and University of California Press, for extracts from *Love and Property in the Novels of Charles Dickens*, by Ross H. Dabney, and *The Rise of the Novel*, by Ian Watt

Chatto and Windus and Pantheon Books Inc., for extracts from *Dickens the Novelist* by F. R. and Q. D. Leavis

Eyre Methuen Ltd., for an extract from *English Historical Documents*, vol. XII (1), edited by G. M. Young and W. D. Hancock

Faber & Faber Ltd. and Random House Inc., for a verse from 'The Geography of the House', from *About the House* by W. H. Auden

Oxford University Press, for extracts from *The Dickens Theatre*, by Robert Garis; *George Eliot: A Biography*, by Gordon S. Haight; *Charles Dickens: The World of his Novels*, by Hillis Miller; *The Dickens World*, by Humphry House; *The Oxford Illustrated Dickens*, *The Clarendon Dickens*, and *The Works of George Herbert*, edited by F. E. Hutchinson.

University of Toronto Press, for extract from 'The Topicality of *Little Dorrit'*, by John Butt, published in the *University of Toronto Quarterly*, no. 29, 1959.

Introduction

Does Dickens lack at the heart of his creative flow discriminative faculties which we rightly expect and find in the works of the other great novelists? As late as 1970 Dr and Mrs Leavis wrote with the sense of championing a minority view in arguing for Dickens's intelligence the capacity for consistent and sustained discrimination at the centre of his art. Indeed they hailed him as 'the Shakespeare of the novel',[1] yet found it appropriate more or less to dismiss nine of this Shakespeare's fifteen fictions, including all the works preceding *Dombey*, as self-evidently not offering 'a providently conceived whole, presenting a major theme'.[2] (If I propose to myself in this study a still narrower survey and look only at *Our Mutual Friend*, *Bleak House* and *Little Dorrit*, it is not for that reason.) In fact they generally appear still seriously influenced by traditional assumptions of Dickens's weakness; for example, as in the opening of their chapter on *David Copperfield*: 'It is a long novel, uneven in quality . . . .'[3] Many of us feel the same sort of thing about *Measure for Measure*, but the critical traditions operative in Shakespeare's case oblige us — and creatively — to fight over the issue of the play's unity; we are not allowed almost to assume a less favourable account as a likely premiss.

Or, again, one does not have to go back further in time to find even so great an admirer as Angus Wilson subscribing to a view of *Bleak House* as possessing 'a central defect — the character of the heroine, Esther Summerson',[4] as not only is 'often thought now', but also was thought by John Forster and many of his contemporaries.[5] Yet, with the portrait of Esther, Dickens is evidently seeking radically important narrative effects for his novel's meaning; effects not of an apparently local significance (as might be claimed of 'The Bagman's Tale' in *Pickwick* or Miss Wade's 'History of a Self-Tormentor' in *Little Dorrit*), nor with the unspecified status of the quasi-autobiographical mode when sustained throughout a novel, which incurs the difficulty for the reader of ever knowing exactly where to discriminate between the first-person narrator and the invisible 'silent' author behind him (or her). Surely upon Miss Summerson much of *Bleak House*'s whole success depends. She is not only a major character; by her author's deliberate design, she is made the mediating consciousness of much of the work altogether. In reading her chapters we can only be aware of listening to an unusual voice speaking out of what ought to be a meaningfully idiosyncratic situation. If it fails of that meaningfulness, then the book is half sunk as a work with a serious claim upon the full attention of an adult intelligence. Yet Wilson seems to have little sense of thus opening a hangman's trapdoor under the novel when he is unable to vindicate Esther's 'reporting to us, with an almost intolerable coyness, all the praises that others give her'.[6] And this unconsciousness of just how much (of drastic irresponsibility and failure on Dickens's part) their own recurrent qualifications portend is almost endemic among the Dickens critics. Wilson goes on, in the connection I have adduced, to admit a general 'falsity about women' in his subject and, '(a more serious defect)', remarks the failure of the Lady Dedlock story to connect significantly with that of the Chancery law-suit;[7] but the whole of John Carey's *The Violent Effigy*[8] develops for explicit theme (see his Introduction, especially pp. 8–10) an account of Dickens as an anarchic mind, an artist almost congenitally incapable of consistent thought. And these are among his warmest admirers.

What other author could survive such charges – at least in his reputation as a truly significant artist – if we accepted them for proven? If we had to confess that Jane Austen afforded her male characters only a comparable unreality, or that the two households in *Wuthering Heights* had very little genuinely meaningful connection; if it were frequently agreed that James had founded the Strether of his *Ambassadors* upon a major and irritating misconception, or if *Anna Karenina* by general admission had a merely modest power to disquiet, on account of its developing 'a carefully and methodically symbolized social panorama' (John Bayley's view of the later Dickens fictions by contrast with 'the more disquieting picture' of *Oliver Twist*, of which he writes a powerful positive appreciation[9]), how often would we be disposed to reach those books down from dusty shelves? Yet at the same time, with every passing year of the post-war epoch, Dickens's artistic status, the view of him as a giant among the novelists, has grown and grown.

In so far as it is not simply baffling, the critical schizophrenia in respect of this author leaves us with an image of Dickens as an erratically brilliant man, a genius of fitful insights, capable by turns of profound, disturbing intuitions and the crassest crudities; an artist, in short, from whom we expect an active operation of the creative *intelligence* not so very much greater than from someone who indulges, under whatever mediumistic influence, in an ecstasy of spiritual possession or some kind of automatic writing. It is not that I could make out a case for everything in the Dickens *oeuvre* (I *would* be embarrassed to have to defend everything in *The Old Curiosity Shop*). But I do not think the critical element, the required powerful discrimination at the deep centre of his artistic gift, is lacking in anything like the degree generally assumed or implied.

In the study that follows I offer a reading of *Bleak House* which is frankly grateful for its 'defects' — Esther's coyness, the failure of its various stories to intermesh, and so on — because it finds much of the novel's significance in them. Its apparent faults — of plot, of characterisation — are felt and argued to be telling strengths which have been misapprehended. But the fact of this long history of critical resistance or qualification, which is as much with us today as it was with 'The Inimitable's' first readers, cannot be countered (I believe) so simply. It is a phenomenon in itself with which the admiring no less than the hostile critic must come more amply to terms.

What I have especially in mind is the apparent dichotomy which exists between Dickens's confident genial voice, his tone of (as it were) suppressed high spirits or ebullition just held in check, and the darkness, the recalcitrant and impassable human agonies which he deliberately discovers for us. Perhaps the following instance may recommend itself as representative:

Patriarch was the name which many people delighted to give him. Various old ladies in the neighbourhood spoke of him as The Last of the Patriarchs. So grey, so slow, so quiet, so impassionate, so very bumpy in the head, Patriarch was the word for him. He had been accosted in the streets, and respectfully solicited to become a Patriarch for painters and for sculptors; with so much importunity, in sooth, that it would appear to be beyond the Fine Arts to remember the points of a Patriarch, or to invent one. Philanthropists of both sexes had asked who he was, and on being informed, 'Old Christopher Casby, formerly Town-agent to Lord Decimus Tite Barnacle,' had cried in a rapture of disappointment, 'Oh! why, with that head, is he not a benefactor to his species! Oh! why, with that head, is he not a father to the orphan and a friend to the friendless?' With that head, however, he remained old Christopher Casby, proclaimed by common report rich in house property; and with that head, he now sat in his silent parlour. Indeed it would be the height of unreason to expect him to be sitting there without that head. (*Little Dorrit*, i, xiii, 146)

Is not all this *too* delighting? Is not Casby, the rack-renting landlord who grinds the faces of the poor in Bleeding Heart Yard, lost — swallowed up — in this figure which is positively welcome to us for provoking from Dickens such pleasurable comic utterance? (Not only the last little joke, but the carefully inflated character of all the language here — 'accosted', 'proclaimed' — evokes a humorous response; and the more so in its context for all the other parts of our first long introduction to Casby — i, xiii, *passim* — being amusing.) Is not the disposing of this material in a manner which to some extent at least seems to derealise ('in sooth') the delinquencies at issue a procedure we ought to question? For in plain fact, as *the author himself* shows us, the 'Patriarch' is frightening; a ruthless being in whom a whole range of human sympathies — even of the most rudimentary — are fearfully missing; and he is all the more worrying in that he represents a whole class of people like him.

Examples of what I mean proliferate endlessly, for it is practically the first characteristic of the Dickens voice which is at issue.

We can readily recognise the appeal of a Squeers or a Quilp, for example, as lords of misrule. They are creatures who have found outlets for energies which civilised social relations necessarily constrain. Opposed, however, against the tremendously correct Nicholas Nickleby or the actually debilitated Little Nell, we have the right to ask if in the end these monsters have not walked off not only with some of the imaginative sympathy stirred up by the works in which they appear (as Falstaff does, as do all the great Vice-figures) but with the terms themselves of serious and responsible debate there. If it be objected that *Nicholas Nickleby* and *The Old Curiosity Shop* are those of Dickens's early works where his immaturity counts most for weakness, it remains nevertheless significant that Dickens's writing is all alive in treating of such figures as Squeers or Quilp, the Crummles theatre troupe or Mrs Jarley's waxworks, and is wooden, develops expectable tropes (though it is not therefore valueless), in characterising Kate Nickleby and her aristocratic pursuers or the mendicant girl of the later work. For both novels evidently organise themselves around the theme of innocence turned out of doors to be defenceless in a largely unfeeling world. Do we have a foretaste in these early works, then, of what Professor Garis alleges[10] of the whole Dickens cannon: that its author is brilliant at the isolated theatric cameo, a special music-hall-turn style of portraiture of his own, but that his creative energies are essentially alien to being involved with (or are not concerned to sustain) a living experience of the full human consequences of what he shows?

'The child of [Caddy Jellyby's] marriage [in *Bleak House*]', he says, 'is rather pointedly symbolic, but Dickens's delicacy of touch carries the day', and Garis quotes from the text to show us how graphically Dickens brings the sick little infant before us. Yet he continues,

> The theatricality of Dickens's art makes it possible for us to consent to 'read' the meaning of this symbolic child (who turns out to be deaf and dumb) as straightforwardly and simply as it was invented. Herein lies the advantage of Dickens's obvious rhetorical intentions. For in non-theatrical, non-rhetorical fiction, where there is a consistent dramatic pressure within the scene, we could not contemplate a symbolic figure like this one with anything like the mild pathos which is possible in the Dickens theatre. Consider our feelings about Benjy in Faulkner's *The Sound and the Fury*, who is surely as meaningful — and as intentional — a symbol of bad blood as Caddy's baby. We are not, for Benjy, the sympathetic and pitying audience that we are for the patient hopelessness of Dickens's symbolic figure. With Benjy, we are engaged in a dramatic situation, we participate in the intensities of feeling directly, we *live with him* in an illusion of reality. And, in fact, we watch Benjy dribble and drool and weep, nor are we insulated from disgust by anything like Dickens's theatrical presence, performing these painful things before us. Accordingly, we experience a painfully (and beautifully) intense *complexity* of attitude towards Benjy, which in turn is the necessary preparation for our intense feeling of admiration and love for Dilsey.[11]

Meanwhile a special delight which is very frequently holding laughter in check (laughter of no exclusively wry or sharply satiric nature) is what we bring from reading the larger part of Dickens's work. But that same *oeuvre* continuously offers itself as coming to terms with the hurts and negations of a world which the author himself identifies for us as seriously crippling. How can we vindicate, how even tolerate the phenomenon? It is this, I suspect, rather than the substance of George Eliot's famous objection,[12] that is the hurdle at which opinion has most baulked. There is the sense underlying so much critical caveat, not that Dickens was 'wrong' in deploying strategies of presentation appreciably different from the world-building of other great nineteenth-century novelists, or that his techniques present a physical scene and its human constituents which are simply unconvincing. On the contrary, what I conceive the unsatisfied readers choke upon is the very reality of the universe — and its pains — which he images. *Their* suspicion is that one whole part of his artistic nature is deployed in eluding the fullest kinds of authorial responsibility towards the tragedies and sorrows his fictions so palpably bring before us; that Dickens powerfully evokes human wretchedness only to collapse or divert its claims upon our sympathy and our thought. On the other side, for the further elucidation (or complication) of the paradox, it is just the vitality which characteristically expresses itself in this manner — the manner of the *Little Dorrit* example I have quoted (as also, of course, in other fashions) — which appeals to the Dickens fans.

Are his devotees, therefore, adept at making silent compromises between the moral integrity of their intelligence and some essential (and fatal) undertow of whimsy on this author's part? I think not. To me this typical mode of Dickens's expression, in which the comic is so frequently in play, appears as a function, not of effervescently irresponsible high spirits — though high spirits are legitimately in the case — but from the very centrality, the catholicity of his response to our human situation. The almost continuous activity of humorous vision and comic language rises up as honestly as his graver intimations, derives really from the same order of perception as of the predicaments he describes and of which he tangibly conveys the suffering. (This is a general claim, of course. Like every master, he has his lapses.)

Accordingly I have chosen to look at two of the component parts of the Dickens canon, in and for themselves, in my attempt to make this truth appear. If I dotted from novel to novel I might, as with the wrong kind of Scriptural exegesis, be able to argue any kind of case. 'Distinct General Form Cannot Exist. Distinctness is Particular, Not General.'[13] But my first object of enquiry is *Our Mutual Friend* and for the paradoxical reason that it seems to me the very exception which probes the rule. This novel stands on its own — the more so, given the unfinished nature of *Edwin Drood* — as a kind of semi-alien body in the Dickens *corpus*. What I hold most dear in Dickens is largely missing there; yet I can hardly leave so major a text out of account. Moreover, I believe that, looking at the defections there of the sanity in question, this wholeness of perception which generally informs his work will the more readily (by contrarieties) suggest the essential characteristics we respond to in its author's other achievements; those of us (this is to say) who can find little significant fault with *Pickwick Papers* or *Great Expectations*, *David Copperfield* or *Little Dorrit* under any searching light that modern criticism may swivel upon them. In short it will serve as a fitting introduction to my argument as a whole, by being an appropriate means of reawakening, without too many leading questions or promptings, the reader's own memories of what it more frequently means to inhabit the Dickens world. For I am not concerned to commend any unsearchingly implicit faith in his judgement and creative processes, and my study begins with that book not only by way of expressing an approach to them which is other than fondly credulous, but also in the hope of focusing the issues with which the Dickens *oeuvre* comes to terms.

Of course, such premises granted, I well recognise how the disparity of this later book gives an air of insecurity to my general case. It might be supposed that the alien modes – in characterisation, in the narrator's address – which we meet with in the more powerful and convincing parts of *Our Mutual Friend*, the intimations markedly other there than what its predecessors ripely affirm, half collapse this defence of Dickens as the protagonist, in his previous novels, of a comic art which is fully responsible to many of the largest and most serious human concerns. If the Master himself left 'behind' him the intuitions of his earlier achievements and their characteristic modes of expression, who are we so amply to endorse these things – as truth-telling, as unblinkered accounts of reality – as this essay seeks to do? But a significant object for discussion is that *Our Mutual Friend* does not succeed on its own terms. Separate features of it are convincing and potent, but in noticing their failure to integrate we are still talking about sanity, and must leave our judgement about the authority of the new directions Dickens was taking towards the end of his tragically abbreviated life as much suspended as speculation about the nature, as about the ending, of his very last novel.

In Chapter 2 I look at *Bleak House* with the purpose of showing just how sustained and uncompromising the vision – the characteristic Dickens voice and view – is. For, if *Bleak House* cannot be defended from the charge that in large part it is an amateurishly misconceived enterprise or a job that has been half botched, my claims for the instinctive operation of a strenuous intelligence at the heart of his artistry (for all Dickens's *real* lapses) are presumably in ruins. This was a work executed, after all, in the years of his maturity; it was a major undertaking devised (at the most conscious level) with care and executed over no rushed period of time.

Then I examine *Little Dorrit*, which in respect of the case for the Dickens voice seems to me his masterwork. No less severe an account of our human life, this novel probes yet deeper into its constitution, synthesises the finest perceptions of the earlier books and vindicates finally the tone which invests itself and its predecessors. It does so by (as it were) engaging 'head on' with the problem this introduction has attempted to raise. What was in some sort instinct earlier in Dickens's narrative posture has now become metaphor, theme, a fully articulated fable. Dickens here shows all his cards. To the question 'Does the comic confidence immanent in so much of his language — the barely suppressed ebullience that underlies, as in the reader it is evoked by, his most characteristic idiom — arise from the very wholeness of his response to our human resources?' or 'Is the Dickens comic tone, amidst so much powerfully mediated darkness of the social and the personal life, a perception of resources which are really there?', the chapter on *Little Dorrit* in which this enquiry comes to rest argues an affirmative view.

Such are my reasons for looking at these works rather than the earlier volumes, the comparative depreciation of which in recent years (as much by neglect as by critical fiat) is depressing. It is not that I am less enthusiastic to write about *Pickwick* or *Oliver Twist*, but that space is limited.

Of course in the last analysis we cannot argue one another into likings. The widespread resistance to Dickens's genius as an agent of serious and fully responsible thought is now well over a century old. Though it has lately tended to take cover (in the face of the neap-tide of adulation more recently accorded this writer, especially in the universities) it still exists. And, if it constitutes an unprejudiced response to his novels, then — *vox populi, vox Dei* — it may well be the correlate of real insufficiencies in the works, insufficiencies which philosophical or temperamental weaknesses in such admirers as myself idly hinder our recognising; it may be the devotees and not the non-jurists who suffer from a mental block. Certainly an obstacle of the kind is somewhere in the case. But, when we consider the history of taste, we have to redefine the very term 'prejudice'. There are only too many instances of whole traditions which have acted like armed eunuchs of a harem before the curtained and obscured entrances to other major *oeuvres* (the fate of the metaphysicals or of early English studies in the eighteenth century, for instance). We have to remind ourselves that the principles of neo-classical criticism in Renaissance Europe, whether among the contemporaries of Michelangelo or the courtiers of Louis XIV, tended to be not hotly debated ground but the specula through which whole generations naturally observed and evaluated the artistry with which they were presented. The supposed 'unities' of Aristotle radically formed part of the very pulse or breath itself of the perception of the literate through entire epochs. It is just possible that a whole society has brought to the Dickens texts assumptions which make much of what the novels actually do and say invisible. The veiling has taken place before; and the fabric with which it has been done may be of no such superior quality as has been predominantly supposed. We have all the tokens of just such an occlusion being in question; the same sense, as possessed by eighteenth-century readers of Shakespeare, that here is work informed by the highest kinds of energy (and intelligence) yet with lapses or failures which our critical faculties cannot accommodate; indeed, rather, the feeling that here is work for which our critical traditions and equipment are insufficient.

The readings offered below do not claim any special authority. But they are reflections of a spontaneous, instinctually felt experience of these fictions and in that sense at least they compete with the suffrages which, Dickens's work being in question, have with similar honesty been doubtful and hesitant, partial and seriously qualified.

Note on abbreviated references

In all that follows, reference to the novels is (with one exception, noted below) to the ('New') Oxford Illustrated edition (1948–58). Reference is by book or volume number, in small capital roman figures (if the given text has been so divided by Dickens), followed by the chapter number, in lower-case roman numerals, and then the page numbers, in arabic numerals. Thus, II, xvi, 409–11 in a reference to or following a quotation from *Our Mutual Friend* signifies Book II, chapter xvi, pages 409 to 411, in the said edition of that work; and lxiii, 847 in a reference to *Bleak House* (not divided by books or volumes) means chapter lxiii, page 847, of that novel.

References to *Dombey and Son* are to the Clarendon edition of Dickens (this volume edited by Alan Horsman, Oxford 1974); but the form of the references follows the same principles as given above.

1 *Our Mutual Friend:* The Rhetoric of Disaffection

I

Our Mutual Friend deserves more respectful consideration than it has received from what may be called the George Eliot school of criticism. Of that, Henry James's original contemporary review in *The Nation*,[1] though particularly stringent, is representative, with its reliance on what at that date (1865) are already orthodox assumptions about the kind of realism proper to the novel as an intelligent art form. When he objects that 'A story based upon those elementary passions in which alone we seek the true and final manifestation of character must be told in a spirit of intellectual superiority to those passions . . .',[2] he offers us, as over the larger part of his essay, mere assertion (i.e. about one given artistic method being solely allowable). By contrast, the exuberant affirmation of G. K. Chesterton[3] hardly takes account of palpable differences of tone between this work and its predecessors, differences which constitute a difficulty with which the book recurrently confronts us and of which it is surely impossible for the attentive reader not to be aware: namely, that of relating, one to another, the fictive modes by which its interests are presented. Such a reader must find himself asking, 'Is this really one unitary (and therefore meaning-full) vision of life, when we are given on one side, for example, Mr Boffin enacting his charade of miserdom as in the pantomime version of a fairy-tale and on another the kind of realism which portrays — with a beautiful closeness of true-to-life imitation — a new social type in the languid aristocratic aimlessness of Eugene Wrayburn and Mortimer Lightwood?'

Equally misplaced seems its treatment at the hands of the New Critics. One can well perceive how Garis has come to find 'their over-emphatic and misleading excitement about Dickens's symbolic structures not . . . a way of defending the success of the late novels but rather . . . a means of evading the issue'[4] (which is effectually 'the essential failure of each novel as a whole'[5]). Representatively, J. Hillis Miller approves a not very definite theory of the tale's thematic region: '*Our Mutual Friend* is about "money, money, money and what money can make of life" ',[6] and systematically exhibits a through-running train of symbols and narrative technique. Yet there is much in the novel which does not answer his purposes (whether in the essay I have cited or in the chapter on *Our Mutual Friend* in his full-length study of Dickens[7]), and — again, representatively of this whole major tendency in modern criticism (*The Dickens Theatre* instances the work of Edmund Wilson and Lionel Trilling as other examples[8]) — this is simply ignored or even made to disappear by being twisted into the given Procrustean shape of the scheme he imposes upon it. (Not but that I am grateful to him for certain local observations, see p. 57 below).

Professor Garis's chapter, however, scarcely offers a closer scrutiny, for being subsumed to a total account of Dickens with which his study challenges not only these present-day critical habits and estimates but also the Dickens achievement itself. According to him, 'Dickens is a great genius, a great artist'[9] (in some fashion he seems never to define really and fully, especially in its compatibility with his other contentions), but he is also a fundamentally unserious one, an author who, as continuously as he registers the darker aspects of human life, betrays them by a delight in the sheer process of his performance (as author) which is all-engulfing. His art is the art of the exhilarated and exhilarating stage monologuist, the interest and enjoyment of whose performance derives from its ingenuity, of which, in this art, performer and audience alike are uniquely conscious. It is of the very nature of the Dickens experience that its first palpable feature is the presence of the narrator's powerful personality, or that we fail really to wonder — i.e. gape with embarrassment — at the historical fact of his public readings, as we should certainly do in the case of George Eliot or Tolstoy if we were to learn that they had done the same with their works. The primary and essential pleasure in reading Dickens is that of observing a brilliant performer in his full *persona* of majordomo of the literary festivities dominantly and triumphantly at work. What the novels give us (as Garis sees it) is a series of brilliant theatric charades, which we would be prigs not to delight in, but which do not deserve the kind of consideration elicited by any comparably characteristic episodes in 'Fielding, Tolstoy, Henry James, Flaubert, Joyce' (for instance),[10] because they are not organised parts of a sustained movement or fully pressured application of responsible thought. (The inescapably discrediting character of Garis's study becomes plainer with each of his successive chapters as it wars against the pretensions not only of the various critics but also of the Dickens manner itself, in its general manifestation[11] and as an individual achievement in the respective separate cases of (particularly) *Bleak House, Hard Times, Little Dorrit* and *Our Mutual Friend*.[12]) *Our Mutual Friend*, Garis argues, is marred not only by the endemic faults and contradictions inherent in its predecessors; it is also seen to be self-defeating in being informed equally by the 'intention to make our flesh creep and also to write with quiet good manners: . . . not a happy combination'.[13] Dickens has here apparently attempted to write more self-critically, more 'tastefully' even, than hitherto (with an eye to that congenital gap — between offered, morally serious authorial intention and actual, irresponsible theatrical performance — which mars all his other works except *Great Expectations*);[14] and 'what tastefulness in the theatrical style yields is sadly like the genteel finish of academic landscape and genre painting'.[15]

To Garis's general thesis my own view is radically opposed; and, though I do not myself enjoy *Our Mutual Friend* very much (that I do not do so is, I believe, partly a consequence of just what is locally successful in the book), it seems to me a more challenging work than any of these various approaches suggest. Once we have come to acknowledge those features which are effective and disturbing (the portrait of Headstone, say, or the ingenuity of the authorial manner in the 'Social Chorus' scenes), we find ourselves faced with an important, if unexpected, aspect of Dickens's thought which, in any study of his works that attempts to say something generally valid about the world-view implicit in his utterance, cannot fairly be ignored or wished away. At the same time we must equally recognise that the novel does not justify the endorsements of a Chesterton or the New Critics, who have failed to see how relatively poorly or occasionally, as art, it is realising a unified theme, or bringing into significant relations intuitions which remain largely opposed and uncombined.

Part of my purpose in this chapter, then, is to demonstrate its dividedness, the ways in which one creative purpose or informing idea—emotion seems to be undercut by another at the novel's very heart. If we are dissatisfied with it, that (I believe) is the cause. But my larger intent is by this means also to adumbrate those characteristic tendencies of the Dickens perception which, in contrast, actually fill

us with an exhilarated sense of moral triumph or ethical joy, and I seek
to do this precisely because they are more characteristic.

For all its real differences, *Our Mutual Friend* evidently purports in
essence to be what each of the other novels of Dickens's middle years
constitutes: an examination of the condition of contemporary English
society, an enquiry – by extension – into the human condition as
such and the possibilities for the innocent, or at least the less
corrupted, individual life within the dark world these works
discover. This is to be undertaken by the fable well summarised in
Ross H. Dabney's lucid study:

> The main plot . . . concerns a mercenary marriage set up by the
> will of an immensely rich dust collector – a marriage which
> eventually takes place when changes in their situations and
> character have allowed the parties to it to love each other
> disinterestedly; the subplot is about an indolent purposeless
> young gentleman morally redeemed by the love of a working girl,
> whom he marries in defiance of the not quite united voice of
> 'Society'.[16]

A polity sick with the lust for money, its economic organisation
rooted in a grotesquely inflated valuation of what in itself is mean and
wretched; the incuria of contemporary government and administration, as they determine the quality of the human environment and
the lives of the poor; social barriers of a highly artificial and
destructive nature: these ideas are represented in the history of Old
Harmon and his domestic circle at the significantly named Harmony
Jail; in the social life of the Veneerings, the Lammles, Podsnaps and
their 'friends'; in the ordeals of Lizzie Hexam, Betty Higden and 'Miss
Dolls'. And at a first glance the principal stories (as accounted such by
Dabney's summary) are indeed, like several other component parts of
the work, more successful than the earliest reviewers tended to allow.

Such reviewers[17] found the whole Harmon story of exchanged
identities, as of the secreted wills, straying perilously near absurdity.
Its extravagance was signalised for them by such a chapter as II, xiii,
where the supposedly dead young heir wanders about the backstreets
of the London wharves neighbourhood considering all his adventures
and developing his present resolutions as it were almost openly for the
benefit of the reader's otherwise undispersable ignorance. But for me
the failures there are more technical than radical. The long soliloquy is
incredible because no one can accept that any man would talk to

himself in prose so ordered, with arguments and reflections so detailed as this:

'When I came to England, attracted to the country with which I had none but most miserable associations, by the accounts of my fine inheritance that found me abroad, I came back, shrinking from my father's money, shrinking from my father's memory, mistrustful of being forced on a mercenary wife, mistrustful of my father's intention in thrusting that marriage on me, mistrustful that I was already growing avaricious, mistrustful that I was slackening in gratitude to the two dear noble honest friends who had made the only sunlight in my childish life or that of my heartbroken sister . . . . ' (Ibid., 366)

This is simply not a credible mode of speech for the kind of colloquy with the self here alleged; but the fundamental psychological truth of John Harmon's situation and his inward debate is as iron or adamant. What is rehearsed for us is a history of extreme brutality, of emotional deprivation in the first degree. Like his sister he has been rejected by his father for daring to oppose his bad designs (in his sister's case, the loss of their parent's financial support has led to her own and her husband's death). After an infancy that would have been wholly loveless but for the ministrations of the Boffins – and we account *his* turning out decent very much to the credit of their early example – the boy has been packed off first to a Brussels school, then to South Africa. This is the story of a melancholy man, disconsolate after the fashion of *Little Dorrit*'s Arthur Clennam (who also, significantly, returns to London to take up his inheritance at the beginning of *his* story), and it is hard not to feel in both cases that their past exile in a distant land is a correlative expression of the emotional as well as physical situation these men have endured; their isolation as much in as outside the *domus et urbs* of their youth. South Africa – like Belgium – is merely a named blur here.

John Harmon has come back not at the enticement of his new legacy in its pecuniary character but to put that much larger inheritance which is the 'first world' of his experience (to appropriate T. S. Eliot's term) to the question. We could almost claim for him what Eliot says of his Tiresias in his note to section III, line 218, of *The Waste Land*: 'although a mere spectator and not indeed a "character", he is yet the most important personage in the poem, uniting all the rest. . . . What he sees, in fact, is the substance of the poem.' The hero

who is the 'mutual friend' of the novel's title (Mr Boffin so names him
to Mrs Wilfer in I, ix) *is* of course a 'character', a major protagonist in
its action, but the unique significance of his part in it is his being at
once agent and spectator, both of and outside the world with which
he is again engaged after so many years' detachment from it. His
affronting the ways it subordinates the creative-instinctual features
and imaginative possibilities of the social life to the inert and
intrinsically valueless is critical from the first. Old Harmon has died
having deliberately contrived a challenge to that moral superiority at
the prompting of which his outraged son first left him: namely, can
the younger man avoid being implicated in the ethics of the world all
around him, in the morality of which his parent's career was so
unrelenting an embodiment? This is the point of the miser's bequest
and the match he has tied to it. Will his son be corrupted by the
prevailing money-lust, will he contract loveless and dishonourable
nuptials — for all his fine professions of the earlier time against his
father's tyranny in the case of his sister's marriage for love — given so
impressive a temptation to withstand as the apparent legacy of the
dust mounds? (And of course if he *does* defer to the all-compromising
condition of their inheritance, the dead testator has arranged, by a
refinement of irony, to despoil him of his money-gains — i.e. with his
plot of the second will, the discovery of which, in the sifted and
cleared dust-heaps, will pauper his 'heir' again.)

If the issue were as simple as this the sane course would be equally
evident and easy: to have nothing to do either with the lucre or the
girl (whom as yet John Harmon, we must remember, does not
know), to keep merely at his 3000 miles' distance. But London
remains the only world in which he is rooted, from which he derives,
and he has to come to terms with the fact of his childhood and the
nature of its society if he is ever to lead any kind of uncrippled adult
life. What other possibilities exist for him than those he attempts to
open up by coming back to England upon his father's death, when
here is his language background, his native milieu — and of course it is
our own culture, a major one — the original soil (even if it be
corrosive dust) of his entire constitution as a social being? One thinks
of Aristotle's *Politics* on this issue: 'But he who is unable to live in
society, or who has no need because he is sufficient for himself, must
be either a beast or a god . . . .'[18] So it is no measure of improbability
that we should see him resorting to the extreme courses he
undertakes; I mean, with the 'Julius Handford' and 'John Rokesmith'
disguises. These have become necessities of his situation, which in

turn impressively represents the problem this part of the novel is to centre around. The whole purpose of his hidden probatory life hereafter is to find the answers, in a personal drama, to the challenge which is recurrent and central in Dickens's fiction: what can be thought, known and achieved by the sensitive mind, by the responsible individual, who inhabits a human world informed by so many bad values? *Can* any significant fulfilment, particularly fulfilment via personal relations, attend him? For Rokesmith – Harmon, like Arthur Clennam, draws a blank at the idea of the solitary existence. Both plainly come back to London as men who are unhappily lonely.

This theme of the destructive parental relation or legacy ramifies, and one thinks not only of that tormented 'Young Person' poor Georgiana Podsnap, or of Bella Wilfer, in whose dreadful mother's discontents something of her own unhappiness, acquisitiveness and self-will has surely originated. Lizzie Hexam and Jenny Wren's stories express the degree to which birth into this society tends to confer inextricable difficulties which fundamentally inhibit hopeful living.

Lizzie, for instance, can only be dispossessed by her situation of those fulfilments which ought to characterise her life as an adult (and beautiful) young woman. Her origin, the fatherhood to her of 'The Gaffer' and the river alike, make it 'not simply' a matter of compassion towards the parent she loves that she should remain with him; though to participate in his dreadful trade wounds her deeply. Repudiating him, we are shown, and with him his way of life, would be a disavowal of her very beginnings, her psychic roots. In this aspect of the matter Hexam is unanswerable when he argues,

> 'How can you be so thankless to your best friend, Lizzie? The very fire that warmed you when you were a baby, was picked out of the river alongside the coal barges. The very basket that you slept in, the tide washed ashore. The very rockers that I put it upon to make a cradle of it, I cut out of a piece of wood that drifted from some ship or another.'   (I, i, 3)

The basic elements of *her* 'first world', as of her primary affections – for her father, for the waterway – make up a burden of guilty dependence by which she would be disabled whether or not she had ever personally sculled for him; which likewise the nature of her position compels her to do. Her importance and rarity among the novel's *dramatis personae* is exactly her moral refinement in the midst of such an environment; yet by the same token these felt origins and debts can only weave around her whole moral consciousness a web of difficulties incapable of resolution. She participates in something truly ugly if she embraces the terms of the life in her river-home. She is unfilial, hypocritical, ungrateful, she commits negations – self-denials – deep and dangerous if she disavows them. Retreat of a different kind from that of merely running away is thus enforced, a withdrawal from the outer to an inward existence which in meditating introversion further and further disables itself. It is part of the quiet fidelity to psychological truth which is so characteristic of Dickens and which used to go so often unnoticed among the critics that already by this period of her existence in which we come to know her her most intent living is done in daydream and reverie, staring at the coals of the fire in her father's hovel (see I, iii, *passim*; and note the illustration 'Waiting for Father', at 160–1).

The Gaffer's death makes only a very limited kind of simplification. While he is alive she is constrained by the knowledge that she is 'in some things a stay to father, and that if I was not faithful to him he would – in revenge-like, or in disappointment, or both – go wild and bad' (I, iii, 29). (To have such an influence is her highest hope for her own future at the beginning of the tale.) With the passing of her father she is more than ever thrown in upon herself and her need to 'expiate' the past. Out of this desire to 'compensate' (as she puts it) for her domestic background, she goes to work in the City, living with Jenny Wren, whose own parent was the son of one of the Gaffer's objects of professional interest, and who is

'. . . employed by the house that employs me. . . . This poor ailing little creature has come to be what she is, surrounded by drunken people from her cradle – if she ever had one, Charley.'

'I don't see what you have to do with her, for all that,' said the boy.

'Don't you, Charley?'

The boy looked doggedly at the river. They were at Millbank, and the river rolled on the left. His sister gently touched him on the shoulder and pointed to it.

'Any compensation – restitution – never mind the word, you know my meaning. Father's grave.'   (II, i, 227)

The man with whom Lizzie falls in love is disabled in a complementary manner. His own alert wits find his background in its

different fashion so despicable that there really seems to him to be
little in life to live for. After all, the human dimensions he has most
largely known are those of 'M. R. F.', and

> 'M[y] R[espected] F[ather] having always in the clearest
> manner provided (as he calls it) for his children by pre-arranging
> from the hour of the birth of each, and sometimes from an earlier
> period, what the devoted little victim's calling and course in life
> should be, M. R. F. pre-arranged for myself that I was to be the
> barrister I am (with the slight addition of an enormous practice,
> which has not accrued) and also the married man I am not.'   (I, xii,
> 146)

Wrayburn's pose is really a mirror-image of the role-playing which
goes on throughout that ambit of society which his position as
'M. R. F.'s' son makes open to him. The 'Stucconian' dinners are
theatric occasions in which no one really meets anybody; each person
encounters elaborate − if to the intelligent eye, fairly transparent −
personae. Yet the *dégagé* young lawyer is sympathetic in a way
Mrs Veneering is not, because his mask is a reaction against, not with,
the environing behaviour; it is the only means he knows (as such, half-
courageous in him to adopt it) of fighting off the acknowledgement
of deep loss, pain − of, essentially, despair.

> 'It is very quiet,' said he.
>   It was very quiet. Some sheep were grazing on the grass by the
> river-side, and it seemed to him that he had never before heard the
> crisp, tearing sound with which they cropped it. He stopped idly,
> and looked at them.
>   'You are stupid enough, I suppose. But if you are clever enough
> to get through life tolerably to your satisfaction, you have got the
> better of me, Man as I am, and Mutton as you are!'   (IV, vi, 690)

If we ask where this hopelessness has originated, we can usefully turn
again to Dabney, for the clear synopsis he gives us of a later episode:

> When Eugene has married Lizzie and his father has seen her, all
> goes well. Mr. Wrayburn, a connoisseur of beauty, asserts that
> Lizzie's portrait ought to be painted; he tastes the claret he has been
> served and says, 'My dear son, why do you drink this trash?' −

a question 'tantamount in him' — Eugene later says 'to a pater-
nal benediction on our union, accompanied by a gush of tears'
[IV, xvi].

But when this critic goes on to draw the conclusion that

> This outcome is consistent with the class assessments of *Our Mutual
> Friend*, which ferociously attacks new money and the upper
> bourgeoisie but allows decency and honour to the representatives
> of the old gentry — Eugene, Mortimer Lightwood, the Rev.
> Milvey, Twemlow. Although capable of arranging advantageous
> marriages for his children Mr. Wrayburn accepts with grace the *fait
> accompli* of his son's marriage to Lizzie, and furthermore is able to
> understand his son's action and to appreciate Lizzie's true excel-
> lence when he sees it[19]

it seems to me he has lost sight of his own emphasis upon the
significance in the novel of what he calls Dickens's 'obsession' with
the idea of 'inadequate or evil parents'.[20] What have we been given,
in the passage he has just enlisted, but a glimpse of a lifetime's
emotional starvation? To which the most likely response — or rather
the best that can be hoped (and it is disastrous, of course) — is just the
kind of flippant outlook we find in Wrayburn junior: a pose and
attitude designed to keep at bay all open committed discourse and
relationship with other people — and with that the possibility both of
having to acknowledge the deep wound this kind of background has
meant, this kind of relation, and any other hurts of a similar kind that
life may offer.

Eugene is a brilliant portrait of the upper-class English scion as he
has perhaps existed to this very day; the product of an education and
tradition which famishes the affections. The 'my dear son' in the
given instance is ruinously a mere form of words; like the other's 'my
respected father'. If there is any tie between Eugene and his parent
more than the most mechanical, then its proper idiom was long since
abolished by, or perverted into, this manner of speech, which can pass
a remark about claret in the immediate face of an introduction to the
younger man's new bride. Irresponsive and irresponsible habits of
utterance, as of thought, are now therefore the very pattern of
Eugene's soul; as we see from his behaviour towards Lightwood,
whom he knows for a true friend and a centre of sincere feeling and
loyalty towards him and with whom he can nevertheless refuse to

engage in serious conversation when the other urges it (II, vi).

Lizzie's sincerity makes short but delicate work of the powerful convention in most (respectable) novels of the age[21] that women are somehow unconscious of having impulses which make them capable of being seduced. The whole riverbank conversation between her and Eugene is centred on her impressive wholehearted openness of address and her lover's difficulty in matching it, Lizzie insisting that she herself has an identity as worthy to be taken seriously as her visitor's (IV, vi). Wrayburn is plainly as much attracted by her possession of these qualities, which he has so much missed elsewhere in his experience, as to her good looks. But it goes against the grain of all his sentimental education in a world of very un-Platonic 'forms' to believe that he would not discover what he deems (as a result of his upbringing) to be the proven insufficiency of human enjoyments even in wedlock with this unusual woman:

> ' "You wouldn't marry for some money and some station, because you were frightfully likely to become bored. Are you less frightfully likely to become bored, marrying for no money and no station? Are you sure of yourself?" Legal mind, in spite of forensic protestations, must secretly admit, "Good reasoning on the part of M. R. F. *Not* sure of myself." '   (Ibid., 696–7)

Yet he cannot give her up. She has come upon his experience as an uncharacteristic entity and called in question the very terms of his outlook:

> 'You don't know how you haunt me and bewilder me. You don't know how the cursed carelessness that is over-officious in helping me at every other turning of my life, WON'T help me here. You have struck it dead, I think, and I sometimes almost wish you had struck me dead along with it.'   (Ibid., 692)

So we come back to Lizzie's predicament, with the knowledge of that in Wrayburn which aggravates her difficulty. If he is neither to leave her alone nor to propose marriage, there exists the other possibility of a love affair. According to his ethics – those, representatively, of the upper-class blade – it is legitimate for him to make love to a girl from the lower orders without being responsible for the consequences (to her). The painful irony for the observing reader is that marriage to each other, with its *commitments*, is the one conceivable way in which both could begin to live positively at this point in their arrested and entangled careers. The insistences of 'the dark backward' upon Lizzie's supposed moral debts to it, for example, would be counterbalanced by her new responsibilities, obligations (as a wife, possibly as a mother) with at least as peremptory a force.

It is part of her being like any heroine a personality to whom things can happen importantly that Lizzie refuses to devalue the quality of her attachment to him either by agreeing to a temporary (i.e. partial) liaison or by being willing to forget this her great love and take up at some future period with another man; just as it is a similar mark of the profound loyalties which inform her nature that she is not prepared to forsake the company of her natal river either in the City (cf. ii, i, the conversation between her and Charley already quoted, the fact of her regular evening stroll there beside the water) or out in her more distant provincial retreat. What is more tragic is that her lover has been so incapacitated in his turn emotionally and morally, and by the social animus against marriage contracted across the class divisions (which barriers Lizzie also wishes to defer to), that his attitude should make frustration the issue between them. For the important initiatives rest with him. (It is important for us to keep in mind the fact that Eugene is peculiarly responsible for this relationship in the first place. He does not accompany Mortimer on that first journey to Lizzie's dwelling (i, iii) in order to render any useful service; he just goes slumming for the evening in a characteristic mood of egoistic aimlessness, on a jaunt which is not informed by any real respect for the people he is visiting.)

There being no valid compromise, she is thrust back into a life of further retreat, is driven away, as is Betty Higden, to whom she likens herself (iv, vi, 694). Her capacities for relationship in the sexual dimension are now, as it were, pre-empted, while the hope of achieving 'restitution' for her domestic past we know to be futile. She has nothing to expiate; it is a prison of the mind to which there as yet exists no liberating key. She becomes effectually a kind of anchoress in her Oxfordshire retirement, ('She would joyfully die with him, or, better than that, die for him', she has earlier declared of herself: ii, xi, 349); we note the little neat bare whitewashed (i.e. cell-like) room in which Bella Wilfer finds her lodging, the minimal individualisation of the adult personnel with whom she toils by day (iii, ix). Her recreation now can be only with the local children, in what to her, as a grown-up looking in, are their simplifying and contracted dimensions of interest and thought. What else can she do, how can she live more fully than this, in a condition which is so paralysed?

Only the near-fatal event of Eugene's 'accident' (IV, vi) can resolve these difficulties. It incorporates the girl and the river together in a catastrophe which spontaneously necessitates the creative acceptance by her of her earlier career. The Gaffer's trade and her involvement in it become an inheritance without which she could not at this naked immitigable moment save the life of the man she loves. The 'criminality' of the earlier years now flies (irrevocably) up the beam in a balance of which she herself is forced to recognise the just measure. It would be a moral monstrosity in Lizzie not to think 'Now Heaven be thanked for that old time . . .', as she makes out with the boat to save her battered lover (Ibid., 699). Likewise there is renewal for Eugene, the assault and his long hovering between life and death mean a major clarification for him; he finds out that his only interest and value in remaining alive are Lizzie and her needs (IV, x). But the extremity of this redemptive act is a measure in itself of the difficulties with which Dickens sees the potentially or actually responsive individual en-meshed by the prevailing ethos and *mores* of the social world he knows; that it should take a premeditated and very nearly successful attempt at murder to perform this enfranchisement for them both. Wrayburn, we are reminded, has been permanently disfigured (IV, xvi, 811).

If in their first elements the John Harmon story and that of Lizzie Hexam and her lover are credible and significant, it is also true that Henry James maligned Jenny Wren when he called her 'a little monster'.[22] Far from being a 'creature of pure fancy . . . belonging to the troop of hunchbacks, imbeciles and precocious children who have carried on the sentimental business in all Mr. Dickens's novels', i.e. a grotesque we cannot reasonably find ourselves 'accepting as a possible person',[23] she has a fully constituted *human* reality which exemplifies in an extreme way the problem of living in this society. Almost uniquely among the characters of the novel she is not only committed to the cause of fair play but also wordly-wise in an effective manner. She has by far the greatest share of shrewd, dry-eyed competencies among the story's personages of goodwill, for negotiating the traps set by the selfish and malevolent. Of this we see examples in her suspecting Eugene's intentions from the very first (while Lizzie still misconstrues them; II, ii, 236, 238), and her stonewalling him later when he tries to inveigle the Oxfordshire address from her; or in her well-collated doubts as to Fledgeby's seeming honesty (IV, viii, 721), which help to extricate Messrs Riah and Twemlow from the money-lender's snares. There, for instance, she has only had Lammle's beating of Fledgeby to go upon (III, viii) and the having heard the 'mature young gentleman's' name at 'St. Mary Axe', but these are enough for someone with wits as sharply trained and alert as hers, to pick out the important hints and develop the connections.

Yet if she 'knows the tricks' (II, ii, 224) of the scavenging predatory world as many of the other good characters in this story do not, it is just because she has been given an education which has also left her more than half a little shrew. Given her father's dissipations and her own physical disabilities she has had to monitor her parent's every ruse like an unsleeping termagant, if either was to be sheltered and fed at all. As a denied child (we are shown) she has sought, by casting her father in the child-part of their relations, to mollify the pain of her emotional famine in this household and the perversity of her role. One result of this is that she is a disappointed parent as well, for all that this strategem, financially as well as emotionally, helps her to cope with their situation. (He brings her nothing but worry, pecuniary distress, and eventually drinks himself to death [IV, ix] – partly with the money with which Eugene Wrayburn has unscrupulously bribed him.) Her heroism in fact is the issue; one cannot say less of someone who by the age of thirteen years has been made to be knowing in the sharp-edged manner Dickens delineates here, without losing her fundamental delight in the virtues of honesty and justice. All her significance derives from her not being the ridiculous affectation or self-indulgence on the author's part which James construed. The real native fineness and delicacy she can show – which in their turn are the more tragic for being the sensibilities which have to endure her entanglements and disappointments – are exhibited at their most helpful in the nursing of Eugene (IV, x: 'The Dolls' Dressmaker Discovers a Word').

To the pain she suffers and the cruel mocks of the neighbourhood's this-worldly children she has responded with the infants and flowers of her visions. Whether these be considered a compensating fantasy or a real variety of spiritual insight is unimportant. Their evocation *is* in part sentimental:

'. . . Such numbers of them, too! All in white dresses, and with something shining on the borders, and on their heads, that I have never been able to imitate with my work, though I know it so well. . . .' (II, ii, 239)

This is weakly expectable and immediately puts us in mind of the effete angelology of so much Victorian religious art. But two important polarities are being held in balance. On the one hand the apparitions have the magnificent innocence of Blake's uncorrupted young, with their desire to express themselves in all-inclusive play and dance (unlike the actual children of her locality), and an approach to her suffering and incapacity which is not pitying or patronising. Given that such manifestations 'appear' to her, these things are the measure of Jenny's intelligence and her moral being's compass. When they touch her apparently they mitigate her pain; a fine insight on Dickens's part (and 'Miss Wren's') into the psychosomatic nature of what is worst in her – as in so much – physical distress; and into the relief, by contrast, which is concomitant in so lonely a life when active mutuality instead, as on these occasions, becomes the embracing feature of the girl's experience. On the other hand, the emphasis falls no less upon its intermittence, upon their leaving her, like Caliban, crying to dream again. We are given, in fact, a classic unsentimental account here of the lonely child – as such; of how its loneliness inwardly develops a charged full imaginative existence which by turns partly compensates, partly works to heighten, its sense of desolate exclusion from the communal life.

The same unhappy duality must be acknowledged therefore in every aspect of her existence. What makes her competent to be (in some measure) successfully heroic in this world, derives from all that makes her life more largely frustrating and disconsolate. The fierce barking *persona* she adopts towards her 'child' and indeed towards most callers is a real and painful perversion, but we recognise in it her only way of coping with the difficulties of her situation. Ineffably pathetic are her fantasies about the 'him' she will one day marry; not only in that such nuptials will probably never come to pass, but also in that a strong foundation of doubt, cunning and antagonism has become her recipe for a securely ordered life in wedlock as well as out of it. Skipping with its crutch between the clattering myriad wheels of the metropolitan streets, the figure of this young 'ruined beauty' altogether expresses, even in its very agility, the degree to which any really effective preparatory education for living in her society comes, to the just and responsible person, at a perhaps too ruinously high price. 'How can I say what I might have turned out myself, but for my back having been so bad and my legs so queer when I was young?' (IV, ix, 732). This is tragically unanswerable.

The representative problem her history expresses and those

embodied in Lizzie Hexam's are effectually subsumed by the John Harmon story. We return to that as to the most inclusive engagement the book offers with what has been thematically raised in these less central plots. For there Dickens has taken over three great ideas of myth and legend: the prince who wanders through his domains in disguise to test his subjects, educate their sympathies, or examine his beloved; the quest-knight who visits the waste lands and there poses the liberating question; and the dying and returning god. These various aristocratic functions are appropriately incarnate in a young man who, *in propria persona*, possesses the sort of wealth which means kingship in this society. Money can do anything here; it has all the privileges of authority, can even purchase a seat in the sovereign legislature, as Mr Veneering does, and the miser's heir has (by rights) an enormous amount of it.

That an affirmative discovery on his part will be expressed in terms of a final wedding, a vindicated and satisfactory marriage for love between this *jeune premier* and the heroine whom as yet he has to prove, does not diminish the seriousness of this drama's typological implications; which in the earlier part of the book are very suggestively sustained. Recalling the attempt made upon his life by the murderous seamen shortly after he came ashore, he talks about having been drugged and bludgeoned so that ' "I cannot possibly express it [i.e. the consciousness of those hours] to myself without using the word I. But it was not I. There was no such thing as I, within my knowledge" '(II, xiii, 369). This is a real death in very truth:

> . . . destitution of all property,
> Desiccation of the world of sense,
> Evacuation of the world of fancy,
> Inoperancy of the world of spirit. . . . '[24]

And again it is important to keep in mind the inevitability of his actions; how, other than by the means he attempts, is he to discover whether Bella Wilfer can love him for himself or whether the cash-nexus must poison every relation; how else is he to 'begin life' (I, viii, 97) as something other and more than simply a 'Genius' who has made 'three-hundred and seventy-five thousand pounds, no shillings and no pence' (IV, xvii, 818–19), which is all the identity allotted to one of the Veneerings' guests? His near-death by drowning looks historically beyond the narratives of the Christian cultus to the fertility rituals of ancient Egypt, say, or Mesopotamia. But, with the figure of Osiris or Tammuz behind him, what we have to confront at this heart of the novel is an anti-type of resurrection story.

In exile from his home, he completes the book's elucidation of the essential moral character of the world it observes, in having put off the tokens of his Royal Birth (the public claim upon his dust-mounds inheritance) and coming upon this society as the Stranger or Outsider whom no one is obliged to respect (and they don't). He exists as no one else among the *dramatis personae* of the novel, outside and looking in upon its various worlds: that of the shabby-genteel Wilfers and new-rich Boffins, of waterside London crime and dusty respect-ability, of violence and order. After a period in the desert of exile, with a maturing life about which we know nothing, like Jesus, he returns in the prime of young manhood, to become an archetypal victim of the social world's scavenging nature in the country of his inheritance. He has been foully slain — as everyone believes — for the sake of the commodity to which all decencies are sacrificed in this com-monwealth, and, after sojourning further, during his crucial hours in and beside the river following the attempt on his life, in the border territory between life and death, he returns thence to work for a moral rebirth of that portion of his Kingdom which is renewable and can be made his Bride. Yet — and this is the tragic intimation of his whole part in the book — the very attempt to break free from his predicament can only aggravate it. Putting the question to these lands at all — is there anything here but the cash-nexus?; can any personal value be found in this environment? — cannot be done without falsifying or even corrupting too much of what he himself seeks to vindicate.

Of his original plan he has to make confession that it had meant to be harmless, 'but clearly the wrong ["the implication of an innocent man in his supposed murder"] could never have been done if he had never planned a deception'(II, xiv, 380). This difficulty of Rogue Riderhood's false witness against 'The Gaffer' he is obliged to circumvent by blackmailing the villain in his own fashion (same chapter); indeed, more generally and largely, 'Julius Handford' and 'Mr. Secretary Rokesmith' are committed to playing on the supposition of a murder (his own) and the fact of one (the Third Mate's) to gain their ends. Well intentioned as these are, such proceeding surely has to be a very doubtful foundation for his creative enterprise in a world disfigured by the trading of others (like Jesse Hexam) in the unhappy deaths which foul the Thames and condemn the lives on either side of it. We cannot but recall how the novel's first image is of a scavenger fishing nameless corpses out of the river. What more potent compressed intimation could be given of the human relations which Dickens now sees as predominant in the world he knows? We have to share in Lizzie Hexam's loathing of her father's profession. It is not just that drowned bodies are sensuously distasteful (somebody after all has got to dredge them up), nor even that he works at a trade and in a milieu where, according to the integrity of the individual waterman, murder itself may be a way of life. It is the ghastly irony of anyone's profiting out of the *felo de se* of those citizens who have been made desperate precisely by the attitudes around them:

> It were too much to pretend that Betty Higden made out such thoughts; no; but she heard the tender river whispering to many like herself, 'Come to me, come to me! When the cruel shame and terror you have so long fled from, most beset you, come to me! I am the Relieving Officer appointed by eternal ordinance to do my work; I am not held in estimation according as I shirk it. My breast is softer than the pauper-nurse's; death in my arms is peacefuller than among the pauper-wards. Come to me!'   (III, viii, 504–5)

This community's suicides' final assertion of their immitigable individuality *is* their very act of self-removal from a theatre of behaviour so cruelly irresponsive to it. But here that ultimate protest is itself merely converted into a means of acquiring hard cash. That is the grimmest turn of the screw.

In his scheme for the improvement of Bella Wilfer, 'the dead heir' gets the 'Golden Dustman' to ape the class snobberies and money-avarice generally abounding, and no reader has ever failed to register as a genuine intrinsic decline Boffin's so dynamic and enthusiastic account of his role of miser-tyrant. Moreover, the wife to whom Harmon finally unmasks (as late as IV, xii) – though Dickens makes little of this, the problem is present with us – might well claim that she never *has* really known her husband for himself; that the device by which each was to marry the other only for the sake of their inherent natures as human beings has effectively obscured those identities. Returning thus again to the primal issues at the heart of John Harmon's strategy, it is difficult not to feel that the naming of a person constitutes a part of his uniqueness which is imponderable only because it may be radical and comprehensive. How much is he the man she wedded, when his name, lineage, position and function in society, and his abode, all turn out to be quite different from what she consciously undertook? The poor fellow is effectually trapped all along – whether or not he recognises it; and that portion of the narrative which most immediately imitates his larger withdrawal from the social life and its bafflements in order to come to grips with his situation is exactly the part in which his deliberating mind is seen as in fact quite lost in a maze:

> He tried both, but both confused him equally, and he came straying back to the same spot. . . . He tried a new direction, but made nothing of it; walls, dark doorways, flights of stairs and rooms, were too abundant. And like most people so puzzled, he again and again described a circle, and found himself at the point from which he had begun. (II, xiii, 365)

If one allows a representative significance to this kind of writing – tellingly charged in being where it is – then one 'wastes criticism upon unresisting imbecility' to speak at length of the jejune conversations that characterise the Harmon couple's married happiness. For example:

> 'Do you remember, John, on the day we were married, Pa's speaking of the ships that might be sailing towards us from the unknown seas?'
>   'Perfectly, my darling!'
>   'I think . . . among them . . . there is a ship upon the ocean . . . bringing . . . to you and me . . . a little baby, John.' (IV, v, 688)

The Bella Wilfer who speaks here is a shrunken, desexualised, eyelash-fluttering minnie. Our problem lies in Dickens's very evidently endorsing this kind of relationship as a satisfactory outcome to complexities far more difficult of resolution than is implied in this kind of language. For my quotation exemplifies no local but an intrinsic defect in the later portion of the novel (I forbear to quote at length in the matter, but see II, xvi; IV, v, xii and xiii, *passim*). One comes to view the gross, even hectoring sentimentalities of the Harmon story's conclusion as heavy colouring-in after the event, an attempt on the author's part retrospectively to establish our conviction of the validities supposedly affirmed by this marriage, the happiness and innocence allegedly achieved in it, which his more local and immediate treatment of John Harmon's perplexities has not substantiated.

We have been shown after all (as in the degeneration of Noddy Boffin) the great dangers which inhere simply in the possession of wealth. Even on the story's own terms the young couple have been as happy as ever they can be, in their suburban dwelling on a modest salary (IV, v), and when Bella there insists she does not want them to have any more money than what they already enjoy, one can only wish her husband would pay heed. He does not, however, and at the end their apotheosis is removal to a great glittering gilded bird-cage of a residence in the heart of 'Stucconia' — where the Stucconian ethics are actively endorsed.

Though Silas Wegg is a comic character to some extent in the manner of Dickens's great eccentrics, yet he is not so liberating as to be exempt from real responsibility for the ugliness of his world. But the most significant feature of his nemesis is that at the end Boffin and Harmon have him pitched — as a punishment and a disgrace — into exactly the kind of 'scavenger's cart' that has made their fortune; a gesture which one might almost call Podsnappian, and especially disturbing in men whose experience ought to have meant to them (if any clarifications have been afforded by the course of their recent adventures) a stronger awareness of the difficulty, or rather the destructive easiness, of taking up simple ethical postures like that.

The same sort of failure in authorial intelligence or responsibility characterises Dickens's treatment of the Lizzie Hexam—Eugene Wrayburn story — specifically *its* 'happy ending', which does not begin to take account of what it will mean for this couple to 'fight it out', in Eugene's phrase, 'here, in the open field' of the British social snobberies (IV, xvi, 813). They will in fact have a deadly time, two hapless pariahs in a world of rigid class-distinctions and caste-taboos. Their problems have only begun, but the novel is nearly silent on this score.

II

This is the recurrent tendency of *Our Mutual Friend*. Again and again it offers us important issues expressed, as to their principal features and initial development, in a truly challenging manner. The Harmon story alone is only one 'raid on the inarticulate' here which is distinctly 'new' in the Dickens *oeuvre*, and warrants some more consideration for this book than the brief dispatch it gets in *Dickens the Novelist*[25] — a work of which the essential (and grateful) premiss is its authors' concern to take the whole development of Dickens's thought seriously as thought. Nevertheless, while several major elements in the novel begin by portending a sensitive and scrupulous reticulation of meanings fully grasped and presented, comprehensive and profound, we find them recurrently plunging thereafter into alien defiles, becoming incoherent, weak and decentered.

From a Marxian point of view, for example, there should be a powerful interest in Dickens's portrait of Messrs Venus and Wegg; the nature of those two characters, their environment and relations. Were they to ply their cunning against Boffin and then against each other so that in the end all three, consumed with avarice, had lost the entire Harmon fortune, we should have before us a suggestive, though simplified, paradigm of the contradictions inherent in the capitalist system as regarded by the German socialist classics of this same period; the more remarkable in an author who, for all the motley heterogeneity of his reading,[26] had never studied them or owned their influence. Venus's 'little dark greasy' emporium—workshop lies at the murky centre (Clerkenwell) of the world's first industrial trading metropolis and is as such a pregnant symbol of the nature of the economic structure and personal interchange in its society; just as its owner's name is an ironic commentary thereupon. (Venus, the Eros that is also the first-born child of Wisdom and Power, is here not even infernalised into disordered sexuality — unorganised lust — but diminished into the self-endorsement of his pallid romanticism, his being in love with 'love'.) It is impossible to believe that the 'articulator' is as much actually attracted to Pleasant Riderhood for herself as for a means of indulgence in his private cult of sensibility. In three words, he enjoys his failure as a suitor, and what his shop really tells us about the interest of the world it represents in faithful sexual love is neatly demonstrated:

Concurrently, Wegg perceives a pretty little dead bird lying on the counter, with its head drooping on one side against the rim of Mr. Venus's saucer, and a long stiff wire piercing its breast. As if it were Cock Robin, the hero of the Ballad, and Mr. Venus were the sparrow with his bow and arrow, and Mr. Wegg were the fly with his little eye. (I, vii, 78—9)

His trade exists to satisfy people's wish to be detached from living in the cherishing of dead, unitary but inorganic life-images, untroublesome substitutes for the independently-centred and therefore disturbing real thing.

We may think, likewise, of reification in the Marxian sense when meeting with the autonomous 'life' of 'the crafty Silas's' wooden leg. We note how when the taxidermist greets Wegg at their first meeting in the novel (and he greets the more human part of the fellow with the reluctance of his own shop-door — ibid., 78), it is as the appendage of his disassociated and now defunct member that his visitor can have an interest for him. Where 'a Hindoo baby' (ibid., 79) has very much the same status and function as a 'stuffed canary' (ibid., 80) — which is to say it has become a curio, ornamental 'art' of the most trivial kind — remarks such as these become apposite in a way that goes beyond their speaker's intention:

> ' . . . Get your head well behind his [the stuffed alligator's] smile, Mr. Boffin, and you'll lie comfortable there . . . he's very like you in tone. . . .' (III, xiv, 580)

The very fact that by ordinary standards Venus proves not an out-and-out villain, a completely egoistic rogue like Wegg, and that he comes down on the side of honesty against his partner in crime, could show him for a still more damning representative of the bourgeois morality in this phase of modern capitalist development — again, on the classic socialist view. Keeping a shop that deals in death, cherishing its darkness (his eyes shun the light), evidently asking not too many questions about the provenance of some of his work-materials, he is personally gentle, not indecent by certain measures; but his whole economic and personal interest is absorption in a life which is essentially necrophiliac. Yet we are asked to believe that his role is ultimately not that of an accomplice in the cash-nexus morality. With the implications alone of the articulator's shop and its alligator's head, Dickens himself has given us the rectitude of Boffin, as Venus helps the 'worm of the hour' outwit the other 'Friendly Mover', in no flattering manner. But he patently endorses Venus's later part in the story as honesty *tout court* rather than a subtle, if unconscious, switch of allegiances between participating in one mode of cash-worship and in another. When the taxidermist alerts the seeming flinty miser to his danger from Wegg's scheme, we are asked, unreasonably, to believe and applaud. But what feature is there in Venus's character and situation, as developed up to this time (III, xiv), to make us find it representative and likely in him — out of *his* world, which is so much of the essence of its total ugly environment — to be honourable in such a fashion? A piece of authorial legerdemain has substituted a new, more scrupulous character for the original Venus of I, vii.

Dickens might for that matter have made Wegg a truly ominous figure, boding ill in a much more dangerous, even frightening way, as indeed he seems to have been half inclined to do:

> For Silas Wegg felt it to be quite out of the question that he could lay his head upon his pillow in peace, without first hovering over Mr. Boffin's house in the superior character of its Evil Genius. Power (unless it be the power of intellect or virtue) has ever the greatest attraction for the lowest natures; and the mere defiance of the unconscious house-front, with his power to strip the roof off the inhabiting family like the roof of a house of cards, was a treat which had a charm for Silas Wegg. (III, vii, 501)

But Wegg is hardly able to strike us as an 'Evil *Genius*' when we are shown so early in his plotting the folly with which he has 'over-reached himself . . . by grasping at Mr. Venus's mere straws of hints, now shown to be worthless for his purpose' (ibid., 500— 1) or the easy competence of insight with which Boffin sizes up and dismisses the hopefully predatory Lammles (IV, ii). Indeed Father Shea has advanced the theory that the introduction of Venus and his shop sidetracked Dickens's original intention, a more impressive one than what that critic finds actually worked out.[27] This in his view was to protray not only Wegg but also either the Lammles or the Veneerings (more probably the former) making an attempt upon the Golden Dustman's fortune; an attempt which presumably, in its beginnings at least, was to have known some success. Given the actual progress of the novel as we have it, 'The vision of Mrs. Boffin's "Fas'nable Society" scrabbling for "coal-dust, vegetable-dust, bone-dust, crockery-dust, rough dust and sifted dust — all manner of Dust", could no longer be actually dramatized; it could only be implied.'[28]

So that some things in *Our Mutual Friend* are left undone, unestablished; others are overplayed. In the Wilfer family there are all the 'ingredients' for an extension of the novel's meanings; Mrs Wilfer's style of pride, her 'Lavvy's' sort of impositions, are significantly congruent with the values we meet in the Veneering circle or even in the boasts of Rogue Riderhood (his 'sweat of an honest man's brow' claim). They provide an importantly realised context for Bella's motives to have risen out of; they embody the money-dilemma of the novel as a whole (wealth means corruption, but the lack of it means unhappy constraints) in a difficult complicated way that we need to encounter, i.e. outside environments almost exclusively unsympathetic. Mr and Mrs Boffin visit them to solicit Bella's removal into their guardianship (I, xix). Bella visits them from time to time (e.g. II, viii; III, iv). Bella visits her father in the City (III, xvi) and ultimately makes him an accomplice to her wedding at Greenwich (IV, iv). The reader is in fact always visiting these people; but at no point do they step out of their place on the margin of the action and its significance. By contrast we could recollect the part of the Peggotty family in *David Copperfield* to see how little the Wilfers 'earn' the amount of coverage and treatment they receive at the author's hands. What they have to tell us about shabby gentility is useful but limited and this is rendered up on our first acquaintance with them (I, iv).

It is of a piece with these deflections of significance that the novel is a field for polemics which yet dissipates the passions of polemic. In the High-Society scenes of *Our Mutual Friend*, for example, we are offered an account of a human group in which no real principle of community consists: it is a sort of fatuous echelon or *corps de ballet* which is instinct with dullness, with intellectual and moral vacuity; its very rituals oppose generous and feeling values. Veneering claims everybody for his oldest friend but really has no friend at all. Lady Tippins goes to the Lammle wedding-breakfast because 'she has a reputation for giving smart accounts of these things, and she must be at these people's early, my dear, to lose nothing of the fun' (I, x, 118). To Podsnap other people are either extensions of his personality licensed by him (II, iv, 253) or they are objectionable entities to be thrust out of sight and mind.

Such figures ought to be capable of alarming us, as their equivalents certainly are elsewhere in Dickens. The issues expressed in the story of the Harmon dust-mounds, along with Dickens's open raillery against the traffickings of the stock-market (at the beginning of I, xi), ought to assist in constituting a sustained indictment of the economy and society under review. The trouble is that we can be thoroughly right-minded about the practices permitted under the 'New' Poor Law, for instance, as is the author in his *Postscript (in lieu of preface)*. Yet that angry postlude, for all its historical justification, does not rescue his book's actual achievement, cannot retrospectively reinstate the kind of fierce indignation which his earlier works made so to rage in us but which this novel has failed to awaken. Edgar Johnson offers what is a recurrent account of the tale in finding in it a social criticism bleaker than ever before.[29] The author certainly purports to be flaying the opulent inhumanity of the governing stratum and the standards of the finance capitalists. But, while he exposes for entirely worthless (and joyless) the very social fruits as established in 'Society' for which thousands are forswearing the ties of man with man in this observed Victorian rat-race — and such are evidently his conscious intentions — much of the cutting-force of the satire and caricature that are present in these scenes is dissipated in the action.

There is no want of aggravating criminality in Podsnap's replies to the challenges of the 'stray personage of meek demeanour' at his dinner-party (I, xi). But our sole experience of his actual social operations, whether as a 'Marine Insurer' or anything else, is to find him collaborating with Mr Twemlow to rescue his innocent (if dim) daughter Georgiana from the clutches of a couple of fortune-hunting rogues (the Lammles). In the process both men thwart the marriage-for-money scheme of Fledgeby — *the* master-usurer of this whole fictional canvas, who, with his combination of weakness and meanness, ought to be portentous and threating enough. For we are willing to believe that the tribe in which the counters of exchange have become autonomously important to the extent shown here lays itself most open to the brutish propensities symptomatised by the worried sexlessness (his continual feeling for an unincipient moustache), the feeble jaw, small puny build and ratty little eyes of the vicious money-lender. But we hardly find the real 'Pubsey and Co.' persecuting anyone other than members of the irresponsible high society — except Mr Riah, whose collusion in his employer's detestable practices is an artistic weakness of a much simpler kind: it is not credible.

In fact to our considerable relief Fledgeby draws the sting of the Lammles, and they, representative as they are of the dire upper-class parasitisms, assist in foiling those of his cruelties which deserve no tolerant ackowledgement — to Riah and Twemlow — before they depart for their dreary punishment of a future in Calais.

Much of the detail in the 'Society' chapters supports the idea that this social stratum is thus continously turned in upon itself to become its own disablement and penalty. But a matrix of economic disorder of which the principal observation is that it is self-frustrating rather than anything else hardly arouses in us the degree or kind of moral outrage which *Little Dorrit*'s account of the *beau monde* stimulated. Indeed, this incoherence of the parts expresses itself still more radically because, for all that John Harmon's earlier history is instinct with highly charged meanings, there is little which at the level of plot or story interweaves that tale with the practices of Fledgeby, the difficulties of Mr Riah or his dolls'-dressmaking friend. What Fledgeby is and what his business undertakes *is* all-symptomatic of the social world Harmon must cope with in returning home. But Dickens's failure to make the various elements of his narrative tell through one another by being brought into more organic relation (so that, to remain with this example, the Harmon and Fledgeby stories are not further developed and illumined by really intermeshing at any stage) is nearly absolute.

Just as there is no visible connection between Fledgeby's spider-like dealings behind the community scene and the finances of Jenny Wren (in fact he agrees to her buying some of her work-material cheap at his counting-house), so, though some of Veneering's guests are offered to us as quintessential representatives of the mushrooming finance capitalism, we see neither 'the Contractor, who is Providence to five hundred-thousand men', nor 'the Genius of the three hundred and seventy-five thousand pounds, no shillings and no pence', nor any other associate of these scenes perpetrate violation — direct or indirect — in the careers of, say, Lizzie Hexam and her like, wholly committed as the 'Stucconians' are to money values. Lady Tippins hardly stirs up anything like the degree of anger in us with which we would react if the results of her enterprise in canvassing for Veneering and helping to establish a circumlocutionary Parliament of monstrous apathy were more substantially concreted. We never actually behold Mrs Higden assaulted by the indignities of the workhouse existence for which that Parliament is responsible, by contrast with the degraded Old Nandy of *Little Dorrit* (I, xxxi) — nor is Podsnap seen to harass her. The 'Society' personages and the administrative ranks they form are ugly enough; but like the Wilfers they are outside the action of the book. (This, by the way, was the primary criticism of the 'social chorus' chapters made by E. S. Dallas in his contemporary review of *Our Mutual Friend*, in *The Times* for 29 November 1865.[30] The 'social chorus has no connexion with the tale in which we are interested and is of importance only as representing the view of society on the incidents of the story as it comes before them'.[31] This was the notice, we must remember, which Dickens admired so much, in spite of these caveats, that he made the quite exceptional gesture of presenting its author with the manuscript of his novel.[31])

In fact we are hardly shown the life of the poor as primarily a matter for concern at all. The emphasis in down-town London is on its dirt, its ugliness and its criminality – however comically presented:

> All things considered, therefore, Pleasant Riderhood was not so very, very bad. There was even a touch of romance in her – of such romance as could creep into Limehouse Hole – and maybe sometimes of a summer evening, when she stood with folded arms at her shopdoor, looking from the reeking street to the sky where the sun was setting, she may have had some vaporous visions of far-off islands in the southern seas or elsewhere (not being geographically particular) where it would be good to roam with a congenial partner among groves of bread-fruit, waiting for ships to be wafted from the hollow ports of civilization. For sailors to be got the better of were essential to Miss Pleasant's Eden. (II, xii 351)

The discourse there is complicated and deserves a long page of analysis. But we may remark as the most dominant of its intimations an ironic tone which is rather happy than anfractuous; though the humour here would have to be more astringently satiric, less felicitiously easy, if this passage were sustaining a really keen-edged social criticism.

It *is* comic in this way exactly because 'sailors being got the better of' is something of which we do not have to take the humanly painful measure here or elsewhere. The only mariner we know to have been imposed upon, at these Limehouse premises, is Harmon-Rokesmith, whose drugging in Pleasant's shop, followed by his attempted murder, he has taken as a heaven-sent opportunity to develop his scheme for putting his position in the world altogether to the test. Later, when he approaches the hovel again (in II, xii), with the purpose of playing another part and clearing Jesse Hexam's memory of slander, it is *his* imposing upon them that is wholly successful.

Out in the country the concern of the rural folk for the wandering Betty Higden is limited, and faintly adumbrated. Her fears of being at large in a hostile world are perversely justified, not at the hands of wealthy or socially elevated extortioners, administrative boards or pauper wards, but by Rogue Riderhood, another member of the working classes (if he can be said to work). There is no indication of the clientele at the 'Six Jolly Fellowship Porters' being commercially or otherwise exploited in their daily lives. It is rather the case that Miss Potterson, who is after all a solitary spinster, has to exert the force of a powerful personality upon them in order not to have the hospitality of her tavern abused (I, vi, 60–6, *passim*). Three of the local community are ultimately proven murderers (of John Harmon as they thought, of the Third Mate actually); those who are unemployed Dickens never expatiates upon (i.e. as being in need of help to work, unlike Plornish the plasterer in *Little Dorrit*), and the scavenging portion of the riverside fraternity all dwell under permanent suspicion of earning their money in a very dark way, not out of sheer necessity but out of unwholesome tradition. From the first Lizzie Hexam has made it clear to us that her father could have got a different job (as, for example, in I, iii, 30, paragraph 5).

If we ask why all this material 'defaults', as it were, I think we find our answer in the novel's nearly unqualified success: the sustained and largely uncompromised portrait of Bradley Headstone. In the schools where people of his kind, like Charley Hexam, have 'first learned from a book' (II, i, 214), the Bible has all representatively been converted from being a universal compendium of vitalising history and poetry (and therefore a great enablement of thought) – the whole education in itself which it was for so many poor people in Bunyan's generation – into a means of further enslavement to the orthodoxies and delinquencies of the age:

> For then, an inclined plane of unfortunate infants would be handed over to the prosiest and worst of all the teachers with good intentions, whom nobody older would endure. Who . . . for a moral hour . . . [would be] drawling on to My Dearerr Childerrenerr, let us say, for example, about the beautiful coming to the Sepulchre; and repeating the word Sepulchre (commonly used among infants) five hundred times, and never once hinting what it meant.
>
> . . . . The adult pupils were taught to read (if they could learn) out of the New Testament; and by dint of stumbling over the syllables and keeping their bewildered eyes on the particular syllables coming round to their turn, were as absolutely ignorant of the sublime history, as if they had never seen or heard of it.   (Ibid., 215)

This is important; exceptionally, it does relate to what we are shown at Mr Podsnap's dinner party (I, xi). Given that at least officially the

New Testament carries with it the ultimate sanctions, the final power to proscribe or endorse behaviour in Mr Podsnap's culture, we may well ask how he can vindicate the *status quo* which is challenged upon his 'hearthrug . . . among the heads of tribes assembled there in conference' by 'the stray personage of meek demeanour' (evidently the novelist himself who has entered his novel very thinly disguised; how would such an intelligence ever be invited to a Podsnap party in the first place?). When this antagonist mentions that 'some half-dozen people had lately died in the streets, of starvation', and asks, 'was dying of destitution and neglect necessarily English?', Podsnap is sincere in his terrible answer:

> 'And you know; at least I hope you know . . . that Providence has declared that you shall have the poor always with you?'
> The meek man also hoped he knew that.
> 'I am glad to hear it,' said Mr. Podsnap with a portentous air. 'I am glad to hear it. It will render you cautious how you fly in the face of Providence.'

What we are made to see is that knowledge itself is conceived in this polity as a closed system of established propositions fixed for all time with inert significances. In so far as various schools of political thought (of course powerfully backed by those with a vested interest in traditionalism) have authorised the view that such and such is the meaning of the St Matthew text, then that is taken to be its unquestionable intention. Thought and imagination, like Mr Podsnap's conception of the arts, are purposeful only in so far as they bring the achieved lifeless definites of these established propositions into mechanical and foreseen relations with each other; in so far as they are degraded, in effect, to being the Fancy of Coleridge's definition, not as they exert upon the dead counters of posited 'facts' the pressure of a fresh enquiry from a more alertly attentive, more 'esemplastic' kind of intelligence.

All this is exemplified in the dreadful-pathetic Miss Peecher and her Mary Anne, for whom conversation is a set of grammatical rules (II, i, 220—1) and geography is 'a refresher of the principal rivers and mountains of the world, their breadths, depths and heights' (ibid., 221), rather than what it ought to be for the school-children in her care: a study which relates to the degeneracy, under the ill-planned spreading sprawl of the new suburbia, of their own environment (ibid., 218).

Headstone experiences all these things as some of the conditions of a very personal imprisonment. His educational career has been the only way open to him of leaving the world of his orphan boyhood; and how cramped and brutish that world was we have made acquaintance with in the Gaffer's hovel and the London waterside low life. Charley Hexam's experience is evidently, and successfully, meant to represent to us the indigences of his teacher's earlier days and his present alternatives; what effectually he must return to if he cannot maintain his current position. But we have equally been shown what it costs in human, imaginative terms, this sole enfranchisement out of inured pauperdom into his role first as student and then pedagogue in an education-system of which the fundamental concepts mate with the lucidities of the Podsnap drawing-room.

The death-in-life-like nature of those orthodoxies needs no further characterisation, but what they really mean in terms of human mutuality — something which after all Bradley is supposed to be seeking in its most intimate manifestations when he is anxious to make Lizzie Hexam his wife — is glossed for us in the final meeting of the teacher and his most 'successful' pupil:

> He looked at young Hexam as if he were waiting for a scholar to go on with a lesson that he knew by heart and was deadly tired of. But he had said his last word to him.

What that lesson is Charley immediately rehearses for this, the only human being other than his sister who has ever befriended him:

> 'It is,' he went on, actually with tears, 'an extraordinary circumstance attendant on my life, that every effort I make towards perfect respectability is impeded by someone else through no fault of mine! Not content with doing what I have put before you, you will drag my name into notoriety through dragging my sister's . . . and the worse you prove to be, the harder it will be for me to detach myself from being associated with you in people's minds. . . . However, I have made up my mind that I will become respectable in the scale of society, and that I will not be dragged down by others. . . .'   (IV, vii, 711–13)

Lizzie however is possessed of an attraction over the schoolmaster which is 'the ruin — the ruin — the ruin' of his old conceptual framework (395) and therefore the whole man's unmaking. The scene (II, xv) in which he begs her to marry him is very painful — and not principally on Lizzie's account. Harassed and distressed as she is there, she is able to think and speak clearly for herself. What stands out is that the lettered Bradley, whose life has been formed on educationists' models, cannot. In threatening Eugene at the height of his passion, he can only repeat his name. The point about language as control, organisation and even exorcism (of the passions, their creative direction) could not be more lucidly available to us: 'A worse threat than was conveyed in his manner of uttering the name' (i.e. with no verbally predicated intention of outrage) 'could hardly have escaped him' (ibid., 399). And the distress of watching these results of the National School discipline is surely aggravated by our sense of the treatment he has received at Wrayburn's hands. Headstone's demented attempt to murder the other man, in the wake of Eugene's airy heartless invitations to Mortimer Lightwood to 'Be a British sportsman, and enjoy the pleasures of the chase' (III, x, 543), becomes partly sympathetic, quasi-allowable. (This again helps to account, I think, for Dickens's not very convincing attempts to asperse the schoolmaster: with, for example, the repeated 'decent' which is used of him at his first introduction; the allegation that he has a dull heavy mind — nowhere substantiated by our experience of him; the reference to his being a 'passion-wasted night-bird with respectable feathers' and 'the worst night-bird of all' — where 'worst' is automatically a word we distrust as null and void, for being a passenger adjective in a key place (III, xi, 555). It must have been alarming to so passionate an advocate of law and order as Dickens to have developed a case which effectually endorses an attempted murder, but the crucial fact is that the author's language is inert when he is trying to alienate us from Bradley, and all alive when he is simply presenting him to us in an immediate way.)

Like John Harmon or Lizzie Hexam or Jenny Wren, Headstone is forced to work out his inward conflict in a fashion which can only be self-defeating. In bringing to extreme exposition his fraught rejection of the ethos of which he has himself so long been a professional mediator, he takes his difficulty to a point of impossible recoil, of now totally inhibited return, for with the act of Eugene's battering he puts himself outside society, casts off irrevocably the codes in which he has grown up. More importantly than anything the law can do to him in consequence, he cannot now (we feel), for better as well as worse, go back to his old way of seeing the world. Hence there are the double ironies running through Riderhood's later visit to the schoolroom:

'And a lovely thing it must be . . . fur to learn young folks wot's right and fur to know wot *they* know wot you do it.'   (IV, XV, 793)

The risk the Rogue takes in saying this consists not merely in hinting his dangerous knowledge of Bradley's guilty secret, but also in reminding the schoolmaster of the intellectual and ethical valueless-ness of his professional dealings. Of a like implication is the brilliant moment that follows when Riderhood amplifies his blackmail threat by invoking just that kind of catechism which stands for 'education' here:

'Oh! It's in the way of school!' cried Riderhood. 'I'll pound it, Master, to be in the way of school. Wot's the diwisions of water, my lambs? Wot sorts of water is there on the land?'   (Ibid., 794)

— as if 'the divisions of water' is an intelligent way of thinking about the 'seas, rivers, lakes and ponds' around us! Yet it is absolutely of a piece with the learning procedures of contemporary Academe, at least at this social level, and with the cramping rituals of thought intrinsic to the society of which they are a part.

But there is also another matter at issue. In Headstone's passion for Lizzie something is out of scale even with the urgencies themselves of an amorous monomania, and it would be comforting if, in the manner of older critics of his author, one could feel that the enlarged kinds of expression he makes to her concerning it (during II, XV) were the consequences simply of an artistic incapacity on Dickens's part to present the relations between the sexes, at their most powerful, convincingly.

Headstone's behaviour and what he says, which is painful because it is so *real*, strangely reminds one of the declarations that pass between the lovers in *Wuthering Heights*. The greater comprehends the less and I am not forgetting such moments as Heathcliff's battering his way out of the Thrushcross Grange of his tamer rival with (all symboli-cally) a poker, or suggesting that Bradley does not want to make Lizzie his mate in every way. Yet in the language of, for example, the comparably obsessed and assailed Phèdre of Racine, there is a through–running and predominating erotic imagery:

Soleil, je te viens voir pour la dernière fois . . . .

Dieux! que ne suis-je assise à l'ombre des forêts!

Quand pourrai-je, au travers d'une noble poussière,
Suivre de l'oeil un char fuyant dans la carrière . . . .

C'est Vénus toute entière à sa proie attachée . . . .

. . . je brûle pour Thésée . . .

and so on. Here in the case of the schoolmaster, who is also reduced to a state of physical illness (IV, xi, 749—51) and criminality by his passion, the various imagery is of impulses which find mind and body, as such, inadequate media for their expression. Jenny Wren describes him as 'a lot of gunpowder' liable to meet with 'lighted lucifer-matches', which implies energies and potential constrained within forms essentially alien to their nature and realisation (as is a wooden barrel which contains saltpetre).

He is frequently represented wearing clothes, particularly a collar, which will not fit him (e.g., II, i, 217), of being half-suffocated (II, xv, 398) or actually choking (IV, xi, 750). If this trait is merely a referent of his fettering within the imposed social norms, or a sort of character-isation (as it were of the simply 'bad', ungoverned will) that Dickens might have lifted out of melodrama, then it accords surprisingly closely and with realistic fittingness to the powerful scene in which Bradley has gone upriver to trail Wrayburn, has decided to murder him and lodges temporarily with the Rogue at Plashwater Weir Mill Lockhouse. The night he spends there is marked by a thunderstorm, which we take for the more expressive of the kind of primary, the literally elemental turbulence within the teacher because his outward form lies so unnaturally still upon his host's bunk (and it is worth noticing here again how Bradley 'had turned up the collar of the rough coat he wore . . . and had buttoned it about his neck . . . though it would have been much easier to him if he had unbuttoned it' — IV, i, 639.)

Earlier (ibid., 637—8) he has had a nose-bleed which, like his action at the time he asseverated his envious hatred of Wrayburn to Lizzie, suggests the blood itself within the man (and all the ideas of impulse which blood represents) chafing and fretting to be free of its limited bodily forms ('"Then," said he, suddenly changing his tone and turning to her, and bringing his clenched hand down upon the stone with a force that laid the knuckles raw and bleeding; "then I hope that I may never kill him!"' — II, xv, 382). And the mysterious, more or other than human, nature which Headstone has to contain is evidently expressed in the violent electric raging around him. Well may the schoolmaster tell Lizzie:

> 'No man knows till the time comes what depths are within him. To some men it never comes; let them rest and be thankful! To me, you brought it; on me you forced it; and the bottom of this raging sea,' striking himself upon the breast, 'has been heaved up ever since.' (Ibid., 396)

More than a world-old lovers' problem seems to be at issue: namely, that sexual intercourse itself does not afford a total identification of the participants one with another, an absolute interpenetration of their bodies and spirits. Headstone seems to have reached a level of impulse of which the sexual appetite is but a symptom. He desires Lizzie, it would seem, not so much with a carnal lust as as a medium whereby to free himself from the imprisonment of his human consciousness and limited corporeality.

> 'You know what I am going to say. I love you. What other men may mean when they use that expression, I cannot tell; what *I* mean is, that I am under the influence of some tremendous attraction which I have resisted in vain, and which overmasters me. You could draw me to fire, you could draw me to water, you could draw me to the gallows, you could draw me to any death . . . .'

That is the significant emphasis. And there is no more talk, in this second interview, of putting her through educational hoops to fit the kind of life on which his ambitions formerly have centred. Rather, in this same fraught episode which consists so much more of a passionate soliloquy on his part than of real interchange between them, we are told, ' "If I were shut up in a strong prison, you could draw me out. I should break through the wall to come to you. If I were lying on a sick bed, you would draw me up" ' – noticeably, not to kiss her, but ' "to stagger to your feet and fall there" '(ibid., 396–7). And we believe him; again, powers are in question quite outside the range of imaginably conjugal relations, energies the play of which the human in itself (*as* figurably *human*) let alone the social, can scarcely endure or survive. And this was surely the issue with regard to the Heathcliff and Cathy of 'The Heights'.

His answer to the tragic dividedness of human beings – separated not only by their moral inadequacy but also in being physically distinct — can only be made the more uncompromising and resolute by what he has come to perceive of the orthodoxies and entrenched codes of his age. But he stands for us, in the supremely powerful scene near the end where Rogue Riderhood insists he should marry Miss Peecher and put himself into a secure position to pay more hush-money in the future than otherwise will be at his disposal.

> 'She's nice-looking' [says the Rogue to him, in recommendation of this substitute bride] 'and I know you can't be keeping company with no one else, having been so lately disapinted in another quarter.'
>   Not one other word did Bradley utter all that night. Not once did he change his attitude, or loosen his hold upon his wrist. Rigid before the fire, as if it were a charmed flame that was turning him old, he sat, with the dark lines deepening in his face, its stare becoming more and more haggard, its surface turning whiter and whiter as if it were being overspread with ashes, and the very texture and colour of his hair degenerating.
>   Not until the late daylight made the window transparent did this decaying statue move. Then it slowly arose, and sat in the window looking out.   (IV, xv, 800)

Beside the power of such writing Dickens's earlier attempts to asperse Headstone show for the mere allegation they are. His first description of the schoolmaster as possessing

> the face belonging to a naturally slow or inattentive intellect that had toiled hard to get what it had won, and that had to hold it now that it was gotten. He always seemed to be uneasy lest anything should be missing from his mental warehouse, and taking stock to assure himself   (II, i, 217)

might work satisfactorily within the discourse of a George Eliot novel (it is remarkably like her rhetoric) but these remarks are insufficient and illegitimate, unrealised and unsupported by the characterisation which determines his actual presence for us in the larger course of the narrative.

The issue has gone far beyond and athwart all questions of social criticism. The success of the portrait of Bradley Headstone as we have it — not as Dickens seems occasionally inclined to try and edit it — subverts what the rest of the novel is talking about, at least in the

stories of its other major protagonists. Its chief intimation is that the
energies represented by the storm or his nose-bleed or the sort of
imagery he uses in conversing with his beloved are the bedrock of
personality as such, the sleeping Kraken which underlies all forms of
what we recognise as human living, whether humane or savage;
something essentially and primarily impersonal and peremptory,
more alien still, more opaque to the civilised imagination, than the
Freudian id. It suggests that an impulse for which our societal term is
merely 'the death-wish' lies at the bottom of human desires, and that
its gratification, when the individual is awake as Headstone has been
awoken, is the largest human fulfilment.

Riderhood's blackmailing is of a piece with the vista which
stretches before his victim, if he resumes his teaching role and
repudiates the authentic experience and severe value of his quite other
yearnings. The vile propositions that the Rogue puts to him are not
only an invitation to be harassed for life by the attentions of an
insatiable criminal (though that has a symbolic insistence of itself
about what a compromise with the social codes involves); it means
more still than compounding in all the important features of living
with the diplomatic and dispiriting, which over the course of the tale
Bradley has come to recognise for what they are.

The Headstone who can thus proleptically age in even contemplating such an accommodation is now resolutely committed to asserting
the most fundamental demands and needs as his experience has
revealed them to him — the need for the dispersion of these energies in
death. Albeit that the symbolically contained world of the Lockhouse
has a warming fire as well as a criminal population, and there is
nothing but cold and ooze beyond its window-panes in the storm
outside, Bradley's staring out of them and then his taking the lock-
keeper down with him into the mud at the bottom of the river is the
real measure of the only way he has found to refuse imprisonment,
not simply by the encompassing social ethos, but in this limited and
separating mode of existence itself which we call human life. The
raging elements or energies within can find their release only in that
kind of dissociation amidst their outward counterparts. His value as a
tragic-heroic figure is beyond that of any other personage in the
novel because he works through to the least compromised conclusion
his radically disturbing view of the human predicament.

And this other, transverse insight which is afforded us by
Headstone's part of the book is in a way supported by the novelist's
manner of looking at the physical environment. The brightness of

Dickens's typical intuitions, we come to note, has fallen from the very air he now beholds.

III

Contrasting the first (vi, 65–6) with the later description in *Dombey and Son* (xv, 217–18) of a district transformed by the coming of the railway, Humphry House has remarked,

> It is interesting to compare this reformer's admiration for what had been done with the plain delight of the earlier description of Camden Town in Chapter VI: the district had then just been rent by the first shock of the railway earthquake which produced 'a hundred thousand shapes and substances of incompleteness, wildly mingled out of their places'. The contrast is not between anything old and interesting and beautiful with the prosaic new which has replaced it, but between the process of change and the achievement. The process truly fascinated Dickens, the achievement merely wins sober moral approval . . . .'[32]

This needs some qualification, however. The material issue is that typically Dickens's energies as a writer are enlisted only where the new vista, like the old, contrives to suggest a larger, more imaginatively feeding environment for the human life within it than would be yielded by any mere catalogue of its various appurtenances. The old scene afforded a rich collection of wonderfully hetero-geneous and suggestively assorted objects; whether 'a chaos of carts, overthrown and jumbled together . . . topsy-turvy at the bottom of a steep unnatural hill', visible geologic strata, or broken-down fencing; while at the same time the author kept fully acknowledged and in view the penury of the place – that its fields were 'frowzy', its waste ground and neighbours alike 'miserable' (vi, 66). So here, in the treatment of the changed locality, the 'improvements' in terms of human need are set up in complex relation with its features considered as they make for nourishment of the life of the imagination. 'Bridges that had led to nothing, led to villas, gardens, churches, healthy public walks' – the latter is a token phrase, betraying factitious thought in that it does not enact its own health. But the train that has carried 'the carcases of houses' and 'shot away into the country' is no mere 'monster'. The ambiguous writing is richly so, for finding a

humanising quality in the environment in both cases. That the old
'Staggs's Gardens' has been able just to 'vanish from the earth' (xv,
217) means that the author sees equivalents in the very nature of the
district for the scenes and transformations which made *The Arabian
Nights* such favourite reading with him as a boy.[33] In chapter xv,
'palaces *rearing* their heads', 'granite columns of gigantic girth',
'warehouses crammed with rich goods and costly merchandise',
'comforts and conveniences all *springing* into existence' (emphasis
added) all witness to the scene's maintaining its inherent qualities of
the marvellous, the gratuitously fecund and liberating for the life of
the spirit which, according to one's view, Dickens uniquely tends to
discover or implant in most of his fictions' environments. (It follows
naturally, for instance, that in both the *Dombey* chapters, and without
strain, the locality is able to be personified as a comic *genius loci*, voiced
with the neighbourhood opinions.)

One of the leading characteristics of *Our Mutual Friend*, however,
is Dickens's inability to discover any such satisfactions in a landscape
very comparably affected by the progress of urban development. If
we look at the purlieus of the schools where Headstone and Miss
Peecher are instructors, this will plainly appear:

The schools — for they were twofold, as the sexes — were down in
that district of the flat country tending to the Thames, where Kent
and Surrey meet, and where the railways still bestride the market-
gardens that will soon die under them. The schools were newly
built, and there were so many like them all over the country, that
one might have thought the whole were but one restless edifice
with the locomotive gift of Aladdin's palace. They were in a
neighbourhood which looked like a toy neighbourhood taken in
blocks out of a box by a child of particularly incoherent mind, and
set up anyhow; here, one side of a new street; there, a large solitary
public house facing nowhere; here, another unfinished street
already in ruins; there, a church; here, an immense new warehouse;
there, a dilapidated old country villa; then, a medley of black ditch,
sparkling cucumber-frame, rank field, richly cultivated kitchen-
garden, brick viaduct, arch-spanned canal, and disorder of frowsi-
ness and fog. As if the child had given the table a kick and gone to
sleep. (II, i, 218)

The actual reference to *The Arabian Nights* in this later passage is
achieved like a currant stuck, however dexterously, into a Christmas

pudding by a deliberating chef. The spontaneous inward vitalising qualities Dickens has traditionally found in similar ambits — or, to put the matter otherwise, the stimulus such landscapes have afforded his imagination in the preceding novels — is here very noticeably curtailed. We are presented in fact, for all that his eye ranges over multifarious and incongruous features (an 'old country villa', a 'brick viaduct'), with a catalogue; each of the viewed objects suggests nothing but itself. The scene's ramshackle character is not presented as, for example, a congeries of partly independent life malignly encroaching on the human world, nor is its 'old country villa' possessed of the enfranchising qualities of some enchanted pleasure-house, or its 'arch-spanned canal' with the liberating dimensions of an Alhambran arcade.

Well may Edgar Johnson remark how 'London itself . . . has become for Dickens what it became for Henry Adams, a barren and stony desert . . . "a hopeless city, with no rent in the leaden canopy of its sky" [I, xii, 145]'.[34] As Johnson intimates, most of the scenes in the capital take place in darkness or gloom at a dismal time of year. There is particularly little description, for any Dickens work, of sunlight, fresh air, renewing Nature, successful (artistically) or otherwise; of any pastoral scene not radically qualified in its character of restorative by the presence of danger or affront (like Mrs Higden's in III, viii, or Wrayburn's in IV, vi). Yet the London of Messrs Nickleby, Dombey or Dorrit was really just as alien a polis by any traditional standards of the acknowledged greenwood. The point is that its dust here is little but mere dust to the author. A promisingly irrational suburban environment he can no longer experience as extra-ordinary in a very literal sense; it has simply become a chaos of 'dilapidated villas, unfinished streets, warehouses, rank fields, black ditches and brick viaducts'. Gone is the perception of such phenomena as constitutive of their own weird, parodic and satisfying civic pastoral, Dickens's spontaneous valleys and grots of jumbled bricks, soot and mortar. The paragraph beginning 'That mysterious paper currency . . .'(I, xii, 144), a famous passage on the scrubby litter of the metropolitan streets, is challenging writing but it is so just because it does not imply the presence behind the objects viewed, or, comprehending them, of a larger reality in which the paper, the wind and dust have a more than one-dimensional character. Indeed there surfaces here a sense of the natural order as unable of its nature to be brought into creative relation with the distinctively human (and therefore social) life within it (the following passage appears so gratuitously, it has still more the character of a determinative statement about the status of human life in the world as the author now sees it):

> The blast went by, and the moon contended with the fast-flying clouds, and the wild disorder reigning up there made the pitiful little tumults in the streets of no account.   (Ibid., 157)

Working against the grain of all that seam of the book which purports to engage with the problems *of* the social life — John Harmon's predicament and adventures, Lizzie Hexam and Eugene Wrayburn's (with Mortimer Lightwood), Messrs Fledgeby and Riah, Jenny Wren and Mr Dolls, the Boffins, Mrs Higden and so on — are intuitions which effectually invalidate it, depths sounded beside which any imaginable social intercourse or societal organisation must anyway appear a superficies of very limited satisfactions and meanings. Beside these intimations, it should not come as a shock to us so much as apparently it does to Johnson that the author can say of Riderhood's recovery from his near-drowning, in III, iii, isolated and fugitive as this 'outburst' may be considered,

> 'And yet — like us all, when we swoon — like us all, every day of our lives when we wake — he is still instinctively unwilling . . . to be restored to consciousness, and would be left dormant if he could.' [Ibid., 503.] *Like us all every day of our lives.* So far has life altered for Dickens since the sunny days when Mr. Pickwick was 'begun in all his might and glory'[35] that he now takes it to be beyond all doubt that only reluctantly do men each day return from sleep to waking.[36]

Yet while we can notice how these two elements of the novel are not integrated, that the author's half-assays at making them harmonise are unsuccessful — the weak endings of the lovers' stories, the unconvincing attempt at criminating Headstone — we have equally to acknowledge a strength, suppleness and activity in the prose of the 'social chorus' scenes, as in those episodes' characterisation, with which the notion of a divided intention or unfocused creative idea is not easily compatible. However much the writer may have been confused elsewhere in *Our Mutual Friend*, what seems to be almost supremely present in these chapters is authorial control itself, the Zeus-like detachment and authority of the observing eye and voice that specially comes into play in these scenes.

None of the personages there to be met with are like Squeers or Quilp, Chadband or Pecksniff, Mr Micawber or even Mr Sapsea. In opinions Sapsea is doubtless the same kind of 'old Tory jackass'[37] as Mr Podsnap. But *Edwin Drood*'s auctioneer also has unconsciously creative flights of imagination (such as the epitaph on his wife's gravestone) which, supremely, individualise him. It must have come as small surprise to the first readers of Forster's *Life* to find that Dickens had seen his way to developing Sapsea's part and function in the novel simply by making him perform in the classic way. I refer to the left-over sheets of manuscript, 'How Mr. Sapsea Ceased to be a Member of the Eight Club'.[38] The more he expresses by simply being, acting himself, the more interesting he becomes because his converse continually greets us with the fresh surprising inventions of a unique imbecility. Podsnap, by contrast, is quintessentially representative – his converse is 'the articles of a faith and school' (I, xi, 129). Possibly he is so egregious and extreme an embodiment of those tenets as almost to tremble into becoming a 'Dickens character', but we cannot say the same of the people who take the floor with him. Lady Tippins, Veneering and Mrs '(wife of Member of Parliament)' (II, xvi, 411), Boots and Brewer, and so on are in themselves boring, not only the repositories of an empty creed and bad values but also imaginatively unstirring. If *they* were to perform themselves for us, tell us their life-story or express their opinions in their own language at any great length, we should throw the book away in disgust at its dullness. Dickens takes them over as seemingly very unpromising materials and – as it were by an enormous deliberate act of intellectual pantomime – turns them into a sort of fantastic ballet of comic relief. There is a real sense in which the 'Society' scenes of *Our Mutual Friend* are interpolations to provide the reader with refreshment between the almost unalleviatedly serious discourse of the surrounding text.

Indeed, Lady Tippins appears more an ally than a threat:

More carriages at the gate, and lo, the rest of the characters. Whom Lady Tippins, standing on a cushion, surveying through the eye-glass, thus checks off: 'Bride; five-and-forty if a day, thirty shillings a yard, veil fifteen pound, pocket-handkerchief a present. Brides-maids; kept down for fear of outshining bride, consequently not girls, twelve and sixpence a yard, Veneering's flowers, snub-nosed one rather pretty but too conscious of her stockings, bonnets three pound ten. Twemlow; blessed relief for the dear man if she really was his daughter, nervous even under the pretence that she is, well may he be. Mrs Veneering; never saw such velvet, say two thousand pounds as she stands, absolute jeweller's window, father must have been a pawnbroker, or how could these people do it? Attendant unknowns; pokey.'   (I, x, 119)

Here the 'horrible old . . . relict' affords a witty description of the Lammle wedding-party as a theatric charade by a band of partly pathetic, partly grim, considerably laughable actors, which is exactly analogous to Dickens's whole treatment of her and her fellows in these chapters. She makes the same syntactical gestures without predicates, participial phrases suspended from a sort of enjoyed contumely; this tone itself is delivered out of a sense of *déjà vu* by one who is supposed to be a typical and absolute adherent of the meaningless social round here observed. So complicated a mode of rejection − this modifying of the tedious, sterile and hypocritical by a rhetoric that affords them real interest, real attraction as pleasantly humorous − is at once taken up in the author's own closely imitative account of the aftermath:

Ceremony performed, register signed, Lady Tippins escorted out of sacred edifice by Veneering, carriages rolling back to Stucconia, servants with favours and flowers, Veneering's house reached, drawing-rooms most magnificent. Here, the Podsnaps await the happy party; Mr. Podsnap, with his hair-brushes made the most of; that imperial rocking-horse, Mrs. Podsnap, majestically skittish. Here, too, are Boots and Brewer, and the two other Buffers; each Buffer with a flower in his button-hole, his hair curled, and his gloves buttoned on tight, apparently come prepared, if anything had happened to the bridegroom, to be married instantly.   (Ibid., 119−20)

And if these quotations are sufficient to remind us of the recurrent note of the narrative tone in the 'social chorus' pages, we should find it all the more significant that Lady Tippins herself, that representative figure at the Establishment boards, has been allowed in fact to become Dickens's partner in a kind of intellectual exercise *in vacuo*; to affect us, at least, very differently from either her earlier avatar, Mrs Skewton, with her menacing vanities in *Dombey and Son*, or that portentous 'Ghoule in gloves', Mrs General, the embodiment of frightful meanings in *Little Dorrit*. In this book Dickens himself no less than

Lady Tippins comes to such events as the Lammle nuptials essentially in order to give 'smart accounts of things, and . . . must be at these people's early . . . to lose nothing of the fun' (ibid., 118).

This may well sort with the failure of a fully engaged concern about the quality of living and thinking among the governing classes of society. Death, the dispersion of the creative human energies upon which their negligence preys, has been found those energies' ultimate fulfilment anyway. But there hardly seems to be any deliberate connection between the nature of the author's attention to these figures on the one hand, and his intimations in the treatment of Bradley Headstone on the other. Where his interest in the Veneerings *et al.* appears to be repaid is in providing him with the means to enjoy a (complicated) exercise of wit. Rather than extending his account of anything else the novel has shown us — unless indeed it is for these chapters that he can be said to have written his book — it is as if the only celebrations that are now self-validating are those of the alert intellect animating its fellows with exhibitions of its range and powers in and for themselves. For this semi-parodic account of the expectable, uninventive, devitalised rituals of the upper classes, has set out its full view of such people and their principles within a chapter; in a sense, within its first page. There is no question here of Dickens's stepping forward and presenting *de novo* his vision of 'Society' and its pretensions or motives as in the past. Not only does the novel's plotting largely fail to substantiate imaginatively the case against these hypocrites and parasites; it is as if the cryptic utterance of these scenes itself serves notice that the author has now settled for a readership of cognoscenti, a 'happy few' whose intellects, being alert like his own and in his own way, make the enforcement of such recognitions unnecessary. The style of address emphasises the monotony of the persons and the vapidity of the *mores* observed. But it also suggests that, if the rest of the world, the larger audience, has as it were at this date to be newly shown or persuaded of the negations inherent in these leading ambits of the contemporary social organism, then the author's Muse is out of patience. In such a case the larger audience is unworthy of a more public self-explanatory utterance; it lies anyway beyond any benefits which the old kind of accessibility of meaning his work offered might mistakenly have been presumed to confer.

In fact few of the original reviewers made the appropriate recognitions. The 'social chorus' chapters were lambasted in the periodicals almost without exception, as caricature both heavy and vacant. The exception was the *Eclectic and Congregational Review* for November 1865. Otherwise the opinions of the *London Review* of 28 October and of the *Saturday Review* of 11 November 1865 are representative. The *Westminster Review* considered the wit of the Podsnap chapter (I, xi) painfully heavy: 'Quid hinc abest nisi res et veritas?'[39] Some of this was the Tory thundering that dogged all of Dickens's creations from *The Chimes* onwards; and Liberal exasperation too with a man who, on the view of the Reform side of politics, refused to allow that things were changing for the better. But E. S. Dallas in his highly favourable notice claimed that the novel's readership was 'perplexed' by this aspect of the tale, and suggested that at least half the reason why the sales dropped impressively between the first and second numbers was that the treatment of these Society folk – for whom he had no good word himself – was alienating in a simple imaginative sense, was artistically bewildering.[40] The significant fact is that, after the steep fall from an initial circulation which had exceeded even his publishers' high expectations,[41] Dickens took no steps to remedy it with any change of treatment or tone in the High-Society phase of the novel, following its introduction in I, ii and iii, in the first number.

Of course some of the earlier Dickens imagination still persists in this work, the more typical idioms of his vision. So far I have strayed into almost letting this aspect of *Our Mutual Friend* go by default. But there is, to name one instance out of several, the wonderful scene in which Silas Wegg is reading to Boffin and Venus about misers, and the two Friendly Movers, after the brilliant sexual image of Wegg's wooden leg 'gradually elevating itself more and more' under the table, both fall into a 'kind of pecuniary swoon' (III, vi). As usual with Dickens's richest humour, the comic vision there is at one with the most attentive kind of ethical discrimination. Simultaneously we are made to recognise and reject, and are hilariously freed from, the equivalence by these two men of the one kind of fulfilment with the other.

There is the marvellous blotched epergne on Mr Podsnap's table, announcing boastfully to his dining guests, 'Here you have as much of me in my ugliness as if I were only lead; but I am so many ounces of precious metal worth so much an ounce; – wouldn't you like to melt me down?' (I, xi, 131).

The answer is emphatically, no, we wouldn't; not for the world. The hideous ornament testifies so egregiously to its own fatuity – i.e. that of its owner – as to be a wonderful insult to him in the very heart of this camp of the enemy; a fine representative reproof, a rich witness to the un-melt-downable nature of the opposing truth, which is the value of beautiful things being not amenable to monetary measurement.

Likewise the Snigsworth engraving which we meet at III, xvii, 620:

> Mr. Twemlow's little rooms are modestly furnished, in an old-fashioned manner (rather like the housekeeper's room at Snigsworthy Park), and would be bare of mere ornament, were it not for a full-length engraving of the sublime Snigsworth over the chimney-piece, snorting at a Corinthian column, with an enormous roll of paper at his feet, and a heavy curtain going to tumble down on his head; those accessories being understood to represent the noble lord as somehow in the act of saving his country.

The peer in question is of course only a lightly characterised entity on the very edge of the novel. Nevertheless, such as it is, his figure embodies those values which in the social world at large depress the intelligent, the sensitive and the humane. Hurtful governing-class vanities are what Dickens is tilting at in this and the other offered images of him; but our laughter is modified in any propensity to harshness or strain at such a point, because the more and less than human in the world is shown refusing to collaborate with his outlook, representative as it is of the insanity of Snigworth's whole social group.

Plainly (to put the point with a laboriousness precisely missing from the felicitous original) the Corinthian column is not the least bit affected, as his tenantry might have good cause to be, by his snorting. He can defeat and destroy the values this ancient monument suggests, he can expurgate its own loveliness and the style of thought and achievement, higher and nobler than anything for which he stands, that it signifies. But it is not going to bow down to him, this stele, or compromise itself. He cannot refute it. Likewise the 'heavy curtain' is going to extinguish his enormous gesture of superiority in importance, domination, glorious opinions (*et cetera*); a gesture of which the whole 'full-length' engraving is itself the embodiment. Thus the native gormlessness of his attitude, expressed in his posture, is made its own refutation; his destructive arrogance is repaid with interest by the figure it makes him cut in this most self-regarding likeness. There is real cause, then, for thanksgiving *here*; as we shall feel with a deep breath after studying the effects of Victorian class-snobberies or 'respectability' on the careers of Bradley Headstone and Lizzie Hexam.

But that is not all. Snigsworth *is* 'sublime' as well as supremely stupid. At whatever pitch the reader may receive these intimations, the ancient pillar is also a monument to the passing of all civilisations; the heavy curtain is the curtain of death which must extinguish the good as well as the parasitic. Any posture which ignores our mortality or the evanescence of all our works after us, be they never so fine, is scarcely an attitude of full attention in the face of things. In certain cases it might support a philosophy criminally irresponsible. There are names in history more resoundingly redolent of vast achieved cruelties and abominations than Lord Snigsworth's, who have had their big schemes for a permanent cultural achievement, an impression upon the living human clay which was designed to be ineffaceable. But the insouciance here under review (as we have seen, the object of comic remark for its inert fatuity of outlook) is surely a measure of human dignity too. If our lives are to accrete values and achievements at all, what response are we to make to death which *doesn't* take a lofty line with it, a sense of our individual selves being exempt from its snuffing − and cleansing − operations? (That also, as we have acknowledged, is clearly part of what is registered here with a beautiful un-self-trammelling complexity.) 'The ogre will come in any case', said Joyce, but the posture of this poltroon as the ogre waits to drop on him is in its symbolically *human* aspect its own vindication. It is our triumph, the more satisfying in that its totally unconscious type of heroism is expressed in the very stance which protrudes all Snigsworth's destructivenesses as a representative personage. Thus it may be said that one of the most vacant discreative figures met with in the tale attests all unconsciously matters which make for a delight in us that has no trivial level of operation.

But in *Our Mutual Friend* such affirmations are fugitively afloat in an unrelated medium. The felicities of the writing in the 'Society' scenes arise from Dickens's having reduced all their action and talk to a parody of itself, a slightly surrealised pantomime; indeed, there are several places where it is as if the action is going forward on a television screen and he has leaned forward and switched off the sound, in order to show the essential inanity of these people's movements and customs. Such a case is the following; yet, when the author talks of Podsnap's guests as 'bathers' in 'haunch of mutton vapour bath' (I, xi, 134−5) after his daughter's birthday dinner, a stubborn reader may legitimately query, 'But what do such images signify, politically – socially – in any connection? What does the bathing metaphor tell us? And are people the more readily to be conceived as proper objects of satire because they are bald or 'sleek-whiskered'?'

> There was not much youth among the bathers, but there was no youth (the young person always excepted) in the articles of Podsnappery. Bald bathers folded their arms and talked to Mr. Podsnap on the hearthrug; sleek-whiskered bathers, with hats in their hands, lunged at Mrs. Podsnap and retreated; prowling bathers went about looking into ornamental boxes and bowls as if they had suspicions of larceny on the part of the Podsnaps, and expected to find something they had lost at the bottom; bathers of the gentler sex sat silently comparing ivory shoulders.

We take the evident point, of course: that the pleasures of the powerful and great in this society are but sad poor pretences at such. Yet J. Hillis Miller's commentary is equally valid:

> What had been initially only a metaphor turns out to have overwhelmed the reality and transformed it into its own insubstantial mode of being. The result is a realistic scene whose triumph is to force us into an unrelieved tension between an attempt to imagine the naturalistic reality behind the words, and a recognition that there is no naturalistic reality anywhere here, only a verbal realm in which it is quite possible to have bathers in the drawing-room . . . .[42]

What is not in question is an attempt at perceiving the scene for some kind of intrinsic character of its own, which is 'out there' beyond the author's head. It is, rather, a self-gratification on Dickens's part, albeit apparently satiric in tone, which the reader has to recognise as a kind of intellectual callisthenics precisely because the 'irony' does not open itself to interpretation. We have lost sight of what the bald realities may be, which are supposed to be ironically animadverted.

So that we are given not even a dialogue reserved to the enlightened, but a private language which in the last resort is impermeable. The wryness of these chapters, their terser address, had done more even than to serve notice of a possible authorial impatience with *us* (the more clearly when such a tone is sustained through the entire scene in which Mrs Lammle and Mr Twenlow are in fact sealing a disinterested errand of mercy – III, xvii). The author, in dominating these episodes so noticeably, as it were with a brilliant high-wire solo performance, has entirely obscured his own position and identity.

The portrait of Twemlow will serve as a simple instance of this. In different chapters we are shown him in different ways; whether 'deliberately' or not we could only say if we knew to what end. In I, ii he is a bewildered repository of the Veneerings' new-rich impostures. It appears to be his *innocence* which accepts dinner-invitations from them without questioning their way of life, or the means (shares-dealings) by which they have come to their wealth. Here he is a comic – pathetic victim, whose brain is alternately 'softened' and 'hardened' in its attempts to grasp the rationale of his hosts' apparently reasonless behaviour (ibid., 6 and 9, for example). In I, x it is with a gentle ragging that Dickens actually endorses 'the poor little harmless gentleman' as a fellow who has had romantic inclinations, who still has a large heart, and who failed in his own generous and disinterested love at an earlier epoch. Yet this considerably sympathetic characterisation moves out of focus when the paragraph closes, ' "No Adorable at the club! A waste, a waste, a waste, my Twemlow!" And so drops asleep, and has galvanic starts all over him' (ibid., 118). There we are moved off, at sudden speed, to regard him detachedly as a mere object, a kind of representative item in the exhibition of social beings whose stale expectable rituals make them contemptible. At one point he has a 'delicate and sensitive and tender spot behind [his] waistcoat' (II, xvi, 409); at another the emphasis falls towards the essential irresponsibility and inhumanity of a man who can find the talk on matters so humanly significant as he has just shared with Mrs Lammle an interference of no grateful kind with the apparently more important issue of his digestive processes (III, xvii, 624).

Who would be disposed to quarrel with either position? Both are just, as far as they go. Twemlow has his decencies and also his part as a collaborator among these higher ranks. His plea for true gentleman-liness at the end is both impressive and vitiated, one would have thought, by his sitting down to dine with such people in the first place. But we can hardly feel that seeing Twemlow whole, as it were in the deliberately ambiguous and complicated manner of a late Henry James fiction, is the sort of process this book has been written to subserve; not least because the other characters, John Harmon or

Silas Wegg, Lizzie or Eugene (for example), do not elicit that kind of observation. So that, with the case of this relatively minor but so subtly drawn portrait, we find ourselves ultimately in no position to know what it means. It is like the final word of the entire work, the 'gaily' on which Dickens concludes the last of his 'social chorus' episodes (IV, xvii), where it is not self-evident that Mortimer Lightwood has cause to repair to the Law Temple in that vein of spirits after the dinner-party at which his friend Eugene and Eugene's bride have been traduced. He has been gratified, certainly, by the support for decent values in Twemlow's outspoken utterance on their behalf at that so representative Establishment table, but it has been equally evident that Twemlow and he are a tiny minority; they shake hands at the end in their isolation. 'Gaily' is really a private word, intimating some hidden state of mind, on the part of Mortimer and his author alike, which the reader cannot penetrate.

It is the same altogether with the novelist's stance behind the chapters in which these people figure. Their characterisation collectively, each contrasting element in the prose, leaves us looking for the-truth-which-is-to-be-observed, the sought constatation of significance, as down an infinite hall of mirrors. Full control is implied in the sheer amount of authorial presence here, the remarkably supple, delightedly secure flexibility of the narrative voice, but not to any recognisable narrative purpose or thematic end.

Whatever the phenomenon means, one recognition we do bring away; that the features which predominate in *Our Mutual Friend* are the very reverse of those generally characteristic of Dickens's art. Here the emphases fall upon the attempt at the new life (with the Harmon-resurrection story) which (effectually) fails; upon death as welcome liberator for the intrinsic energies and tensions of the essentially human, seen as unhappily yoked; upon the primacy, as to value, of a creative world which is private to its author. There are hidden realities elsewhere in his novels, obscurities which are important, but they are not of this kind; i.e. that of an artist who has had supreme confidence in a fully public voice, now choosing to speak in public to himself. In the former works, indeed, the chief characteristic of the Dickens art has exactly been his authoritative handling of experience in a very accessible idiom, its confident intimation that the nature of experience is such that this public idiom, these tones as of a bard in a highly unified culture, are an appropriate measure to bring to it. Likewise that the new life is possible, and that the energies of the essentially human can be not only fleetingly invigorating, but also harnessed, in a fashion permanently delighting and self-justifying, to its realisation.

Discriminations as to the value of the alternative visions are pointless, at least from a critic. But we have the right to remark, in the case of *Our Mutual Friend*, Dickens's failure to make his material unify, and to ask whether that suggests, on his part, the quality of seeing life steadily and seeing it whole which so astonishingly informs his earlier productions.

2 *Bleak House:* The Hidden World

I

It is a representative problem we meet in reading *Bleak House* — representative of the book's rich method and achievement — that we find it hard to discover in the principal stories it tells us satisfactory 'objective-correlatives' for what we have been shown by the novel at large. Lady Dedlock's history seems to be the occasion for most of what appears. (Even Mr Chadband figures, ultimately, as the spouse of 'Mrs Rachel', the nurse who was a final connecting link in the trail of exposure Tulkinghorn traced between Sir Leicester's honoured wife and her secret unacknowledged child – see liv, 733.) And her tale is, of course, a deliberate and not unmoving reproach to the hypocritical ethics of Dickens's society, the false concepts of honour and fidelity prevailing there. But we have little sense of her predicament crystallising or precipitating the novel's meaning. We can only claim that at any given point it incorporates and qualifies all the work's other intimations, if we wilfully forget its failure to be of abiding import to us as we are actually immersed in the book.

The main reason for this is that the baronet's lady herself fails to engage our imagination. Her portrait has what, by any standard, are its patent successes. At her first appearance (ii, 8 ff.) her frozen reserve seems the outward expression of a full individuality pregnant with very interesting suppressions. With his initial account of the scenery at Chesney Wold mediated through her vision of it on a 'miry afternoon' when 'The adjacent low-lying ground . . . is a stagnant river, with melancholy trees for islands in it . . .' and 'The view from my Lady Dedlock's own windows is alternately a lead-coloured view, and a view in Indian ink' (ii, 8, 9); or with his repeated use, as narrator, of the forms of a punctilious etiquette ('My Lady Dedlock says . . . my Lady Dedlock has come . . .'), Dickens intimates an *ennui* which has for its centre a troubled consciousness that runs deep.

Our interest in the veiled life thus suggested is renewed on occasions
like the scene in chapter xl where the Dedlock family are gathered in
the gloaming of their ancestral seat and Lady Dedlock, looking
through the window, broods upon her wrongs at the hands of
Mr Tulkinghorn:

> The debilitated cousin supposes he is "normously rich fler.'
>
> 'He has a stake in the country,' says Sir Leicester, 'I have no
> doubt. He is, of course, handsomely paid, and he associates almost
> on a footing of equality with the highest society.'
>
> Everybody starts. For a gun is fired close by.
>
> 'Good gracious, what's that?' cries Volumnia with her little
> withered scream.
>
> 'A rat,' says my Lady. 'And they have shot him.'   (xl, 569)

And if Dickens by these means makes it possible for us to share as
irresponsibly, if not so salaciously, in the indulged curiosities of either
a Guppy or a Tulkinghorn, then it serves us right if we are
disappointed later in finding her story and nature so trite after all. This
would be appropriate indeed in a novel which goes as far in its efforts
to convict us and to convict itself – in certain respects – as I hope to
be showing further on.

Yet the convincing, imaginatively impressive Lady Dedlock
appears too intermittently and inconsequently to evoke a more than
tangential interest in her case. For all her other appearances, her ability
to have an independent inward life to show needs, finally, the
conviction of such episodes as, say, her interview with her daughter in
Chesney Wold Park at the time of Esther's convalescent stay in
Mr Boythorn's house. Here we are to meet the Honoria Dedlock of
her own conception, free – like Miss Flite with the 'wards in
Jarndyce' (iii), or Gridley with anybody – to give voice to the great
thought by which she is apparently possessed, her account of herself,
without social restraint. Yet there is nothing in this chapter which
does express a unique self. Her impassioned laments could be straight
out of a contemporary novelette; and it does not much mend the
matter to argue that, since Lady Dedlock has ruinously imaged her
life in the role of Fallen Woman as conceived by Victorian
respectability, this is appropriate. Not only has Esther's part as
colloquist in the scene also dropped out of the same fictional sphere,
but in addition the quality of language there in question is not
noticeably 'placed' in the rest of the book. ("O my child, my child, I

am your wicked and unhappy mother! O try to forgive me!" . . . "Dear mother, are you so resolved?"', and so on – xxxvi, 509–11).

An inimical reader (one, say, wearied by pleas on behalf of Dickens's lapses) might here insert the critical Morton's Fork of some such 'defence' as the following: 'Oh, but Dickens's imaginative failure with the Fallen Woman is recurrently a failure, as in this case, of performance. Lady Dedlock is clearly conceived to possess a centrality in the novel which its author hasn't the resources – morally, expressively – to substantiate. Yet we are after all, aren't we?, talking about the *intention* underlying *Bleak House*.'

I would rather acknowledge all that can be argued against the characterisation of Lady Dedlock. For the fault here in question is a *felix culpa*. On any straight view, the immateriality of her inward life is an artistic wound; but if it had not happened, Dickens would not (I believe) have written a work as profound as he has done. It is partly owing to the displacement of this personage – her character and her story – as the centrifugal interest of the whole, that something still better has come to pass than an (albeit excellent) novel of more restricted range and accountability.

This kind of failure is characteristic of the Dickens genius, and a frequent condition of the Dickens success; there are 'non-centres' of a sort in most of his novels. (In reading *Martin Chuzzlewit* do we really follow the development of young Martin's sentimental education – as such, as it affects him – with a panting absorption?) But if I choose to examine such a phenomenon as it operates here, in *Bleak House*, I do so not in any attempt to make some general theme (as it were running through the whole Dickens canon) appear. The 'device' of the unoriginating centre is used to other ends in the other novels. I am simply trying to show by reference to a specific case that Dickens's critical–creative instincts deserve a general environment of greater respect than can be said to accompany the debate upon his books even in our day; and that we can only critically acknowledge the significance of his achievements if we are willing to entail in our aesthetics of The Novel some conditions and qualities of performance that traditional criticism has tended to displace, and displace unjustly.

If, then, we do not hang breathless upon the gradual enchainment of the discovery of Lady Dedlock as Captain Hawdon's one-time mistress and as implicated in the murder of Tulkinghorn – if this compound interest is not our chief experience of the book as story and as fictive debate – how much more can be said for Esther

Summerson's part in it? On A. E. Dyson's view she has just this function; she is the magnetic pole of our imaginative involvement in *Bleak House* and the whole novel primarily constitutes (as we are to come to realise) an answer to her 'godmother's' attitude (iii) and to the question 'Esther Better Not Born?'[1]

Yet, if Dyson be correct, why does the book derive so little impact from what is, after all, its use of ancient and in themselves profoundly suggestive motifs: the story of the child who has lost (and who later finds) his/her true parentage, the consequences to the parents and the encompassing social organism of that discovery? Half the world's myths, most of its folklore, reverberate with these great themes. Yet their vibration in Dickens's book is really of the weakest. From the first, suspense is at a minimum. The hints of Esther's connection with Lady Dedlock are broad as early as the scene in the Dedlock church (xviii), or again during the younger woman's musing on the — to her — specially interesting features of her mother's appearance in chapter xxiii. When the truth is finally stated between them (xxxvi; cited three paragraphs back) it modifies neither the action nor the issues of the book, comes as no shocking revelation which reorients the very terms of the heroine's developing outlook. (Of course, for contrast we could cite Pip's situation in *Great Expectations* when he discovers the identity and purposes of his real benefactor.) The failure of this relationship to make a serious qualification of *Bleak House*'s case (I mean the novelist's whole world and train of thought as hitherto exhibited to us) expresses itself simply at the level of plot in the fact that there is nothing for Esther to do about her mother's embarrassed position, now or later, as both of them well recognise; nor is there anything Lady Dedlock can do for her. Dyson claims that by her very existence the younger woman constitutes a threat to her mother's security; and that this is the pivot upon which the novel's meanings hinge. Esther is certainly haunted by this fear (from xxxvi onwards). But we cannot be so haunted, for her position is in fact almost irrelevant. She could have died at birth for all that Tulkinghorn cares or ultimately needs to know about *her*. Certainly it is true that Mr Guppy first stumbles upon the trail of Lady Dedlock's 'guilt' by uniting her picture, at Chesney Wold and in Jobling's room at Mr Krook's, with Esther's likeness. In turn Mrs Snagsby has (un-wittingly) contributed some of *his* (Guppy's) perceptions in the affair to Tulkinghorn's store of suspicion and dangerous knowledge (see the recital of her 'wrongs' in liv). But the teeth of the trap the lawyer has been ready to spring upon his aristocratic client's wife have been many and various in their provenance, and we are never induced to suppose that, but for Guppy's part in the jigsaw of revelation, the solicitor's incriminative activities would have been confined to dim guessing. In fact the major items of Tulkinghorn's information are quite other than this knowledge of Esther's likeness to her ladyship; something he (like Sir Leicester) is never shown to remark. Yet, if Esther's mistaken sense of being a threat is crucial, why in that case does the author fail to dramatise his action around the question, 'Will Mr Tulkinghorn be still more dangerously empowered by discovering the present identity and whereabouts of Lady Dedlock's child?' Dickens never makes the possibilities for that kind of tension tell. Just as the lawyer is first apprised of Lady Dedlock's past not by anything Esther does or figures in but by the baronet's wife herself recognising a piece of her former lover's handwriting in Tulkinghorn's possession (ii), so likewise it is Hortense, not Esther, who finally forces the issue and provokes Lady Dedlock's long fatal flight, by murdering him. (We are never, for instance, made to wonder whether Esther has committed the deed – though on Dyson's reading she has as good a motive as her mother in having as cruel an anxiety to allay.)

All this subsumes into our larger general sense of not reading the novel essentially for its account of the changes in Esther's fortunes. We are very far from indifferent to them; the question is one of degree. Yet, as with her mother, it is difficult to look back on this book as *principally* the stimulus of an avid attention on the reader's part to her hopes, her interests, the registering of her vulnerabilities. Her childhood hardly takes possession of the reader's involvement in the manner of Copperfield's much longer (and more uncertain) juvenile adventures; nor is the rest of the novel the story of her adult life in the way that *Great Expectations* organises itself, for intensity of interest and direction of significance, all around the fortunes of the continuously developing hero of that later work.

Whether we account the offered occasion of *Bleak House*'s developments to be Lady Dedlock's, or Esther's history – or (the ultimate anti-plot or failed plot of the novel) the Jarndyce cause in Chancery (see the discussion of this below, pp. 100–11) – we find ourselves drawn by these stories into a world where behaviour can be observed, only to remain in an ultimate way inexplicable. These 'failures' in the accomplishment of Dickens's apparent enterprise – to tell us about the real inward Honoria Dedlock in a manner which will satisfy, to develop a tremendous yarn out of the closing phases of the egregious Jarndyce case, or to make Esther Summerson the great centre of the work's capacity to absorb and engage our interest – sort tellingly with the impermeability of most of the lives in the novel's world.

There is the capacity on the part of its well-intentioned characters to assimilate the delinquencies of their acquaintance. Mr Jarndyce accepts with the only stoicism possible – quiet indignation – the workings of Chancery. But confronted in other respects with palpable evidences of his society's sickness as a society – the plight of Jo or of the children of 'Coavinses', or meeting a domestic offence such as the fate of the Jellybys – he dematerialises these encounters with outrage by such devices as his 'East Wind', or his 'Growlery', tactics of indirection which would seem to relieve him from getting trenched down in open warfare with the general irresponsibility of his world. (The 'East Wind' trick obscures the authorship of the wrongs, his 'Growlery' dissipates *in vacuo* the energy of his righteous anger.)

We may go further, and hold him responsible for some of the ugliness. Skimpole is manifestly more destructive and cruel from within the security of John Jarndyce's patronage than ever he could be otherwise. Without Esther's guardian, arrest for debt would long before have diminished the ability of this 'innocent child' to prey upon others.

Caddy Jellyby has been brought up in a hard school. She needs no remonstrance as to the injustice of her mother's behaviour. But to the deadly origin of her husband's, and therefore her child's, tragic debility she is blind; blind, we may think, with a strange perversity. It is she alone who by sheer force of native intelligence and resolution has repudiated Mrs Jellyby's horrible irresponsibilities. Yet, no less than the infatuated Prince Turveydrop, she applauds and slaves to meet the demands of her criminally parasitic father-in-law.

To say that this blindness is the function of a self-distrust inculcated by her former experience of the parent–child relation would be generous enough and in another novel, as it were, probably appropriate. But here it is factitious. The gap is unexplained between the dotage of which Caddy is but too happy an admirer in the Turveydrop household, and the lucidities which have been radically and with conscious deliberation embodied in her clean break with her monstrous mother. Dickens does not suggest, with implications however fugitive, the essential cause of the discrepancy in Caddy's conduct.

A supreme example of these abdications of critical intelligence is the behaviour of Ada Clare. Inwardly no less harassed by Richard Carstone's profligacy of money and opportunity than his other relations, she effectually encourages him in his most ruinous courses, not least his fatal entry into the Chancery suit, by accepting his waywardness and becoming the principal apologist for his terms of reference with the rest of his friends; as if so intelligent a young woman could express true loyalty and love by adopting, in every point, the desperate fatuities of a person of inferior discrimination and will (recognised by her as such, no less than by Mr Jarndyce). Among all her fiancé's acquaintance (for he comes to anathematise their guardian's counsel) she is ultimately alone in possessing a real opportunity of compelling his application in a creative and hopeful career, rather than one which is visibly destroying him; and she must know this. She has simply to insist that he honour the original terms of the agreement made between them (xiii): namely, that Richard would first prove himself by steady application at a profession before claiming her hand. With her acquiescence in his mania, she seals his doom, her own (as a widow) and that of their child which is to be fatherless. And rationalisations after the fact – this is in fact what people do, a person can have all the right-minded views and yet not translate them into her own conduct – does not take account of the way in which Dickens withholds from us Ada's psychological history in the case.

There was no intelligible reason earlier, for that matter, why the Bleak House menage should not have been implacably horrified at Richard's very first suggestion of going into the law – given his propensity to be attracted to the 'family curse' as Jarndyce had already named it; still less, that that same guardian should arrange his apprenticeship with solicitors who are the reverse of hostile to the Chancery proceedings as flagrant denials of justice. It is the Lord Chancellor who alone characterises Rick's conduct in the severe terms really appropriate to it (xxiv, 336); that same Chancellor who cheerfully presides as an honourable individual (cf. his personal appearance and conduct towards the wards in Chancery in iii, 30–2) over an endless series of extreme judicial travesties.

We are not justified in giving these discrepancies an entirely mystic significance. Dickens is clearly intending to show – and his theme is enlarged in *Little Dorrit* four years later – that there is a general conspiracy of complacency among the privileged classes, which includes the intelligent as well as those besotted with the virtues of 'the system' (Kenge, the Dedlock relations, and so on), about the nature of

the society over which they preside. Nevertheless this acknowledgement will not carry off all the vexed question of Tulkinghorn's or
Bucket's motivations for what we see them do.

We can postulate all sorts of motives for the lawyer's long-
achieved and elaborate harassment of Lady Dedlock. But, as Bucket
himself remarks — the detective who is everywhere (either in his own
person or those of his myrmidons) and who knows everything which
can be elicited or deduced by investigation — 'the deceased . . . was
deep and close; and what he fully had in his mind in the very
beginning, I can't quite take upon myself to say' (liv, 727). Several
possible causes are hinted one way and another. Tulkinghorn may
have desired a hold over his victim from sexual or financial motives,
he could have longed to revenge a lifetime's suppression, no less of his
intelligence than of the truth in the interest of his dim aristocratic
connection, with a spectacular scandal of his own unravelling. It may
be a simple unalloyed thirst for power that pricks him on; or, more
profoundly, a general, impersonal malignity (though necessarily
specific in its realisation) born out of the recognition, at bottom, of his
whole life's essential purposelessness. We are reminded of his one
friend,

> a man of the same mould and a lawyer too, who lived the same
> kind of life until he was seventy-five years old, and then, suddenly
> conceiving (as it is supposed) an impression that it was too
> monotonous, gave his gold watch to his hair-dresser one summer
> evening, and walked leisurely home to the Temple, and hanged
> himself.   (xxii, 306)

In Tulkinghorn's case, this motivelessness may have a particular
significance. For myself I believe that the largest implication of Iago's
role in *Othello* is of the poison within, the Moor's latent capacity for
self-destruction. Likewise in the sinister lawyer of Dickens's novel we
see embodied in one of its deepest-grained representatives the
autonomous malignities of the settled social order and its prudential
forms in the contemporary world. Yet in both cases we denature the
author's achievement if we do not also acknowledge these men's
phenomenality as human beings, as presented personal entities. From
the ultimate mystery of their motivation there come reverberations
as of ultimate spiritual nullity — almost as far removed from hatred as
from love. If we are unwilling to talk about Iago and Tulkinghorn as
devils, it may be simply because we are concerned to pay tribute to a

more inward, three-dimensional account of the diabolical psychology, on Shakespeare's and Dickens's parts respectively, than the European tradition has tended to incorporate in its thinking about infernal life.

Much can be brought forward from the text to support any or all of these positions — the grounds of argument, I mean to say, as to the root causes of his behaviour. But we argue precisely because none of the evidence is finally specific enough, just as there is no discernible reason for Tulkinghorn either to delay or to bring forward the exposure of his hostess's secret when the timing of that revelation is discussed between them at Chesney Wold in xlviii ('Closing In'; see 661).

Certainly Tulkinghorn is pretty firmly placed in his moral aspect; with all the black-rook imagery and the like, he is plainly a bad man. Bucket, however, while he hardly possesses the implications we have glanced at in the Lawyer's case ('What you know, you know'), nevertheless has the same ability to baffle analysis as to the springs of his behaviour and a still greater impenetrability of ethical commitment. Dyson almost vitiates his good and necessarily long account of the disquieting ambiguities in this character's conduct thus:

> Like Jaggers, Bucket poses problems which clearly teased Dickens. What are the ethics proper to a detective? When (if ever) can lying and treachery serve higher truth? How far need a man's profession commit him to guile? Bucket is a man of natural friendliness and good nature who uses these qualities most unscrupulously in his work. To all appearance, they become, therefore, their diabolical opposites, a proof that warmth and good nature can never be 'known'. . . . The technique of breaking down a victim by friendliness and imaginative empathy points to one of the most frightening roles in modern literature and life . . . .[2]

For Bucket is more disturbing still than this, because we cannot moralise about him. If he is wittingly responsible for Snagsby's being imposed upon as an involuntary and unconscious coadjutor in Tulkinghorn's illicit researches (xxiii and thereafter) then he is a ruthless cad. We are shown the domestic discord which the poor law-stationer and his household suffer in consequence and cannot resolve: Mrs Snagsby's suspicions of his relation to Jo; his own — well-founded — terrors of being involved in a stupendous, dangerous mystery, of which the unknowability most undermines him; and

Guster's distracted fit, brought on by her mistress's final exasperation in the matter, which ultimately prevents Bucket and Esther reaching Lady Dedlock in time to save her (lix). But we cannot be certain that, at that stage in the course of Tulkinghorn's detective action against Lady Dedlock, the police officer actually supposes his monitor to be investigating her past for any purpose extra-judicial and unethical. In assisting him he may have had a natural reliance upon the emphatic respectability of the lawyer's whole former career; though, again, the full irony is that he does help Tulkinghorn, whether or not he realises it at the time, with an enquiry that has no meaning or value in English law (i.e. pre-marital sexual relations are and were no indictable offence, nor of any professional concern to a member of the police forces). Dyson remarks that

> Bucket . . . is chiefly responsible for Sir Leicester's stroke by his method of breaking his news. The mystifications, which in a lesser detective tale might be *frissons* intended solely and permissibly for the reader, become psychological torture in a context as rich as this . . . there are hints of some subtle if unpremeditated class-revenge in the relish with which he always calls Sir Leicester 'Sir Leicester Dedlock, Bart' . . . .[3]

Quite. We cannot avoid this suspicion. It must assail our whole attempt hereafter to bring the detective's inner nature into focus. But it takes its place with the other, equally viable, and therefore equally uncertain, motivations that Bucket's conduct is able to suggest. If Dickens does want us to watch the inspector playing cat-and-mouse with his appalled auditor of a baronet in a private class-skirmish of his own (this is all in liv), then he has overplayed his hand. The writing is too deadpan in a context where every other character's innermost feelings are fully dramatised: those of the stricken Sir Leicester, those of the flashing-eyed Hortense, those even of the Smallweed and Chadband visiting-party of blackmailers, rapacious and intense. There is not the whisper of one smallest Jamesian hint to refine the suspicion – I mean, that which is offered in Dyson's account of the scene – and bring down behind it the authority of the narrative, which is here omniscient. Bucket *may* be a 'famous whist player . . . with the game in his hand, but with a high reputation involved in his playing his hand out to the last card, in a masterly way' (liv, 724); yet the inhumanity of this professionalism, if such it be, is followed by the page on which he can be seen trying to prepare Sir

Leicester carefully for the terrible blow which he must suppose the
revelation of Lady Dedlock's past conduct will prove. The springs of
the detective's behaviour appear to be amply observed for us, only in
fact to be most largely obscured.

This trait ramifies wide and far in the novel. There is the double
nature of Boythorn, Jarndyce's friend. He is a man of intemperate (and
therefore essentially anti-social) expression, yet he has extremely
gentle (i.e. social) manners. He is a neighbour who sets mantraps
(albeit 'humane' ones) on one side of his garden in a strongly
contested affair of a goat, and who yet grows Eden within its walls
(see the description in xviii, 247–8). We find Sergeant George's
assistant Phil Squod unable to approach any object in their shooting-
gallery directly, but 'limping round [it] with his shoulder against the
wall, and tacking off at objects he wants to lay hold of, instead of
going straight to them' (xxi, 303). The nervous tics of other
characters in Dickens's novels usually have some accountable cause,
psychological or pathological. In *Little Dorrit*, Abbey Flintwinch's
cateleptic deportment and her glazed staring eyesight follow with
observable naturalness from the condition of residing through many
years in Mrs Clennam's gloomy house under the rule of her hard
employer and her ferocious husband. Her disabilities themselves
reflect and inform us of the ambit in which she moves.[4] But there is
nothing deducible in this sort from Phil's tactics. Bleak House itself (I
mean the building) is a child's paradise. It combines the most
satisfying diversity of accoutrement and structure with no suggestion
of the labryinth (see the description in vi, 65–7). Yet its new owner,
whom almost any cruel tidings send hurrying into his 'Growlery', has
retained the bitter name given to it by its previous occupant, his
cousin Tom Jarndyce, a wretched suicide ruined in the Chancery
cause very much as Carstone is ultimately ruined. Even the all-
cautious Guppy, watchful over the interests of number one with his
whole language drawn out of legal practice, has his successful
attendant parasites in Tony Jobling and young Smallweed, whose
habit of letting him pay for their victuals it never seems to occur to
him to challenge.

At the same time the whole novel is in process of affording us a
strong sense of the failure of the social life. It is impossible not to be
powerfully affected by the vision of deprivation in the London slums
which Dickens gives us with his Tom-all-Alone's — or out at the
bricklayers' by St Albans; by the plight of the children of 'Coavinses',
or by that of 'Nemo' (Captain Hawdon). We cannot fail to be

exasperated at Mrs Jellyby's neglect of her family, the hypocrisy and patronage of Mrs Pardiggle, the general parasitism (as expressed in the persons of the Smallweeds, and Vholes), the whole legal confraternity (and its imitators, like Krook). Chancery represents an entire social—political system; as Dickens is the more careful to make clear by showing us Sir Leicester emphatic in his support both for the legal *status quo* and for that of corruptly elected and irresponsible 'Buffy—Cuffy', 'Coodle—Doodle'-style administrations.

So much of this failure is effected by people who 'should know better'; or, which comes to the same thing, is countenanced by them. The problem Dickens confronts is that of a society where there is no lack of human or material resources but which is yet so delinquent. The Lord Chancellor is not himself simply a villain. Rather, he has a firm intelligent sense, which Carstone's friends dangerously lack, that Richard should be faced with relatively strict censures and insistences early (this is expressed in his voicing the same — xxiv, 336) if he is to have a chance of making good at all. His Lordship is thoughtful and provident indeed, in his more private relations (again, we remember his kindness to the wards in Chancery in iii). Yet he never speeds up judgement in Jarndyce and Jarndyce, he is never 'brought to officially recognise the existence' of the Man from Shropshire, nor does he ever call Miss Flite's plea before the bench.

We even meet the paradox among the gentry. Sir Leicester Dedlock's personality would seem to be wholly exposed. The loyalties of the baronet are brought before us by Dickens with a marvellous richness and fully defined by him:

> Sir Leicester is content enough that the ironmaster should feel that there is no hurry there; there, in that ancient house, rooted in that quiet park, where the ivy and the moss have had time to mature, and the gnarled and warted elms, and the umbrageous oaks, stand deep in the fern and leaves of a hundred years; and where the sundial on the terrace has dumbly recorded for centuries that Time, which was as much the property of every Dedlock — while he lasted — as is the house and lands. Sir Leicester sits down in an easy-chair, opposing his repose and that of Chesney Wold to the restless flights of ironmasters.   (xxviii, 394)

This is from Rouncewell's first visit to the baronet and deserves a practical exegesis running to several pages. I must be content with a paragraph. That which is of cardinal value in the Dedlock traditions has suddenly surfaced here in its native aspect. The most crucial feature of the new industrial society, of which the ironmaster is given to us as a considerably attractive spokesman, may well be its capacity to mechanise the life of the spirit (Carlyle's fear). The problem of bringing our contemporary environment, for instance, into intimate relation with the ever faster diminishing experience of life in time as a function of a maturing natural order is now so acute that Dickens can only be regarded as visionary—prophetic in here opposing *this* aspect of the best in the Dedlock traditions to the new order embodied in the hopes and 'restless flights' of Sir Leicester's visitor. Nonetheless the failure of the old aristocracy to acknowledge their own mortal participation in the natural round, the partial spuriousness therefore of their vaunted attachment to the agrarian life-rhythms and feudal social structures (like all other men they die, and therefore as a governing class they should properly have respected the urgent human — which also means animal — needs of all other men): this is present too. The insufficiency of Sir Leicester's complacent consciousness of 'that ancient house', 'that quiet park', 'those gnarled and warted elms', is before us, whether from the immediate hint in the text (the 'easy chair') or because we have already been shown that vista as an ambit of unrecognised desperation. This was the significance of its very first treatment in the book; as Brian Cox has demonstrated in his full account of the symbolic implications and emotional contours of the third paragraph of ii, where Lady Dedlock is looking out over Chesney Wold in exasperation at her dishonest position, her childlessness, and the emptiness and flatness of her existence. As Cox, in his article in the *Critical Quarterly*, II, no. 1, (1960), remarks of that passage, 'Dickens's great descriptions of places and people attain their peculiar hold upon our minds because every detail fits into an imaginative pattern'. We are introduced to Chesney Wold, and indeed the fashionable world, with that evocation of the 'flooded park', the 'soaked deer', the 'lead-coloured view' and 'sweating oaken pulpit' (in the ecclesiastical repository of Dedlock attitudes), because the possibilities of a vigorously creative aristocratic role in the development of society have been abdicated or lost sight of. In like fashion, even though Sir Leicester has married a commoner of no fortune, and has done so for love, he and his wife have not borne a child.

'An honourable, obstinate, truthful, high-spirited, intensely prejudiced, perfectly unreasonable man' (iii, 9), like 'Conversation' Kenge he is strictly fair according to his lights; and those lights are not hopelessly limited in certain relations. He is utterly even-handed in his dealings with the ironmaster, about the future of Rosa and Watt. Along with his class indeed (represented by the assembled cousins to whom Mr Tulkinghorn propounds his menacing parable — xl, 571 – 3), he rejects the very idea of any interference in private matters of the heart between a husband and wife, on the part of any outside agent armed with whatever ethical fiats. In the event, this charitableness — so lacking in the High-Church Mrs Pardiggle's proprieties *or* even Mr Rouncewell's (who is evidently a northern puritan), let alone in Mr Tulkinghorn's investigation — is exactly what he extends to his wife at the height of her disgrace. Yet this same aristocrat who is so powerful (albeit that he is now the pillar of an order which is being displaced) assists in corrupting the suffrages which give Britain a parliament that does nothing for the likes of Jo the crossing-sweeper. And as for Kenge, who evidently would sooner cut off his hand than fail in any duty, the country's system of equity is a very great system, a very great system' (lxii, 843).

To acknowledge these characteristics in either personage as typical and credible (which they emphatically are) is yet — in a context where so much is veiled of human motivation — only to be thrown back on the central and recurring difficulty which the book propounds. We are given, after all, no psychological case-study as to why these men should think and behave like this. We even have no specific insight into the reasons *why* Mrs Jellyby campaigns in a fatuous and unmeaning manner for the alleviation of spiritual darkness far away which she does not understand, rather than (in a much humbler spirit) its very real equivalent, and with it desperate material inanition, within her native shores and indeed almost under her feet. Somebody who can seek to organise the ludicrous undertakings she and Mr Quale have on hand (e.g. iv, 41) — 'a project . . . for teaching the coffee colonists to teach the natives [in Africa] to turn pianoforte legs and establish an export trade' — is at least evidently conscious of her society having at its disposal wealth and forces historically unprecedented for actually getting large schemes accomplished. And of course this novel, begun in the year of the Great Exhibition (1851), is no less redolent of the new resources of industrialised society in the person, manner and interventions, in the Dedlocks' life, of Mr Rouncewell the ironmaster.

Expressing itself brutally, however, in the crowded industrial slums of the new age and the negligence of contemporary government, the old human problem abides by which our planet has been plagued all along: the enormous failure of will to make our resources tell creatively – our resources spiritual and imaginative as well as material; social and corporate as well as individual – in the private and communal life. All these people we are shown, and those whom they represent in the entire spectrum of society, have but to put their shoulders to the wheel speedily to encompass powerful changes for the better in every dimension. Yet, though they can individually possess insights or decencies or commitments of a kind which should induce such activity or work to alter opinion in the very spheres where they have influence, they do not do so.

I have suggested earlier that John Jarndyce retires into his 'Growlery' in order to avoid the pain of a more fully recognised enmity to his society. A comparable interpretation will account too for his habit of diminishing Esther with pet names of a kind which minify the adult and the female in her nature ('Dame Durden', and so on). But this is never certainly intimated by the text. These ideas are only hopeful guesses, rationalisations after the fact, which show for the more random and insubstantial when there is so much else to rationalise. We believe in Jarndyce and in all the other characters. The very fact that in almost every case there are several possibilities of motivation, of which we are so aware, secures their credibility. But the failure of any single one of these possibilities to achieve authority gives us the novel's ultimate image of the absurdity of the failure viewed everywhere in the story: its 'absurdity' in the sense of the modern 'existentialists'. For this our historic defection as a species from realising individually and corporately the full positive potentiality of our human nature *is ultimately* mysterious and impenetrable.

'Quite an adventure for a morning in London!' said Richard, with a sigh. 'Ah, cousin, cousin, it's a weary word, this Chancery!'

'It is to me, and has been ever since I can remember,' returned Ada. 'I am grieved that I should be the enemy – as I suppose I am – of a great number of relations and others; and that they should be my enemies – as I suppose they are; and that we should all be ruining one another, without knowing how or why, and be in constant doubt and discord all our lives. It seems very strange, as there must be right somewhere, that an honest judge in real earnest has not been able to find out through all these years where it is.' (v, 58)

As Mrs Leavis comments on this passage, 'It is . . . the laws of human nature and the society that man's nature has produced as the expression of our impulses, that constitute what John Jarndyce calls "the family misfortune".'[5] And our inability to trace finally the springs of these characters' behaviour not only offers us an image of the great ruining *manque* in human affairs. It does so in a manner which baffles all possibility, on our part, of absorbing or muffling this perception in aesthetically enjoying it.

Miss Flite says of her life spent in the Chancery court, ' "There's a cruel attraction in the place. You *can't* leave it. And you *must* expect" ' (xxxv, 498), which imitates what in itself it is to be alive. We all go on living day after day on the expectation or in the hope (however irrational) of some great vindicating experience, some epiphany which will illumine the dark places of our lives (again, our existences corporate and individual), which will justify the chaos, make coherent and meaningful the drudgery of our past consciousness – like Miss Flite's long cruel years of waiting for a judgement. (To make *them* bearable, let alone her future – even were the Chancellor to hear her plea and award her many times what she asks – she really *needs* a Second Coming.)

In like manner we have to go on reading *Bleak House*. We need to wait upon any possible development of the Jarndyce cause because such may express its essential origins; what it is in the nature of things which could so have brought about all this legal obfuscation and malpractice. How can a civilised Chancellor preside over, and therefore connive at, the cruel disastrous Chancery procedures (and all, by extension, which they represent in society at large)? Moreover, development might after all reveal in the business some available justice which is not dependent upon the local insufficiency of fallen and corrupt human law; the truth of the matter, the 'natural justice' (which at least requires that, however worthy or worthless the various appellants in the case, it should not have been so long protracted without redress) may enforce itself in some redemptive way. But when Jarndyce and Jarndyce finally implodes there is no question of a Royal Commission being set up with sweeping powers and immediate despatch to prevent the like abuse ever transpiring again. Indeed really no development ever takes place. Like the other plots of the novel, the cause in Chancery ultimately collapses, simply folds in upon itself and betrays us to further mystery or at least dissatisfaction.

So it is with the characters of the story. We want to know more of John Jarndyce, Esther Summerson (of her hidden life more anon),

Mr Bucket, Lady Dedlock, Tulkinghorn and the rest; we *have* to go on studying them, for at any moment we may be given to penetrate their natures, to understand them and with them our own deepest mysteries. Our interest, far from being abated, is increased on account of that hidden area in their inward lives, the region of ultimate motivations. Yet we never are given the means ultimately to analyse them to our satisfaction — or relief. The crucial origin of their various incongruities of judgement (like the Chancellor's) in thought, speech and behaviour, remains in the most radical aspect as much occluded at the end as at the beginning.

If Dickens did not suffer from a 'falsity about women' (Angus Wilson's view, quoted earlier[6]), if Lady Dedlock had a fully realised or realisable personality (to instance the essential 'flaw' in *her* case), *Bleak House* would be a different kind of book which, owing to its essential *procédés*, would probably tend to subvert its own case. Given the triteness of her revelations or her ending (trite not in the sense of being unmoving, but of inspiring us with the complaint, 'Is this all that Honoria Dedlock's frozen impassivity has curtained, this mere tale of a 'disgraced' female with so ordinary a secret!'), we are thrown back upon a more wholly reconstituted sense of the mystery of human behaviour. Were she to have the sort of penetrable reality the lack of which criticism deplores (or, if it is friendly, tends to skirt around), the image of living which the novel offers us would be vitiated by its own nature as the portrayal of characters and a scene that could be properly analysed and explained. There would be a fundamental implication in the very method of the work that we can and do come satisfactorily to terms with the general failure of the tribe, or that we happy few, the readers, can escape the general burden. The very process of perception entailed would confer upon the author and his audience a special status as exceptions to the imaged rule, would leave them somewhat like unconvicted demi-gods overviewing a comprehensive lapse among mortals in which they do not themselves tragically participate.

Dickens is not representing a total anarchy (such perhaps could hardly be imaged anyway) and his novel works, like other novels, by means of language and action that are ordered. But he is concerned to make a fable of our essential human predicament and in a manner we are not able to muffle or absorb with the means traditionally afforded by some of our usual privileges as readers, sitting outside a fictional action and perceiving its underlying causes.

In one phase of the work after another, we are not able to ignore the life which is hidden; nor can it be exposed and known. Of itself, this veiling brings into active play the irritant intrinsic to living itself, the 'absurdity' of human life as defined before. On one hand, there is its 'cruel attraction': 'You *can't* leave it. And you *must* expect.' Complementarily we have the impenetrable occlusion of ultimate motives in a world where we desperately need to diagnose the fundamental failures which have created so limiting a social organism as the novel also makes us acknowledge. We are caught throughout in a powerful unremitted tension: that of having to study the problem of the failure — the endemic human lapse — without being able to penetrate the hidden world of ultimate motivations which it implies. And by these same means the novel keeps palpable the problem and disgrace of our existence in a fashion we cannot dodge, continually convincing us of our own complete involvement therein.

To a large extent, then, the reader is rendered vulnerable, with his usual privileges as a sharer in the author's omniscience and something of his foresight curtailed; though, again, as we find with living itself, not completely. (In that resides the difficulty. Would not total bafflement mean a certain larger release from what we understand as consciousness?) Alongside the massive 'density of specification' which here, as everywhere, is the Dickens hallmark — an enormously concreted world substantial to all the senses — goes the impenetrability of the leading characters and the failure of their stories to crystallise into a meaning which will explain it (i.e. the world) in a manner which will satisfy. As readers we are reinvested with something analogous to the defencelessness and the innocence life itself may well be deemed to impose upon us — the life, namely, which exists outside the covers of literature, in which we run unexpectedly into door-jambs or break our legs; an organum as solid, definite, and to a comparable degree uninterpretable.

Yet this — again, like life itself — also reduces us to making other, simpler acknowledgments within the framework and delineations we *are* given. There has been brought before us the essential illogic of our condition as it expresses itself in the baffling tragic problem of our moral inadequacy. Yet the book not only restores us to wakefulness about this insufficiency and this dilemma; its fictive processes (of the kind we have examined) harmonise with the characteristic Dickens modes of narrative and human portraiture, to make equally freshly palpable to us the creative illogics of life, those elements and features also inhering in this so–defective world, which of their hopeful happier nature make the issue so exasperating. (For, if there were no love, goodness, beauty or interest in living at all, would the game be worth the candle?) *Bleak House* is more and other than merely 'disconcerting'. Dickens images all the human centralities.

II

Muffled and blurred, subverted to some degree or compromised in another as it may well be, all that is honourable, warm and generous in John Jarndyce, Mr Snagsby, the Bagnets, Sergeant George, Mr Boythorn, and so on we have to accept with the more implicit faith just because their behaviour in certain aspects is opaque. The deaths of Gridley and Jo can be described as sentimentalised only if we want Dickens permanently to sustain, like most of his successors in the English novel – like, most emphatically, James, who sustains it without a 'drop' in the whole course of his *oeuvre* – a discourse which all the time contains irony, humorous detachment, comic distance, an inassailable poise of balanced recognitions. And he does possess a narrative mode infinitely flexible; but these episodes are necessary in order entirely to assure us that the author has a hand to show; that, behind the detachment constituted by these essential and requisite sophistications, there is a deeply committed humanistic personality for whom the varied tones, the comic perspectives and humorous distance are ultimately what they purport to be: a means of endorsing mutuality in an immediate human context and not, by any slightest possibility, a technique which finally leaves it (this in the very last resort) somewhere at arm's length.

> 'Let me lay here quiet, and not be chivvied no more,' falters Jo; 'and be so kind any person as is a-passin' nigh where I used fur to sweep, as jist to say to Mr. Sangsby that Jo, wot he known once, is a-moving on right forwards with his duty, and I'll be wery thankful. I'd be more thankful than I am aready, if it wos any ways possible for an unfortnet to be it.'   (xlvii ['Jo's Will'], 644)

These – our own experience of contemporary down-town children, or our readings in nineteenth-century sociology, will lead us to suppose – are hardly the authentic accents of a boy allowed to grow up in a state of savagery such as Dickens has recurrently adverted as Jo's portion and his character (see, for instance, xvi, 220–2; xlvi, 627–8). Yet if we feel that the sweeper's articulateness here, for a lad so fully deprived, betrays a factitious sentimentality indulged in by the author at this point, I think we have brought expectations and inhibitions to the text which do not discover a real gap in the narrative or test a genuine failure of its strength, but displace our actual experience of it. The only licence here is one of idiom; the boy's inward workings in themselves, albeit thus expressed, are wholly believable. (And if he is not allowed this stylised articulateness, how can they be made known? So many of Mayhew's waifs and strays, one suspects, speak *oratio obliqua* in his reports of his interviews with them,[7] not because he has no very faithful ear for rendering the various speech of the London streets, but because a really alien, hostile and incomprehensible environment — as it is for the likes of Jo — will take its toll no less in language than in everything else; and Mayhew has chosen rather to translate — which also means bowdlerise — their idiom for his readers than have them miss all contact with the London poor.) Like his first lesson in the Lord's Prayer, Jo's speech has a genuine poignancy and honest pathos because its affective qualities — testimony of good intentions, innocence, vulnerability and so on — are only partners with its expressiveness of futility.

All the most distinctive incursions into his existence that we have witnessed have been effectually assaults of the irrational and unintelligible; the highest irony consisting in that they are so not only for him, on his blinkered unschooled view, but in an absolute sense. In one respect it is even arguably kind of Bucket (seconded in this by Snagsby) always to urge Jo to 'move on' and to keep him doing so; he might otherwise have to meet a regular charge of loitering. Bucket's attitude may be the best that he as an officer of law can find by way of compromise with a human recognition of this society's ineptitude (so far as it is expressed in law) at dealing with such indigence. It might still further conceivably be read, this recurrent 'move on' instruction, as embodying (although not consciously and deliberately) a *preparatio evangelica*: 'Under the law all sin. Move on!' (see below, part III of this chapter, for a discussion of the role of law and gospel in *Bleak House*). But on the largest view, which must take account of how it immediately affects Jo, there is nothing but heartless fatuity in the requirement, exactly because he has no real home, place, role to move on from, or to.

Mr Snagsby's half-crowns are as valuable for their delicate affirmation of human sympathy (perceived as such by the boy) as for their material assistance, but their principal effect for us is to point the failure of any coherent scheme of maintenance for the sweeper —

whether in terms of his being given a fair start in life as of human right (regular food, housing, education, companionship), or a proper return for the service he renders the community. Significantly he is the only agency, from beginning to end of the story, to make any attempt (with his sweeping) actually to improve the condition of Tom-all-Alone's. So that the law-stationer's money-gifts can only heighten the urchin's deepest sense of bewilderment at a social environment which is in one aspect generous (and generous in a humanly immediate, feeling and delicate way) and more generally pitilessly unaiding with the sort of blank amoral indifference of the weather that finally leaves him a prey to the smallpox infection. When Lady Dedlock, by his guidance, visits her former lover's horrible grave, the pain of the episode (as apart from its deliberate nausea) springs much more out of the quality of intercourse between its living protagonists than from the poignancy of her bereavement or Captain Hawdon's condition.

'You mean about the man?' says Jo, following. 'Him as wos dead?'

'Hush! Speak in a whisper! Yes. Did he look, when he was living, so very ill and poor?'

'O jist!' says Jo.

'Did he look like — not like *you*?' says the woman with abhorrence. . . .

'I'm fly,' says Jo. 'But fen larks, you know. Stow hooking it!'

'What does the horrible creature mean?' exclaims the servant, recoiling from him. . . .

The servant shrinks into a corner — into a corner of that hideous archway, with its deadly stains contaminating her dress; and putting out her two hands, and passionately telling him to keep away from her, for he is loathsome to her, so remains for some moments. . . .

She drops a piece of money in his hand, without touching it, and shuddering as their hands approach.

(xvi, 223— 5)

These reactions are not the less tragic for being inevitable and in a real sense justified. ('Orthodoxy ought to / Bless our modern plumbing: / Swift and St Augustine / Lived in centuries, / When a stench of sewage / Ever in the nostrils / Made a strong debating / Point for Manichees.'⁸) The conduct of a woman who herself is mightily oppressed with inward and outward harassments and who elicits our sympathy as such here embodies the irrationalities for Jo of his whole existence, the seemingly general attack upon his consciousness which all of life is for him. She seeks him out and yet recoils; she gives no reason for visiting this grave nor why, as an alleged 'servant', she can afford to pay him a gold sovereign for his slight trouble; she treats him as an object of loathing and yet relies on his guidance and good faith. Perhaps the single most valuable or necessary acquirement that has been denied Jo from his lack of either a fully incorporated role in a genuine society or of 'education' in the narrower modern sense is the ability to rationalise – however erroneously, however fantastically – other people's behaviour. When the tough, spry little character (newly fortified, we may remember, by some good meals at Mr Snagsby's expense) perishes of the smallpox which Esther Summerson survives, it is hard not to feel that his entire constitution has collapsed at last, not only under the strain of the virus and the bad weather, but also under the constant pressure of the problem of the *Bleak House* world, our acquaintance with which I have already canvassed, but which by him is experienced at its most unmitigated and filterless: that of being a self, an (in his case literally) houseless entity, bombarded, as with visible Democritean atoms, by a ceaseless flux of incoherent behaviour, demands, reactions; experience from all sides which, because it is so harshly total in its uninterpretability, can be felt only as assault.

A start is made on his education, of course – within his last few moments of life. The Lord's Prayer could stand for a type of men's attempts to make the randomness and incoherence of experience tolerable and negotiable. But its broken meaninglessness for Jo at this epoch of his career fully counterpoises any notion of his making a new start. 'The light is come upon the dark benighted way' – yes, but only seconds before he is 'Dead!', and an angry reproof to the social governors is the emphasis with which the chapter concludes. The irrelevance, which is in larger part to say the tardiness, of Woodcourt's attempt to introduce into the boy's experience these ideas for a coherent and sustaining relation between the self and the Other is more than locally ironic. It is but too believably representative an act of a mid-century evangelical radical, this rehearsing of the Lord's Prayer as a kind of superstitious talisman, no less efficacious for being a completely meaningless form of words in the ears of the individual involved. Jo in the role of trusting parrot at the end of his career does not make an actually ugly sight; but it is pathetically inept, and in a manner that modifies our experience of other, comparable intimations in the rest of the tale. This, we find ourselves remarking, is why Dickens keeps Allan Woodcourt so much on the margin of the novel's action. His real virtues – his greater intelligence, not least, than Mr Jarndyce or Esther, his dedication of himself as a doctor among the poor to the hard work of heroism, his total loyalty to decencies which are so much lacking in Mrs Pardiggle or Mr Quale – derive from one of the best of the high-ethical ideologies (that is to say, the evangelical radical) at work in this society. Yet this itself is shown to be not enough. 'Il faut cultiver son jardin' is effectually Woodcourt's response to the total social problem, and, of all the *dramatis personae* in the story, his own is the strongest case from which to argue for it; the quietest and most dignified dedication to essential rather than fraudulent values. But this episode of Jo's death develops our sense of these commitments and this intelligence – very fine as they are – as being finally insufficient, matched against the full in-adequacy of the surrounding environment. Woodcourt turns out to be an Albany uttering, at a moment of deepest outrage, a wholesome platitude.

Recognition of these truths, however, only serves to throw into yet deeper relief the claims of Jo's status as a human being, and nowise mitigates the value or moral beauty of the sympathy with his plight which is shared by those attendant upon his last illness and refuge. The scene, like the visit to the children of 'Coavinses' in chapter xv, possesses the capacity radically to challenge us for a response from the mind and heart together free from spurious emotional restraints of a kind we concede to in so very much of all our other living and reading. Across the artificial and destructive barriers in the social and the inward worlds, an endorsement of certain loyalties and commit-ments is compelled. Mind and heart, to renew the terms, are har-monised, not compromised, in such a case as this, where the novel-ist has not fallen victim to unsifted or undigested emotion (as is the case with his position *vis-à-vis* Little Nell from the beginning of *The Old Curiosity Shop*, let alone at her death). The reader's own unity of affirmations – of sympathy, of indignation – does not signalise an eclipse of judgement. In sharing this singleness of response with the other ministrants at Jo's deathbed – Messrs Jarndyce, Snagsby, Bucket, Sergeant George, Phil Squod – we do not suspend our critical awareness of their opacities, perversities, compromises; even of their past co-operations, however slight (and Inspector Bucket's has not been slight), in the total process which has brought Jo to this pass. But it is a counter-challenge to any notion of 'benevolence' or 'human brotherhood' as terms and experiences themselves discredited by the contact we are also being given by the novel with the hiddenness (and therefore unmedecinable nature) of the very springs of human behaviour. If we wish to dislodge or discredit such a response, we have to explain away the actual experience of many readers, not all of them of the dimmest or least scrupulous, as of an enfranchisement in such scenes as this of Jo's death from a series and modality of human intercourse — I mean, the everyday consciousness and reciprocities of many of us — which is thus defined by Dickens's treatment of his material, and felt by the reader, to be considerably less than sufficient. The successful 'sentimental' episodes in Dickens have the very trick and taste of 'calling' more rather than less of 'the whole soul of man into activity'. And Dickens's evident belief in the latency of these more generous, open, selfless capacities in so many participants of the human heritage is thus approved by the event.

To say all this is not to leave diminished the more humdrum but no less grateful decencies represented in Esther. Our most serious difficulty with her is that everything she does and thinks is predictable — that is, not just in character, as a virtue of portraiture, but of a too specifically foreseeable reaction at all times: the mark of significant limitations. She does not have the advantages, by Dickens's design, of David Copperfield or Pip, both of whom are the only mediators of their world to us (and who are given complete possession of the full Dickens range of tones and intelligence), who are not 'cases' (writing as they do throughout from the vantage-point of experience and adventures which have achieved their purgation or illumination), and who are principal active protagonists in their own stories (but for her discovery of and hospitality towards the stricken Jo, in xxxi, Esther sets very little of the tale in motion; her role is most largely that of a spectator).

Nor is her speech, the speech she reports within her narrative, informed by so rich a cultural inheritance as that of Jeanie Deans — to instance another heroine who winds her way, clutching at the clew of 'simple' innocence and duty, through a labyrinth of traps and dangers. In another environment, even in Mansfield Park say, which is an ambit really distinguished by delinquencies no less grave, she might figure as insipidly unoriginating. But then in *Mansfield Park* (the novel) the ultimate social consequences of the irresponsibilities

and insensitivity we are shown are in certain directions suppressed;
there is no actual Tom-all-Alone's, no fully presented death of Jo. In
the context of the general moral chaos of the world Esther mirrors, a
chaos so fully embodied, we recognise in her limited imagination the
inescapable concomitant of certain fixed perimeters, for conduct, of
which the definition and rigidity are welcome. We can want to shout
at her for advising Caddy to consult her mother again in the matter of
her marriage – a bad mistake; but her unimaginative 'straightness' is
on all other occasions a blessed relief beside the Protean inventiveness
of deceit which characterises the morality of the Smallweeds, the
apologetics of Kenge, the 'closeness' of Mr Krook or the procedures
of the Chancery lawyers, representative as those traits are of features
of living severely grim in the larger social world.

There are capacities still more widely diffused which Dickens
celebrates, however; and the first of these celebrations, for intrinsic
value and continuous inherence through both his narratives (but with
especial exuberance in the 'impersonal' narrator's portion of the
novel), is his embodiment of the human personality as self-creating in
an impressive degree. We have, for example, this presentation of the
neighbours of Messrs Krook and Snagsby in Cook's Court, Cursitor
Street:

> Now do they [the reporters of the newspapers] show . . . how
> during some hours of yesterday evening a very peculiar smell was
> observed by the inhabitants of the court, in which the tragical
> occurrence which forms the subject of that present account
> transpired; and which odour was at one time so powerful, that Mr
> Swills, a comic vocalist, professionally engaged by Mr. J. G.
> Bogsby, has himself stated to our reporter that he mentioned to
> Miss M. Melvilleson, a lady of some pretensions to musical ability,
> likewise engaged by Mr. J. G. Bogsby to sing a series of concerts
> called Harmonic Assemblies or Meetings, which it would appear
> are held at the Sol's Arms, under Mr. Bogsby's direction, pursuant
> to the Act of George the Second, that he (Mr. Swills) found his
> voice seriously affected by the impure state of the
> atmosphere. . . . How this account . . . is entirely corroborated
> by two intelligent married females residing in the same court, and
> known respectively by the names of Mrs. Piper and Mrs. Perkins;
> both of whom observed the foetid effluvia . . . . (xxxiii ['In-
> terlopers'], 457–8)

This is not (as it happens) strong writing, but it is very recognisably and representatively Dickens's in that, though it uses a satirical device, deflation is far from being its only, or major, effect. It is of course amusing and we do assist at an exposure of the pretensions of these public entertainers: the reporters, the landlord and his performing artists. Yet in their very belief that the whole style of their professional discourse is the appropriate idiom for intercourse with their public — whether or not it can fully impose itself upon that public as the accredited mode of their normal quotidian consciousness — they express an innocence and a sort of consecrated view of personality which is exhilarating.

Bogsby's neighbours and the newspaper's readers all know to some degree or another that theirs is no district of human paragons. Yet such pretensions as are expressed in this sort of language are the very means by which decent behaviour ever comes to be at all. I must maintain the fiction that my neighbour is a being of unmessy, elevated mind, lofty aspirations, highly civilised consciousness, noble habits (and of such characteristics in themselves Bogsby *et al.* evidently deem the language with which they fill the newspapers the appropriate tokens), if I am to treat him with any respect. A god's-eye view into his (or her) imagination's inmost workings from minute to minute would leave most of us irreconcilable misanthropes, sickened Gullivers. It is in the gap between the inward darknesses of almost every human consciousness and the bright (though partly spurious) human pretensions that we constitute the materials for beauty, value, love in our experience or conduct at all — constitute them absolutely and authentically. The enormous active collaboration of ordinary people in this process — this perhaps most healthful of all human processes — Dickens continuously registers, and always with evident delight:

Mrs. Piper pushed forward by Mrs. Perkins. Mrs. Piper sworn.
    Anastasia Piper, gentlemen. Married woman. Now, Mrs. Piper — what have you got to say about this?
    Why, Mrs. Piper has a good deal to say, chiefly in parentheses and without punctuation, but not much to tell. Mrs. Piper lives in the court (which her husband is a cabinet-maker), and it has long been well beknown among the neighbours (counting from the day next but one before the half-baptising of Alexander James Piper aged eighteen months and four days old on accounts of not being expected to live such was the sufferings gentlemen of that child in

3

his gums) as the Plaintive – so Mrs. Piper insists on calling the
deceased – was reported to have sold himself. Thinks it was the
Plaintive's air in which that report originatinin. . . . Has seen the
Plaintive wexed and worrited by the children (for children they
will ever be and you cannot expect them specially if of playful
dispositions to be Methoozellers which you was not your-
self). . . . (xi, 147)

Like Mrs Gamp's conversation, Mrs Piper's whole idiom, her superb
'bad' English, is designed to represent her way of life as more
coherent, better managed, more informed by all the properties of a
high decorum – learning ('Methoozeller'), a wide linguistic competence (the 'Plaintive's air in which that report originatinin') and so
forth – than it actually is. But in putting forward these pretensions
she is complimenting her audience and inspiring them to treat her and
each other as participants equally in this nobler, more enlarged and
humanly responsible reality.

Much the same principle is operative in the case of Mr Chadband.
Most of Dickens's hypocrites are so famously enlivening just because
their dismissal of the ordinary range of reaction and expression, the
eccentricity of their developed roles, bears witness to an important
freedom of self-creation on the part of the race as of the individual.
Mr Pecksniff, Mrs Gamp, Mr Micawber would all figure as
dangerous rascals *tout court* if Dickens were solely examining what
makes for order or disorder in the society which *Martin Chuzzlewit*
and *David Copperfield* reflect. But when his scheme also takes in
question what creative forces there are inside the human psyche as
such, even within so moribund a social order as is expressed in these
novels, then their sins become practically venial beside the value of
what their outrageous *personae* betoken as enterprises of human
energy and creative power.

Mrs. Snagsby in tears.
'Or put it, my juvenile friends, that he saw an elephant, and
returning said, 'Lo, the city is barren, I have seen but an eel,' would
that be Terewth?'
Mrs. Snagsby sobbing loudly.
'Or put it, my juvenile friends,' said Chadband, stimulated by
the sound, 'that the unnatural parents of this slumbering Hea-
then – for parents he had, my juvenile friends, beyond a doubt
– after casting him forth to the wolves and the vultures, and

the wild dogs and the young gazelles, and the serpents, went back
to their dwellings and had their pipes, and their pots, and their
flutings and their dancings, and their malt liquors, and their
butcher's meat and poultry, would *that* be Terewth?'

Mrs. Snagsby replies by delivering herself a prey to
spasms . . . . (xxv, 360– 1).

This free-flowing spate of quasi-Biblical verbiage strikes us as the
more expressive of an inward creativeness in that Dickens sees
Chadband not so much as the product of a series of social causes, but as
a phenomenon in the philosophical sense. It is evident that Esther
Summerson is significantly conditioned by her environment. Half of
all that is important in her conduct and self-expression is the unhappy
consequence of the loss of her parents and of her bad early days. Yet
the fact that Chadband is representative of a class of people who make
a cosy living (emotionally as well as materially) out of exploiting the
contemporary Nonconformist taste for 'edification' by no means
fully accounts for his having these maryellous flights of ridiculous
oratory at his disposal. The eloquence is a *donnée* of his nature; which
does not mean that we find him the less credible. His credibility as a
personage is sustained by the unfaltering coherence on its own terms
of his inflated speech and behaviour; or, should one say, the almost
unfaltering coherence? The attempt to blackmail Sir Leicester
towards the end (liv) is perhaps a little too blatant. But his wilder
flights of emotional and religious imposture earlier, exordia from
which he clearly derives as much satisfaction as from the victuals and
cash they rake in for him (and that for the reason that he is a creative
artist in human conduct), are wholly believable. It is all part of the
beneficent paradox of eccentricity in Dickens, operative here, as
elsewhere, to counterpoise the intimations of 'mere' darkness – the
ubiquitous inertia, inhumanity and neglect. Chadband's force and
value in the book's debate is that we recognise in his performances an
essentially human capability affirmed in (albeit perverse) employ-
ment. He signifies the degree to which men have it within them to
disregard the regular, diplomatised forms of living; forms, after all,
which have not done much for Tom-all-Alone's.

If we take, at random, the first description of 'the fashionable
world' and Lady Dedlock's position inside it (ii), or the introduction
of Cook's Court, Cursitor Street, and its history (x), it is worth
noticing that Dickens is doing for his readers what Mrs Piper or the
reporters later perform for *their* audiences.

Sir Leicester is twenty years, full measure, older than my Lady. He will never see sixty-five again, nor perhaps sixty-six, nor yet sixty-seven. He has a twist of the gout now and then, and walks a little stiffly. He is of a worthy presence, with his light grey hair and whiskers, his fine shirt-frill, his pure white waistcoat, and his blue coat with bright buttons always buttoned. He is ceremonious, stately, most polite on every occasion to my Lady, and holds her personal attractions in the highest estimation. His gallantry to my Lady, which has never changed since he courted her, is the one little touch of romantic fancy in him.   (ii, 9– 10)

Peffer is never seen in Cook's Court now. He is not expected there, for he has been recumbent this quarter of a century in the churchyard of St. Andrews, Holborn, with the waggons and hackney-coaches roaring past him, all the day and half the night, like some great dragon. If he ever steal forth when the dragon is at rest, to air himself again in Cook's Court, until admonished to return by the crowing of the sanguine cock in the cellar at the little dairy in Cursitor Street, whose ideas of daylight it would be curious to ascertain, since he knows from his personal observation next to nothing about it – if Peffer ever do revisit the pale glimpses of Cook's Court, which no law-stationer in the trade can positively deny, he comes invisibly, and no one is the worse or wiser. (x, 127)

'Recumbent', 'steal forth', 'admonished', 'sanguine', 'personal observation' – these terms, like the whole nature of the prose in which they are embedded, are of course out of scale with the quality of the phenomena described; or are they? Some people find this kind of writing in Dickens facetious; by implication, one supposes, patronising. But this is not how either of these passages strikes me, whether viewed in or out of their context. What does a real respect for the dead, or for animals, finally consist in, but the fiction (if it *be* a fiction) by which we attribute to them the dignities of which the living humanity is capable. Far from imitating the unhappy patronage of the dead which characterises so much of our ordinary outlook, far from unctuously lowering us all to the level of Peffer's supposed abdications and disablements (as if we were all visiting monarchs on a descending platform inspecting a mine), this treatment of his situation is 'generous, gentle, humble' – in the fully loaded sense of Holofernes (in *Love's Labours Lost*, Act v, scene ii) – not least because it allows for and incorporates a sense of the comic. I can only effectually repeat what I adduced before from Mrs Piper's address or from the copy of the newspapermen in xxxiii. Such an attribution as we observe in these passages, which is the very trick of the Dickens prose at large, of competence, honour, dignity, a whole mode of cognition itself refined, to the dead or to the brutes, has an ironic intention and a humorous effect; but, like all the other habits of speech and conduct by which we dignify our living neighbours, they are the means by which decency and respect and sanctuary come into being or find their expression in the human world at all. The rawest existentialist shifts uneasily at the idea of merely tossing, for requiem, his dead wife's body into a dustbin (even if this were not a hazard to local sanitation); and, while it is one thing for a writer to attempt to present an image of society which is totally honest, it is another if his book also happens to be terribly loveless (I speak now of the love that is *caritas*). This is a question which criticism seems sometimes to lose sight of, and Dickens suffers more than many other authors by its neglect. What does all literary endeavour and philosophical enquiry mean if we only find out enough about our nature balefully to hate ourselves and each other? If that is what true honesty discovers, so be it. But, in that case, living, still less reading about living, has no value anyway. Dickens exposes the fundamental fictions of civilised existence, he exploits them for comic and satiric effect, but he also affords recognition of their healthful properties – as positive values, this is to say, in the society of his day and of any day. His principal mode of discourse, especially as impersonal narrator, is pregnant with the sanity which inheres in the corporate conspiracy there is, in human relations as such, to pretend the health which is so far from informing them.

These freedoms naturally have found an analogue in the nature of the plot; in its not being, as we have already noted, so tightly all-incorporative a mechanism that it almost 'traps' its characters. That so many incidents do not derive their interest exclusively from our concern with Lady Dedlock's difficulties or Esther's fortunes or the development of the Jarndyce cause in Chancery – while these are yet plausible occasions in the first instance for what we are being shown – is a function of Dickens's having solved what I assume to be the novelist's most chronic abiding problem, that of at once 'organising an ado', treating experience artistically and constituting a significance, without denaturing the randomness of life, the independence of his characters, and therefore their human representativeness. For to claim this for *Bleak House* is not to minimise the felt significance of the connections it presents. The unity of interests which ought to, but does not, bind the human world into one wholesome polis of mutually conscientious citizen-relatives, is powerfully focused by the story's unfolding a cross-section view of the contemporary world. (This is why *apologiae* for the coincidences in this novel are supererogatory. They are wholly convincing, in that the reader recognises *ab initio* how the fictional canvas before him is, to appropriate an architectural metaphor, Dickens's view in elevation of the current state of society.) The whole image of human interdependence and the fatal consequences of its being thwarted or obscured, which the novel presents as action (as in Esther's being stricken, and Lady Dedlock's dying, of the smallpox which kills Jo), is marvellously successful.

Likewise, that which in his prose is the element of eighteenth-century Enlightenment rhetoric (derived as much through Fielding as anyone else) is, blessedly, an element; a controlled part only of a very wide range of expression. It is all part of the same, more open registration of human possibility which Dickens's resources of narrative and language are dedicated to tracing. People are perceived more as independent and unexplained phenomena than as they appear in perhaps the majority of novelists — as types conforming to a regular pattern or single underlying essence of human nature.

When Balzac tells us of Wenceslas Steinbock in *Cousine Bette*,

> The poor young man, groaning to find himself dependent on this shrew, domineered over by a peasant woman from the Vosges, was disarmed by her affectionate coaxing and her motherly solicitude for his physical and material well-being. He was like a wife who forgives a week's ill-treatment in the caresses of a fleeting reconciliation[9]

we marvel at the apt and precise definition of the simile. Or when George Eliot remarks that

> In Mr. Casaubon's ear, Dorothea's voice gave loud emphatic iteration to those muffled suggestions of consciousness which it was possible to explain as mere fancy, the illusion of exaggerated sensitiveness: always when such suggestions are unmistakably repeated from without, they are resisted as cruel and unjust. We are angered even by the full acceptance of our humiliating

confessions — how much more by hearing in hard distinct syllables from the lips of a near observer, those confused murmers which we try to call morbid, and strive against as if they were the oncoming of numbness![10]

we respond in a similar manner with a replete satisfied sense of the justice and true representativeness of the observation, its wise closeness to a common human fact. Proust takes the habit of a generalisation to an extreme — a fruitful one, to which most of the time we accord our assent no less than to his predecessors, whether it qualifies place or human character:

> All day long, in that slightly too countrified house which seemed no more than a place for a rest between walks or during a storm, one of those houses in which all the sitting-rooms look like arbours and, on the wall-papers of the bedrooms, here the roses from the garden, there the birds from the trees outside join you and keep you company, isolated from the world — for they were old wall-papers on which every rose was so distinct that, had it been alive, you could have picked it, every bird you could have put in a cage and tamed, quite different from those grandiose bedroom decorations of today where, on a silver background, all the apple-trees of Normandy display their outlines in the Japanese style to hallucinate the hours you spend in bed — all day long I remained in my room which looked over the fine greenery of the park and the lilacs near its entrance, over the green leaves of the great trees by the edge of the lake, sparkling in the sun, and the forest of Méséglise . . . .[11]

I say 'habit' of generalisation, because it is probable that the majority of novelists everywhere have perceived their people and their scenes in the manner here essentially in view. In his Preface to *The Human Comedy* Balzac, with the strictest critical accuracy, can see that he has committed himself to a massive physiology of 'the human heart' ('le coeur humain')[12] as observable in his culture and his lifetime, because he assumes that 'the human heart' is a valid term which will embrace all the various manifestations that are conventionally known as human beings, that their most distinctive features, their most significant properties, are elements held in common.

In that, after all, he simply imitates the rest of us, endorses what we might define in itself as 'sanity'. All but the madmen among us expect the scenery everywhere in our mortal experience to adhere to dependable laws; we relate to our fellow-beings by what we know of our own inward workings. The difference with which I am here concerned is as much one of degree as one of kind, and I am disputing neither the validity nor the enormous success of the modes of portraiture operative in the (I believe) representative passages I have quoted from these authors. The portraitures of Balzac, or George Eliot or Proust (and I am instancing them, of course, pretty well at random as representative giants in un-Dickensian modes) work by developing similes for the conduct and thought observed in their pages out of an already fully assumed, and in fact aprioristically established, psychology. Proust does not *prove* to us that all human mentality is a uniform continuum cut into a million lengths, of the same dishonesties, subterfuges and so on as his characters attempt, unsuccessfully attended by such a narrator, to obfuscate. He presupposes it; not but that his case is in itself so strongly located in the infinite deceitfulness (rather than holiness) of the heart's affections that on that account alone he is a 'wondrous necessary' author.

Yet in Dickens people or things are introduced like this:

She had stopped at a shop, over which was written, KROOK, RAG AND BOTTLE WAREHOUSE. Also, in long thin letters, KROOK, DEALER IN MARINE STORES. In one part of the window was a picture of a red paper mill, at which a cart was unloading a quantity of sacks of old rags. In another, was the inscription, BONES BOUGHT. In another, KITCHEN-STUFF BOUGHT. In another, OLD IRON BOUGHT. In another, WASTE PAPER BOUGHT. In another, LADIES' AND GENTLEMENS' WARDROBES BOUGHT. Everything seemed to be bought, and nothing to be sold there. In all parts of the window were quantities of dirty bottles: blacking bottles, medicine bottles, ginger-beer and soda-water bottles, pickle bottles, wine bottles, ink bottles; I am reminded by mentioning the latter, that the shop had, in several particulars, the air of being in a legal neighbourhood, and of being, as it were, a dirty hanger-on and disowned relation of the law.

(This is a shop with a particular character, perhaps the only one of its kind in the world; not 'one of those shops which . . .' as not only Proust but several of his great compatriot predecessors would tend to describe it.)

There were a great many ink-bottles. There was a little tottering

bench of shabby old volumes, outside the door, labelled 'Law
Books, all at 9*d.*' . . . A little way within the shop-door, lay heaps
of old crackled parchment scrolls, and discoloured and dog's-eared
law-papers. I could have fancied that all the rusty keys, of which
there must have been hundreds huddled together as old iron, had
once belonged to doors of rooms or strong chests in lawyers'
offices. The litter of rags tumbled partly into and partly out of a
one-legged wooden scale, hanging without any counterpoise from
a beam, might have been counsellors' bands and gowns torn
up.   (v, 49–50)

If it be objected that Krook's shop – like his person – is specially
characterised in its eccentricity *for* its failing to exhibit the usual
tokens of the normal ordinary emporium, one could cite – again at
random for their representativeness – the presentation of Mr and Mrs
Bayham Badger (xiii, 173–6), or Mrs Woodcourt (xxx, 411), or the
view of the Iron-country afforded us in Sergeant George's visit there
(lxiii) or even that of the ultra-conventional Dedlock Cousins at
Chesney Wold (for example, xl, 565–8). Though the Coodle and
Doodle factions are represented as a fatuous class whom Dickens
expects his readers to recognise, the whole success of his satire lies in
the metamorphosis of the Whigs and Tories of his day into parties as it
were out of Lilliput or Brobdingnag; in his saying to the reader, 'Take
a fresh look at these people. See them divorced for a moment from
their accepted auras of status and wealth, and examine the logic or
merit of their conduct simply in and for itself. Are their attitudes not
perverse, ridiculous – unaccountable? The mad fantasy of a Coodle
to Zoodle and Buffy to Puffy politics is not mine but theirs.'
    What is recurrently exhibited is a way of seeing people and things,
in both narratives of the tale, as if they were concatenations without
rhyme or reason, odd, inexplicable; perceptions unelucidated by any
commonly possessed key to interpretation. This is not simply a
question of Dickens's marvellous ability to recreate the quality of
childhood-consciousness. The continual tendency to present everyone and everything as much in the character of phenomena that are
unique, unexplained and answering only to the individual laws of
their own impermeable existences, as is compatible with the kinds of
perception permitted by a language-system in the first place – with
all its generalising and universalising properties – goes beyond the
sense it affords us of our seeing these things through one veil less of
authorial intervention and interpretation than we do with other

novelists. It underwrites the whole activity of the tale as metaphor.

III

The modern detective story, of which *Bleak House* is a prototype, is by definition a romance form rather than a fictional genus we can associate with 'realism', even with the realism, strained by other sorts of improbability, which we find in Mrs Gaskell. And the detective-story element here is convincing exactly because its quality as romance is in key with everything else. Dickens can speak of *Bleak House* as a work in which he had 'purposely dwelt on the romantic side of familiar things' (in his Preface to the First Edition – p. xiv of the text used here) not because he has introduced suggestions of the paranormal or preternatural (apart from the step on the Ghost's Walk at Chesney Wold, these are largely absent), but because metaphor is the very staple of *Bleak House* and the essential way in which it constitutes its case. Instead of being acquainted with the largest human possibilities, the freest air, worked out within an ordinary range of likelihoods, we find them imaged in Mr Boythorn's Hesperidean garden (xviii, 247–8), or in the fact that the benevolent John Jarndyce has a fortune which is mysteriously inexhaustible and still more mysteriously untrammelled by the ruinous tentacles of the extravagant extortionate Chancery cause with which he is allegedly associated. We have the same process in the folktale-like character of the narrating heroine's story, with Mr Jarndyce as her fairy-godfather (a function which is doubled, first in his rescuing her in early childhood from a career of misery and then later in his renunciation of her marriage-pledges for the union with Allan Woodcourt which he helps to facilitate). It is this kind of typicality, this kind of representativeness, which is in question with Dickens, and one wounds half the case for this novel if one speaks of the characters and situations in it as if they had the same kinds of correspondence as are implied between the creations of George Eliot, or Hardy, or Conrad, or Lawrence, and the 'empirical' universe outside their books. We read about the personages in Dickens more in the manner of our response to the figures of folklore (whose human appeal and significance are in no way diminished); and we denature the sophistication, rather than the ingenuousness of this text, we miss the very fullness with which it wrestles with its problem, if we think about it otherwise.

Talk about Dickens as 'the Shakespeare of the novel' *can* be both wild and woolly; it will tend to collapse rather than invite new attempts at careful redefinition of both artists' respective idioms. But there is a likeness of the most specific and critically illuminating kind in the simple fact that Dickens and Shakespeare are almost alone in the sheer degree to which both use the elements of folktale in their work and integrate those features (as it were from an earlier phase of mythopoeia than the 'present' each is working in) with all that is characteristically new in the contemporary forms they are using. What is not redolent of the *Märchen* of Dickens's childhood reading[13] is filled out by the conventions of New Comedy (and as in Plautus or Ben Jonson *or* Shakespeare, we are paradoxically more conscious of their function for the relative perfunctoriness or relegation of the love-interest's treatment). Coincidence is 'the point' of Lady Dedlock's story; we accept its manifestations as wholly true, because we are conscious of looking at the story as a cross-sectional view of the presented world. But it is, simultaneously, long-armed. The history of Esther's progress out of orphaned misery into the arms of her Prince Charming is like Duke Vincentio's experiment in 'Vienna' or Prospero's upon his geographically so indeterminate isle, in just precisely not being (though important and cohesive) the unique focus for our interest, the exclusive mode of our attention to the tale, but also to some greater or lesser extent an occasion for showing us everything else; for the revelation of such comic 'types' as Guppy (the fatuous young suitor with incongruous romantic notions), Mr Snagsby (the hen-pecked husband) Mrs Snagsby (the proverbial shrew) and their menage, Grandfather Smallweed (the miser), Chadband (a Methodist Tartuffe) and Kenge (the inadvertent parasite de luxe of this social system); or such dark figures, no less out of folktale than those others were out of age-old comedy, as Tulkinghorn (the motiveless malignant) and Krook (the wizard who finally vanishes in his den, destroyed by the operations of his own necromancy); or of an image of the happy fields (Mr Boythorn's garden) and the *earthly* paradise (Bleak House). All these assist in presenting us with a metaphor of the social life which is not only complex in a necessary way, complex with an *animating* richness of counterpoised suggestions, but also total. Not only has Dickens found, for an image of the disablements of the very poor in his society, the highly stylised figure of Jo; for the significance of the governing classes' negligence, the undiscriminating ravages of the smallpox; for the essential reality of human interrelatedness, the exaggerated, but in the context wholly convincing, fable of the Dedlocks' involvement with people and places that normally they would not acknowledge. *Bleak House* constitutes a metaphor for all of life, for 'the whole show'.

This is why it can begin in the strange (and what would otherwise be arguably irrelevant) manner it does.

Sense and Sensibility and *Anna Karenina* are two of the profoundest investigations we have in the novel form into the problem of the social life; the compromises between it and the individual free spirit which may be deadly and which are, in some mode or other, inescapable. But we are reasonable if we ask whether even Tolstoy's masterwork does not take life *itself* 'for granted', as it were, in examining the problem. We do not have to subscribe to Ian Watt's whole case about 'the rise of the novel' to recognise the justice of his claim that

> The various technical characteristics of the novel [as he has described them in the preceding paragraphs of the chapter[14]] all seem to contribute to the furthering of an aim which the novelist shares with the philosopher — the production of what purports to be an authentic account of the actual experiences of individuals. This aim involved many other departures from the traditions of fiction besides those already mentioned. What is perhaps the most important of them, the adaptation of prose style to give an air of complete authenticity, is also closely related to one of the distinctive methodological emphases of philosophical realism . . . .

In seeking to impress a sense of just these correspondences Austen and Tolstoy are classically representative of most other prose-fictionists in their century, in that they suspend the reader's disbelief by throwing him *in medias res*, by assuming the implicit values (as to the centrality of its characteristic ways of seeing experience) of the established social life of their time; by writing as it were from within the proscenium of its rhetoric. Here are their opening paragraphs:

> The family of Dashwood had been long settled in Sussex. Their estate was large, and their residence was at Norland Park, in the centre of their property, where, for many generations, they had lived in so respectable a manner, as to engage the general good opinion of their surrounding acquaintance. The late owner of this

estate was a single man, who lived to a very advanced age, and who for many years of his life had a constant companion and housekeeper in his sister. But her death, which happened ten years before his own, produced a great alteration in his home; for to supply her loss, he invited and received into his house the family of his nephew, Mr Henry Dashwood, the legal inheritor of the Norland estate, and the person to whom he intended to bequeath it. In the society of his nephew and niece, and their children, the old Gentleman's days were comfortably spent. His attachment to them all increased. The constant attention of Mr and Mrs Henry Dashwood to his wishes, which proceeded not merely from interest, but from goodness of heart, gave him every degree of solid comfort which his age could receive; and the cheerfulness of the children added a relish to his existence.

All happy families are more or less like one another; every unhappy family is unhappy in its own particular way. The Oblonsky household was in a complete state of confusion. The wife had discovered that their former French governess was her husband's mistress and had declared that she could no longer live in the same house with him. This state of tension had continued for three days, tormenting alike to husband and wife, to every member of the family, and to all the Oblonsky domestics. They all felt that there was no sense or meaning in their living together and that any company of people accidentally thrown together in a wayside inn had more interests in common than they. The wife did not leave her own rooms and it was now the third day that the husband had not been at home. The children ran all over the house not knowing what to do with themselves, the English governess had quarrelled with the housekeeper and had written to a friend asking her to find another place. The cook had gone off the evening before just at dinner-time, the under-cook and the coachman had demanded their wages . . . .[15]

The first sentences of *Bleak House* are radically different. While 'London. Michaelmas term lately over, and the Lord Chancellor sitting in Lincoln's Inn Hall. Implacable November weather', may invoke a world of common assumptions, it does so only to displace them. The verbless syntax casts no secure anchor in what follows next,

As much mud in the streets, as if the waters had but newly retired

from the face of the earth, and it would not be wonderful to meet a
Megalosaurus forty feet long or so, waddling like an elephantine
lizard up Holborn Hill

and we are invited to conceive the contemporary social life as itself
one with and part of a much larger stranger reality than we normally
give our human situation the credit for being. The impression is not
fugitive: 'death of the sun. . . . if this day ever broke . . .' (from
sentences five and eight). If we ask why, indeed, the novelist begins his
work with a description of London at all – instead of going
straightway to the Chancery Court – the reason seems to be that he
wants to present a large image of its circumambient world, and that
seen just precisely in an unusual character.

Certainly Tolstoy the myriad-minded is perfectly capable of
looking upon the social experience of modern man with something
of the eye he might have for contemplating the prehistoric inhabitants of the earth. For Levin (cf. *Anna Karenina*, VIII, viii–xix) the
difficulty of meeting the different and incohesive faces of existence is
almost suicidal. Yet, albeit that what is in focus in Dickens's work (as
in Anna Karenina's story) is the difficulty and frustrations of living, at
some level we have to endorse Schopenhauer's view – however
much he may have been discredited in this by later philosophers –
that we, everything, did not have to exist in the first place. There is
something generous in the sheer fact of existence, still more that it has
such variegated possibilities out of which as a race we can make
problems for ourselves. Something of this is being implied with the
figure of the Megalosaurus or the other comic suggestions that follow
it, as throughout Dickens's book as a whole. One of the values to
Dickens of the *Märchen*-like elements in his work – not least in
the characterisation of his people or the description of his
environments – is that they help to constitute a world of 'once-upon-
a-time' behind (as it were) the allegedly contemporary realistic
referents of the text. They serve to inspire us with a sense of the social
existence itself – the phenomenality of it – as part of the total
equation, the candle we debate as to the value of the game. When
Joyce remarked 'the ogre will come in any case', part of his meaning
surely lay in just that use of a terminology which reawakens the sense
that our having these – albeit engulfing, impenetrable – veils to rend
or deaths to meet at all has itself a status, from the sheer 'oddity' of the
whole business (the Megalosaurus), which is a generous and creative
factor in the nature of our human predicament.

If the idioms of their language and the forms of their fables in Austen and Tolstoy tend more to take this phenomenality for granted, that is wholly legitimate of course. I make this distinction only to show how *Bleak House* is not a work we can 'convict' of having an essentially (as it were, a resolutely) negative bias. Dickens's characteristic techniques evoke an open and generous imaginative vision and it is in the context of this dialectic, of the book's nature as a metaphor for the whole of life, that we are to see the role of law and that John Harvey's comment (reviewing the Leavises' book on Dickens) is inapposite:

> Given [*Bleak House*]'s ambition in generalising about the human condition, and the major role assigned to litigation in the generalisation, is it a criticism of the novel that it propagates a wholly negative view of the law's function, and all that law can represent? Across the centuries one could compare it with *Njal's Saga*, another great novel that sees man as a litigating animal, but catches him in the formation of a legal system, and shows why it is necessary to have one (while decisively leaving the last word to individual courage and action). One can say this is not a question to ask, since the law in *Bleak House* is symbolic, but *Bleak House* is not *The Trial*: particular processes of law obtrude, and the large symbolism depends on the Chancery sort of litigation being the activity that does characterise the human race. And is that true?[16]

As it is, the book really starts from the more complex understanding he urges. The very existence of law in society signifies the commonwealth's determination, at some date or epoch in its history, to make predominant the creative and responsible human instincts over those which subvert the possibilities of happiness and meaning in the individual or the social life. The very fact of law's evolution – the corporate resourcefulness *that* implies – should powerfully engender hope of such a project's success deployed to these high ends. Yet Dickens notes, surveying the England of his day, how that act of communal intelligence has not produced real justice, any more than all Mr Jarndyce's real humanity and intelligence is given a satisfactory polemic or finds an adequate social expression. Law here embodies the essential problem with which the novel engages – the almost universal will for creative successful living, the general wish for a happy society, and the no less general failure to realise it. We are 'back with' Ada's pregnant comment, 'It seems very strange, as there must be right somewhere, that an honest judge in real earnest has not been able to find out through all these years where it is' (v, 58).

At its most serious, after all, law arbitrates the right to existence; and we are shown its failure and success in the case of sergeant George, mistakenly apprehended for the murder of Tulkinghorn (end of xlix). Of course a decent society must oppose itself to murder and with due process. Even in the most ideally ordered polity the weight of proof would lie with the innocent man arrested in circumstances which George himself freely admits to be incriminating and with a past record of which he likewise truly confesses, 'If I hadn't gone into the vagabond way in my youth, this wouldn't have happened' (lii, 705−6). But we know more of litigation here than to rely on it as simply a specially dexterous means of making truth appear. What makes George's situation so alarming is that there is no particular wish on the part of those who govern this community to see him hang, no conspiracy (as of a corrupt aristocracy his type endangers or a murderous mob his dignity infuriates) to hound the fellow out of his life for some perceptible reason. It will not be enough to save George that the case against him is only circumstantial, that his character wholly belies the murder charge and that he can provide unimpeachable witnesses to that character. The Bagnets, Esther and her guardian are all recognising equally the inescapable inefficacy of law in such a situation and the arthritic and degenerate processes of it in their society when they appeal to him to brief counsel exactly because 'The mere truth won't do' (lii, 704).

Dickens is perfectly capable of a sustained enquiry into the inevitably bad justice of a social organism which has itself become depraved; which is to say more than 'ordinarily' criminal, criminal as by the standards of societies which neighbour, precede or follow it. Hugh is actually hanged at the end of *Barnaby Rudge*. Sydney Carton has to deputise in that extremity for Charles Darnay at the close of *A Tale of Two Cities*. (The extent to which these great novels dramatise what in our own day are still the most important political issues for the liberal intelligence − as opposed to those revolutionary or conservative attitudes which are less than hard-thinking − has been sadly underrated. In *The Violent Effigy* [1973] John Carey brings to his case against claims for the respectability of Dickens's thought the observation that Dickens is only too evidently excited by the rioting in these books, as indeed by any acts of violence within his experience [cf. p. 17]. This seems to me to have the critical lucidity of, say, viewing Shakespeare askance for being only too convincing in the inward realisation of *his* murderers. *Macbeth* might as well have been indited by Mrs Humphry Ward if Shakespeare could not have dredged up out of the murk in his own rich moral nature the capacity imaginatively to identify and project the internal workings of the regicide. *Barnaby Rudge* and *A Tale of Two Cities* ought to figure on any short list of 'the great "political " novels' just because the extreme concern in their author for social order and sobriety is counterpoised by an appetite for outbreak, violence, bursting the bonds which itself is every bit as impressive. His own consciousness, like his novels, was polarised about the great representative tensions of the revolutionary age in which he lived — the age we still inhabit — and it is that which constitutes his centrality; by that that he can so graphically realise the terrifying potency for weal or woe *and* the inalienable place in the individual and thus society at large, of these passions and instincts in the human inheritance.) He is capable of yet profounder enquiry in this connection. *The Pickwick Papers* develop a remarkable paradigm of the Christian theology; and their greatest strength resides in the unconsciousness of the author's achievement. They come ultimately to show for organised around the question of whether natural justice itself is finally relevant. There again the novelist is unflinching. Dodson and Fogg are sickening and they get off scot-free. Mr Pickwick permanently compromises his honour and the very principle of justice he has been upholding in going to the Fleet, thus saying 'No' to the malpractice of his society, when he pays not only his own but also Mrs Bardell's legal imposts for their release from prison.

But the thematic functions of the legal processes in *Bleak House* are otherwise. The good intentions, the impulse towards clarification and the rule of right reason originally implicit in the very instituting of law are in the event expressed in George's release, which is encompassed by a functionary and major representative of this society's law-system, Mr Bucket. His total, seemingly uncentred and apparently unquestioning enthusiasm of self-dedication to the process of finding out things about people (on the off-chance that it may lead to their or other people's detection in crime) is very disturbing in other relations — not least, as has already been remarked, his willingness to join with Tulkinghorn early in the tale to implicate Lady Dedlock in, at that stage, he knows not what. But here it delivers the wrongfully accused sergeant from his bonds. Any attempt at a large vindication for the codes or procedures Bucket serves, and that also means the equity cases we are given to see, would be pretty factitious. A major point is that George is lucky; which Gridley ('the man from Shropshire') and Miss Flite could hardly claim for themselves. Yet it is equally clear that Dickens is not condemning law *tout court*, nor the various auxiliaries which a law-system inevitably develops (some kind of police force, a systematised process of crime-detection). And in what should be the most alarming juridical issue of the story – will Sergeant George be hanged for a murder he has not committed? – Dickens affords just the complexity which Harvey misses.

Law in *Bleak House* is, like everything else there, a metaphor for the reality which met Dickens whenever he laid down his pen. As with the Circumlocution Office in *Little Dorrit* (and its relation to Civil Administration) Dickens is no more developing a view of it as always and inexorably resolving itself into the perverted functions we are shown than Mr Jarndyce's fortune or Mr Boythorn's garden is an image, on the basis of a simple correspondence, of the way the larger human possibilities will usually express themselves. How could Tom-all-Alone's be taken seriously in hand by government without judicial procedure? – and the author's imprecations in the matter plainly call for such intervention (see, for example, paragraphs 2 and 3 of xlvi, 627–8) without fear of that involvement being necessarily self-defeating (Tom-all-Alone's being a consequence of the will-lessness which leaves so much undone that common humanity urgently requires).

But the legal processes, most of all the Chancery procedures, are the more effective as a metaphor for the prevailing inertia and perversity in the political, economic and ethical leadership of his society because their current condition is itself a symptom of those general diseases. The visits to Mrs Jellyby or from Mrs Pardiggle occur early in the tale just after we are first introduced to the Lord Chancellor's court, because Dickens's satire here arises in connection with the nearly paralysed nature of effective reform in the stricken life of England. (The best brief summary of how stricken it was, with regard to this novel's emphases, lies in John Butt and Kathleen Tillotson's *Dickens at Work*, chapter 7.[17])

The population figures had doubled in half a century (1801–51); the towns, especially London, had become glutted modern industrial conurbations without any effective provision of the amenities for the most fundamental decencies of living. As Owen Chadwick has pointed out,[18] not only the Church but all public services were wholly inadequate to cope with the great new influx and expansion and the new needs which accompanied them; for housing, sanitation and education on a massive scale. Real reform there had been by 1851 (as against, say, the situation of 1818); but not reform on a comparable, which is to say the necessary, scale. In 1848 Parliament finally centralised power in the matter of sanitation to the extent of passing a Public Health Act under which local boards

> were given powers to enforce drainage, provide and maintain sewers, and compel the provision of privies. They could pave and cleanse streets, and provide a scavenging service. They dealt with nuisances, offensive trades, and meat inspection. They were empowered to inspect and regulate common lodging-houses. Under certain limitations they could close burial grounds, provide or control water supplies, and provide public parks . . . .[19]

But the Act did not apply to Scotland – or the City of London(!) – and the local public health boards could be created only if one-tenth of the inhabitants of a district petitioned to such effect or if the death-rate exceeded 23 per 1000. By modern standards and the standards Dickens was seeking (though it was a revolutionary change histori-cally considered) these were hardly measures drastic enough for a terrible situation. The cholera epidemic which followed was a living demonstration of how entirely inadequate was government's con-ception of the problems facing the community, especially its poorer members. A man such as Dickens, rare in his continual patrol of the London streets both far and near,[20] saw on the one side an enormous image of capability; the new burgeoning wealth of the nation as a result of its industrialisation and colonial enterprises, the visible evidences on wharfs and in fashionable salons of the astronomic growth of its gross national product; and on the other, in the dire slums and fetid alleys, in the houseless, schoolless, foodless waifs and strays, a complete failure of any commensurable will or drive in the administrative or governing phases of the national life to deal with the worst of its social concomitants.

Although *Bleak House* presents us with 'the romantic side' of 'these familiar things' we do not lose sight of how much the novel is organised around the unprovided agonies of the new mid-Victorian England. With its scenes at the brickmakers' out by St Albans, its treatment of Jo, of Tom-all-Alone's, its acidic account of Coodle and Buffy, its imagery of disease, what could it be but very emphatically a book about 'the state of the nation' for its first readers, to whom those agonies were within the range of their personal daily observation – whence the great value to critical studies of the *Dickens at Work* chapter with its emphasis on the only too ample and alarming echoes these themes had for a contemporary audience.

The predominating groups in the England of 1851 were still men (and women) with superannuated but ingrained ideas who largely saw the national life in terms either of the old agrarian squirearchies and the social organisation which had reticulated itself around them, or the merchant-oriented order of the old, manageable cities. Contemporary equity law, wholly constituted as it was by a thousand ancient precedents and practices, all unrationalised, had long since become a veritable warren of abuses and was valuable almost exclusively to its practitioners rather than to the people whom the laws were officially made to serve. The counsel and all their professional auxiliaries fared regularly much better than the appellant and defendant in any civil action.[21] Dickens had himself already endured grievous experience of this,[22] and as such it was both a perfect instance and metaphor of *the* social problem: the wholesale failure of vision and of will in those who possessed administrative opportunity to ameliorate the condition of the country.

The sickening characteristic of 'the legal gentlemen' in *Bleak House* is that Vholes, evidently a dedicated predator, is *not* the most representative member of the confraternity. *Their* spokesmen are such as the Lord Chancellor or Conversation Kenge or Guppy; men in whom some civilised standards and taboos actually do inhere but whose talents for creative enterprise outside of the most immediate and local relations, whose intelligence, whose very capacity to see the need for reform (in their case within the domains of the legal system they operate) seems to be benumbed or atrophied by the general hypnosis, the apparent and universal somnambulism which so mysteriously yet so radically determines the nation's life.

If only Dickens *could* have dramatised his problem in terms of the working of criminal rather than of equity law, the difficulty of coming to terms with this impermeable and general perversity would have been less. Were government in his Britain committed to villainy (as in the Soviet Union today) with a penal code deliberately designed to frustrate justice and to torture truth, then he might well have seen in 'the condition of England' a new battleground in the eternal conflict between the simply – or largely – good, and the simply – or largely – evil; a struggle from which the upholders of decency do not always retire with lowered crests or deracinated hopes. But the upholders of at least some kind of sanity here – for example, Mr Jarndyce, Mr Boythorn, even Allan Woodcourt – are themselves, we have seen, participants in the 'sinister trance' whereby the abuses of Dickens's time can be tolerated and of which the general consequences in the national life are so well imaged in the abuses of its legal system that Dickens returns to them again and again in his works with vitriolic scorn and castigation.

Law in *Bleak House*, therefore, is both a metaphor for the failures of government in Dickens's society and for the generic inadequacy of the human race at any date; its failure to make active and effective the promptings of mutuality and responsibility, which is the more baffling in that such impulses constitute so much of what it is to be human in the first place (as various aspects of the novel give us to see and feel in their registration of what one may briefly call the human generosities). Even Vholes and Smallweed are not devils or predators wholly apart. They express the condition into which the high aspirations, of the individual, of society, have fallen; for probity in finance and law, or 'respectability', are no worthless values but they are grimly parodied and distorted in the trades these individuals ply.

It is appropriate, accordingly, in a novel organised round such a metaphor that we meet the motiveless malignities which society has developed (as it has run away perversely from its original ends) in the history of a woman persecuted by a lawyer for no assured reason; a lawyer, like the system he serves, whom she cannot escape even if he be individually destroyed. Tulkinghorn's death only exacerbates Lady Dedlock's situation. We are shown what it is to be born into this world without the sanction of the fallen and perverted social codes. These codes (about marriage, chastity, the need for a 'two-parent family' and so on) had a large value, they originally expressed (again) a human commitment which was responsible and creative. But this commitment has become deflected, the codes have become sufficient unto themselves and destructive. From working to protect the unborn child, they now co-operate to wound him. Law itself sides with 'respectability' (like that of Esther's godmother); Lady Dedlock's child is accounted '*il*legitimate', and that taint, we cannot but feel, lays its hand upon her life from beginning to end of her story. As in her mother's case, Esther has no redress against the all-encompassing fact of her stigmatised birth. The need to justify her existence is a hopeless Chancery-style cause which she carries within herself, before which she appears and at which she pleads, from first to last.

The appropriate image of the wronged innocent in such a community, then, the individual who sees in their proper lights the general social processes for the monstrous abuses which they are, might seem that of an appellant in an equity cause, a plaintiff in an action where the judges and the procedures are unjust. Yet Dickens sees that such a response to the prevailing failures of his society — one of mere protest and repudiation — is hopeless and possibly even suspect. It is hopeless for evident reasons — expressed for us in the fact that the 'ruined suitor, who periodically appears from Shropshire, and breaks out into efforts to address the Chancellor . . . can by no means be made to understand that the Chancellor is legally ignorant of his existence after making it desolate for a quarter of a century'. All he does, as would perhaps be Dickens's own function if his novels were exclusively works of indictment and opposition, is to 'furnish some fun' for the lawyers' clerks, and 'enliven the dismal weather a little'(i, 3—4). By definition, the general catalepsy is deaf. And this attitude would also be suspect because the sickness is all-embracing and to take up a position of simple revolt is to rely upon the authority and support of a moral superiority in oneself that in the nature of the case cannot be accredited. Here again Dickens writes what is so very much a fable for our day, if not indeed for any day. If I wax wroth against the absurdly disproportionate wealth — and profligacy — of the 'Western' nations, do I cut off my own hand for raising unnecessary victuals to my lips fifty-two weeks in the year while thousands die by the hour elsewhere of famine? Each of us who is seriously concerned with justice must acknowledge his participation in its universal failure.

Indeed, in a Christian society, law is or should be seen as itself the very token of that general lapse. Obviously arbitration is better than blood-feuding, just as divorce is better than a really terrible marriage. St Peter recommends obedience to the magistrate in an empire where it cost him his own life as well as those of many of his best friends. St Paul paid tribute to the value of law, again in this civic aspect of the idea, in appealing from the trumperies of the Jews against him to Caesar's cooler-eyed jurisprudence. But at a deeper level such accommodations are and always have been the (literally) desperate measures of a degraded race. The institution of law, whether in early Iceland or in ancient Greece (as celebrated in the *Oresteia*), the establishment of a coherent suprapersonal state arbitrament, is the very token of our race's despair of ever regaining — if we ever trod them — the paths of spontaneous goodness. Our elaborate codified

procedures at their best, excellent as they may be in securing a degree
of justice rather than the very perfection of outrage, compare unflat-
teringly with the instinctive taboos, so rarely infringed by any pec-
cant member, of so many other species. Law is a treaty with the evil in
our nature and almost every reader among Dickens's contemporaries
would have been amply catechised in those letters of the apostle
where the law of God – represented by conscience, the Decalogue
(for that matter the moral precepts in *The Analects*) – is itself
acknowledged as the conviction of a tribe doomed and damned. In St
Paul's epistles the all-revolutionising feature of Christ's living and
dying is His re-establishment of the possibility of grace, a state of
being in which the choice between good and evil is no longer a
problem or a burden, is no longer even really a conscious issue. ('The
Tao that can be expressed is not the eternal Tao.')

We have to acknowledge the religious connotations of 'law' in
Bleak House the more readily because it is remarkable how the book's
treatment of the theme centres at its heart round just that sort of
litigation which is condemned in the Sermon on the Mount. Verses
21–6 of St Matthew, chapter v, might well stand as an epigraph at the
head of Dickens's text:

> Ye have heard that it was said by them of old time, Thou shalt not
> kill; and whosoever shall kill shall be in danger of the judgment:
>
> But I say unto you, That whosoever is angry with his brother
> without a cause shall be in danger of the judgment; and whosoever
> shall say to his brother, Raca, shall be in danger of the council: but
> whosoever shall say, Thou fool, shall be in danger of hell fire.
>
> Therefore if thou bring thy gift to the altar, and there
> rememberest that thy brother hath ought against thee; Leave there
> thy gift before the altar, and go thy way; first be reconciled to thy
> brother, and then come and offer thy gift.
>
> Agree with thine adversary quickly, whiles thou art in the way
> with him; lest at any time the adversary deliver thee to the judge,
> and the judge deliver thee to the officer, and thou be cast into
> prison.
>
> Verily I say unto Thee, Thou shalt by no means come out
> thence, till thou hast paid the uttermost farthing.

Neither Jesus nor his disciples are anywhere above giving advice
which is simply commonsense or good peasant shrewdness; but in
their highly charged context (of at times preternatural revelation –

'The meek shall inherit the earth') it is hard not to see in these verses a whole ethic expressed in a particularised form, rather than a call to sanity which is just prudential. Again the issue is the inadequacy of law, of the commitment to the justice which can be juridically embodied, as a foundation for personal relations. We cannot change the world as individuals but we can so live towards others in our own lives that the essentially law-encoded basis of much human living (I am protected from my neighbour and any encroachment he may make upon me by my citizen's state-invested 'rights') is abandoned.

The key fact is that the Chancery causes we are shown in *Bleak House* have all originated in *family quarrels* – the Jarndyces', Miss Flite's, Gridley's – and at the end of the book 'the uttermost farthing' of the fabulous estate has been absorbed, Gridley has repeatedly been cast into prison and Miss Flite's participation in the ritualised anger which is an equity suit has *had* its judgement in her *not* being given a verdict. Like her waiting upon the Second Coming for the conferring of estates and her life properly to begin she has spent all her time, beauty, talent and promise attending a court where her case – as she finally recognises and concedes – will never even be heard.

Such considerations as these must, I believe, be allowed their part in any examination of what *Bleak House* is telling us about 'the possibilities of goodness in such an environment',[23] and they considerably respectabilise the quietism of Esther Summerson and her guardian; of whom we could otherwise complain that passivity, patience and retirement in the midst of so inhumane a society are obviously easier on who knows how many thousands a year, than they are for the likes of Jo, on nothing. There is evidently a more creative principle than that involved in their approach when the kind of opposition represented in Gridley or Carstone partakes – at more than one level – of some of the worst of the primary social sickness, in a sense condones it and the more deeply impresses it into the fabric of their living. Mrs Leavis commends 'the man from Shropshire' for his fight against Chancery[24] with a commentary which would be wholly just (*mutatis mutandis*) were it applied against the reactions of William Dorrit to *his* incarceration (her husband indeed supplies just such an account in the following chapter of their book. Acquiescence in the Marshalsea is deadly). But the view of Gridley as pilgrim-hero misses the irony of his 'dying testament'; and the Bell Yard chapter (of which Mrs Leavis elucidates the rich humanising properties) is also distinguished by a full account of Gridley's case from his own lips, the opening words of which should be guaranteed to raise the eyebrows of the open-minded reader:

> 'Mr Jarndyce,' he said, 'consider my case. As there is a Heaven
> above us, this is my case. I am one of two brothers. My father (a
> farmer) made a will, and left his farm and stock, and so forth, to my
> mother, for her life. After my mother's death, all was to come to
> me except a legacy of three hundred pounds that I was then to pay
> my brother. My mother died. My brother, some time afterwards,
> claimed his legacy. I, and some of my relations, said that he had had
> a part of it already, in board and lodging, and some other things.
> Now mind! That was the question, and nothing else. No one
> disputed the will; no one disputed anything but whether part of
> that three hundred pounds had been already paid or not. To settle
> that question, my brother filing a bill, I was obliged to go into this
> accursed Chancery . . . .'   (xv, 214)

The irony works both ways, and while the procedures of Chancery
are recognised by us as intrinsically chaotic and destructive, this
quarrel of the two brothers is no less disturbing in itself. To attribute
the grounds of their argument to the random chance of Dickens's
having incorporated the case at short notice and almost verbatim
from the life[25] would be to ignore the question of why the author's
artistry, having sieved through many Chancery suits of long suffering
and deferred judgement in planning his book, should have settled for
this as a fitting exposition of the law's intolerable achievements
Unqualified as Gridley's narrative is, we have to see in the man from
Shropshire a co-original of his troubles; that he and his family were at
the least a bit mean in a matter not worth the kind of division which
plainly lies behind the matter-of-fact tone of his telling. They could
have considered that if his inherited farm was worth so much more
than his brother's legacy (as is implied) then that brother had a hard
enough furrow to plough in beginning life anew with what (whether
in 1851 or twenty-five years earlier) was a scanty capital (the £300).
We remember that the Jarndyce cause originated in the various claims
of different Jarndyce relatives. As soon as Richard enters it personally,
he begins to suspect his guardian of acting in an opposing interest to
his own. And it is impossible not to associate the suit with the
intimations I have just attempted to register:

> 'Why, yes, it was about a Will when it was about anything,' he
> returned. 'A certain Jarndyce, in an evil hour, made a great fortune,

and made a great Will. In the question how the trusts under that
Will are to be administered, the fortune left by the Will is
squandered away.   (viii ['Covering a Multitude of Sins'], 95)

The Chancery actions we are shown exhibit the ruin of people who
have gone to law unnecessarily.

   I do not believe that Dickens is proposing quiescence as the most
valid or inspired response to the rank frustrations and thwartings of
the individual life in this society; though if we could say that his trust
was placed in the larger competencies alleged in the Dominical
admonitions ('the meek shall inherit the earth'), it would be crude to
accuse him of escapism, for in the case-history of these equity causes
he has developed a rich metaphor of the individual's involvement in
the general social failure, and, with that, of the danger of hypocrisy,
the further inspissation of the sickness under attack which is likely to
result in the very nature whose protest is revolt 'pure' and 'simple'.

   Gridley, in fighting his cause in Chancery (as if it ever could reach a
just judgement) is not only opposing a cruel and representative abuse in
the public administration – and with a real element of disinterested
courage that we admire: he is 'taking on' the nature of life itself,
the inevitably unjust state of affairs into which we are all born and to
which each contributes. Hence the appropriateness of the way in
which a Chancery cause in this novel, as frequently enough with the
baldest reality in Dickens's day, can only 'absorb itself in its own
costs', 'lapse and melt away' (adapted from lxv, 867) in the manner of
a human life wearing itself out. The Chancery process images the
dispensation under which we live – its painful inability to afford the
decent providence which is humanity's deepest need and which yet
humanity itself fails to embody and make comprehensive in its own
living. The ultimate failed or anti-plot of the novel fascinates us in so
potent a manner on this account. 'There's a cruel attraction in [it]'
because, however little the Chancery story does actually develop, we
'*can't* leave it'; it might yet reveal the original cause of its problematic
nature (or why it is as it is). However groundless the hope is
continually proved, we '*must* expect' some ultimate resolution which
will satisfy. But its processes, like the problems of the individual life,
can be 'resolved' only in being extinguished; the private existence
perishing in hope of 'The world that sets this [world] right'
(lxv, 871).

IV

In looking at Gridley's conduct with this detachment and endorsing it only in this qualified degree, Dickens does not minimise the brutalities of the world he presents or the difficulty of right action in it for the conscientious individual. The criminality of pococurantist government is harmonised shockingly with the problem of respecting the not-worthless provisions which society has made against criminal behaviour (the regulations of law and a police force to carry them out) in the brilliant episode where Esther finds to her chagrin she has no really satisfactory answer to Skimpole's claim that in making Jo's whereabouts known to Bucket and thus 'moving him on' again (effectually to his death), he (Skimpole) was but fulfilling his duties as a citizen (lxi, especially 830). When all reservations have been duly made about his actual self-centred motives on that cruel occasion, there remains an irrefutable sense in which Skimpole is, all repulsively, right. If we want the capture of Tulkinghorn's real murderer – or, rather, exculpation of the two suspected innocents (Lady Dedlock and Sergeant George) – we cannot deny Inspector Bucket's assiduities in other directions any more than we can have individual members of the commonwealth singly choosing, at hazard, when and where they will co-operate with the police's request for information.

This is but one instance, well advanced in the tale, of Dickens's severely responsible and sustained focusing upon consciousness, intelligence and capacity as themselves in such a context no less a burden (though a more subtle kind of disfranchisement) than the extreme indigence which scars so many lives on all sides. Either one is entirely borne down by the circumstances of the outward world – like Jo, whose predicament, for all that it is expressed in a stylised manner, makes plain to us that his condition of jejune consciousness and that of his kind throughout society is at once its own curse and alleviation (i.e. in some respects – not those of the belly – he does not know what he is missing; see xvi, 220– 1) – or one is not. Like the fabulous dowries or troves, the legacies or magic rings of fairy-tale, the point of Jarndyce's apparently sourceless and endless wealth is to provide us with an image of what it means in this world *not* to be like Jo: namely, to be clad and fed and intellectually developed enough to see this environment for the affrontingly insufficient one it is. His wealth is unaccompanied by any meaningful professional occupation (and to suggest that Allan Woodcourt at least possesses a virtue as well as an advantage over him in that respect is to ignore the fact that, even for his new northern practice, at the end of the novel, the young doctor needs help from the Jarndyce coffers to set up on his own terms of social dedication). The most he can do is to give an individual here or there (such as Esther) a lift, or, in creating his own small corner of limited happiness and decency, to remember the real name of the world outside – which *is* 'Bleak House'. But it is also the appropriate title for the world within; which he acknowledges, as it were, in painting it over the door not only of his own abode but also of that of his ward in her new home. It is in John Jarndyce's situation and performance that Dickens objectifies this part of the problem of being conscious in the face of the general social disaster; the really irresolvable tension between the desire to challenge 'the system' as Gridley does or to defer to it by failing explicitly to recognise the prevailing monstrosities, and to oppose them, for what they are. If the latter is the response of which Esther's guardian is guilty much of the time, that does not diminish the impenetrability of his each particular defecting recognition, every ducked judgement, as in its turn metaphorically expressive of the mystery of the general failures in the human world which I spoke of before. (The other leaders of society have whole 'systems' – the law, Parliament, administration – which they can influence.)

The difficulty of finding some golden mean of a middle way here, such as might be implied by those alternatives in conduct, is overtaken as a critical issue by the fact that nobody does achieve this kind of balance within the tale – nobody, that is, except the author. To write *Bleak House* is to bring all these considerations into fully articulated relation. And of course, while the energic potential of the humanly thinkable is embodied as it is here – by *this* language, *this* fictive organisation – we can no more accept the image of Mr Krook's spontaneous combustion or the themes of disease and failure or of universally abdicated involvement as a whole final expression of that world than we can Macbeth's or Lear's accounts of *their* collapsed universes. The fact of Shakespeare's language is itself a qualifying agent in our perception of what his dramas reveal as action and suffering, and we must say the same for Dickens. But there are also qualifications no less radical which both writers make about the role of author, and Dickens certainly does not see in the creative nisus or its organised and directed action, whether as an individual enterprise or as a social role, something which extrapolates him from inclusion in 'the family curse'.

We may remind ourselves that Mr Jarndyce has no marriage, in the end, and no children of his own; only the already somewhat blighted lives of his adoption. All he can do is to set up idealised ambits (*his* 'Bleak House', Esther's and Allan's in lxiv) to which he gives the very name which Dickens bestows upon *his* undertaking as a fictionist. And Jarndyce talks, as perhaps he has to talk if his sensibilities and responsiveness are not to drive him insane, a comparably ordered and diminished language – 'Dame Durden', 'Little Old Woman', and so on: a language reminiscent of fairy-tale. At every point the metaphors work both ways and Dickens's reliance upon the folkloristic world for so much else in his novel is here itself focused in its two-sided character and embodies a radically ambiguous account of the mind which fathers this account of the society under examination. The novel turns upon itself and we find incorporated in its totality as image and metaphor (for the whole of life), the question of the legitimacy of its author's own enterprise as author.

Esther very evidently embodies Health (with a capital H) as well as sickness. When Diane F. Sadoff remarks that, 'Whereas we once thought of Esther as a healthy alternative to the chaos and corruption of the social world of *Bleak House*, we now tend to think of her as a neurotic anal-retentive with identity problems',[26] she has to speak for herself. Such a dichotomy of this heroine's complex nature is neither fair nor useful. Yet Mrs Leavis has argued incontestably that what we are given in Esther is (among other things) the portrait of a 'case':

> Esther is always true to her own peculiarities but they are not mannerisms: . . . Her submissiveness makes her blame herself whenever as a child she is unsuccessful in winning the affection she craves, but she never criticises the others, so that her submissiveness becomes painful to us, as it was meant to. The psychology of an illegitimate child of her time can never have been caught with greater fidelity.[27]

It is certainly part of the truth about Esther that she has an identity-problem – that, all evidently, of needing to find some justification for the existence about which she was assured at a crucially early date: 'It would have been far better . . . that you had had no birthday; that you had never been born!' (iii, 17).·

It follows naturally from this terrible beginning that she should (covertly) always be attempting to gauge her status as an affectional object in every scene of which she describes her participation. This can come to irritate us. In a chapter where one man sacrifices his hope of marriage with her, and another is made her fiancé against his expectation, Esther is still largely preoccupied (without realising it) in portraying *her* emotions; the devices of indirection by which she appears to silhouette her partners', in fact almost eclipse them beside the throbbing sense of her own selfhood that we are given:

> He was so quaintly cheerful that I could not long be otherwise, and was almost ashamed of having been otherwise at all. When I went to bed, I cried. I am bound to confess that I cried; but I hope it was with pleasure, though I am not quite sure it was with pleasure. I repeated every word of the letter twice over. (lxiv, 855)

That there are nine 'I's there in five lines (of the Oxford Illustrated edition) as she writes about the end of her guardian's hope of marriage with her is a function of her strickenness; the matter is certainly beyond blame. Nevertheless it has its part in her meaning in the work as a whole.

It follows equally convincingly from the nature of her problem that she should be glad to diminish her own life and the life about her. She thankfully accepts names like 'little woman', 'Mother Hubbard', and so forth, her internal dialogue (that of her self with its alter ego) is conducted as between a not really believed-in adult and a young child; and indeed all Esther's language by comparison with that of the other, the 'omniscient', narrator, has its diminished and diminishing quality, as do her attempts at human relations. The generosities which exist between her and Charley Neckett (her little maid whom Mr Jarndyce rescues from indigence in Bell Yard) are grateful indeed and the more moving in a world where such mutuality is all too rare. But the pair of them inhabit a shrunken ambit where what we might normally look to as the spontaneous tones and gestures of developing adult life in them are withheld (see, for example, xxxi, xxxv, *passim*).

All this is interpretable and more than allowable. As a consequence of her dreadful childhood Esther's hold on her self-respect is radically uncertain enough (for all that Mr Jarndyce and her other friends ever can do for her) without her exacerbating its insecurity by facing and negotiating hour by hour the full moral difficulty of life in the world as the novel at large has elucidated it for us. It ought to be enough that she is committed to 'goodness' at all, albeit a goodness of a limited and (in some respects) too-simple kind.

This is present to us in the scene where Caddy Jellyby's baby is introduced (l, 680), of which I gave Robert Garis's account in my Introduction.[28] We feel Esther's limitation in her capacity (as at the brickmakers' by St Albans, when the baby there dies — viii, 108–11) to disinfect the scene of its possibilities of 'a painfully . . . intense *complexity* of attitude towards'[29] the baby with her pity. Considering the nature of pity as such, Garis valuably adduces Tolstoy, of whose account of a visit to the very poor[30] he summarises this implication: 'What is wrong with pity, for Tolstoy, is that it forces an identity, a role, on a human being and therefore denies him freedom.'[31]

There are two issues here. One is simply that in Dickens life is represented in a different, not less valid, fictive mode from Tolstoy's; and, given the nature of these different fictional idioms, there is much we respond to as wholesome and generous in Dickens's presentation of his scene. The other is that, within his 'stock' situation with its 'symbolic child . . . [of] straightforward [and] simple . . . meaning' (adapted from p. 120 of Garis) a full complex life of subtle intimations is going on; for to the appeals of a less sophisticated order of narrative Dickens is marrying the massively complex resources of the nineteenth-century novel-form at this advanced stage in its development (as he is doing throughout most of his *oeuvre*). The troublesomeness is there for us readers (Garis acknowledges it in making his complaint) *in* the neatness with which Esther leaves Caddy's child's tragedy so amply described and yet so little redressed and we do react 'against' her pity for being so inadequate a response. Yet, given that the baby *is* constitutionally weak, and deaf and dumb, what else can she do? (Esther goes, after all, to nurse both the child and its mother.) Part of the scene's complexity is that we are left having to acknowledge how, if Esther had an ampler sense of the irresolvably problematic in life, if she offered us a more satisfying responsiveness, it would actually avail her in this as in most instances — it would avail Caddy's baby — very little.

We would leave the matter at this, staring at the hateful insoluble dilemmas and hurts of our human situation, we might even be glad that to the full implications of what she sees Esther is not awake (given her own problems) if she herself were not so much the repository of occluded motivations that she is. When every probable cause of *her* lapses and *her* defected judgements have been taken into account, there still remain situations where, as with so many of the other characters in *Bleak House*, her conduct or her attitudes cannot be interpreted.

I have already touched upon the perversity of her attitude to Caddy Jellyby's leaving home without her mother's blessing. In enforcing a traditional view of filial obligation where the parental ones have been wholly abdicated, Esther becomes the spokesman of just the kind of loyalty to inert ethical formulae which made her first home so grim and has left her position in society as a whole so cruelly insecure. Yet it was her narrative which, we had previously supposed, presented Mrs Jellyby in a sufficiently critical light:

> Peepy was lost for an hour and a half, and brought home from Newgate market by a policeman. The equable manner in which Mrs Jellyby sustained both his absence, and his restoration to the family circle, surprised us all.   (v, ending)

We find ourselves having assumed the presence of an irony there, which is indeed probably operative, but of which the measure, in face of such an episode as this of Caddy's engagement, becomes indefinable.

Much the same consequence derives from her treatment of Harold Skimpole.

> If I felt at all confused at that early time, in endeavouring to reconcile anything he said with anything I had thought about the duties and accountabilities of life (which I am far from sure of), I was confused by not exactly understanding why he was free of them. That he *was* free of them, I scarcely doubted; he was so very clear about it himself.   (vi, 70)

That seems to carry with it an implication precise enough; we conceive Skimpole to be deliberately placed at that point with the critical tone his nasty parasitism deserves. The 'innocent child' goes on later to talk, however, in 'his usual gay strain' of Gridley's difficulties as providential or of the penury of 'Coavinses' and his children as occasions for a meditation on the sublime fitness of everything, and Esther can then actually conclude,

> There was something so captivating in his light way of touching these fantastic strings, and he was such a mirthful child by the side of the graver childhood we had seen, that he made my guardian smile even as he turned towards us from a little private talk with Mrs. Blinder. We kissed Charley, and took her down-stairs with us . . .   (xv, 217)

It would illuminate much if we could say of Skimpole that for Esther, here, his intellectual ingenuities and moral gyrations portended the same resources of human inventiveness and enfranchisement as we are responding to as readers (and evidently Dickens is himself as author) in the performances of Chadband. It might be so. But as with John Jarndyce's motivations or Mr Bucket's – or Tulkinghorn's – this is simply unascertainable. That the narrator writes in the future of the action she describes and from an acknowledged vantage-point of riper consciousness (in this case, the final proofs of Skimpole's moral nature – lxi, 831) only complicates, it does not dissolve, the difficulty of focusing the historical Esther's state of mind both in its earlier and later phases. For this Esther of xv is also the Esther who addresses us at the end of the book. The woman who could see Skimpole in this strange manner is thus the Esther endorsed *by* the end of the book with its very comparable sort of hesitations. Until she begins 'to think that Richard could scarcely have found a worse friend than this' (xxxvii, 522), her evaluation of the parasite is neither collusive nor hostile but unplaceable.

We can well see why she should be far from ready to blame other people: from a self-evident cause she is thoroughly ill assured about the status and value of her own judgements. And there are occasions when this uncertainty is clearly visible as a consequence of that cause (as for instance at the beginning, when she insists on thinking of her 'godmother' or of 'Mrs Rachel' as 'a good, good woman' – iii, 15– 16). Yet that only amplifies her significance as a personage in this novel's world, part of whose inward life is as hidden as the other characters'; indeed whose life is in one respect the most hidden of all. It is a critical fact of the first importance that we are never given to see her through anybody else's eyes (not even, effectually, the other narrator's; Esther we have to interpret or puzzle out from her own utterance). As 'author' of her own part of the tale, she enjoys very considerably that position's inherently veiled life. Herself a crippled member of a world which bafflingly fails in its obligations, Esther's avoidance of the most harrassing problems of living offers itself to us (both in its nature as an ultimate human mystery in which she participates with all the race, and as the function of a particular disablement open to diagnosis) in a fashion of the most assimilable – the product of her labours as an author.

She is no more the representative of the novelist in any simple way than is her guardian; self-evidently. We are adverted of so much by the differences alone between her voice and that of the impersonal narrator, which by common consent is more assured and secure, more free-wheeling in its tropes. Nevertheless, their roles are paralleled. Where else in Dickens is the task of narration shared to this extent between author and character in any other than first-person narration (as opposed to short isolated tracts of psychological case-history like 'The Bagman's Tale' or Miss Wade's 'History of a Self-Tormentor')? Esther Summerson is herself most largely associated with the actions she portrays *as* their story-teller. The fact that the conventions of the novel – this novel – leave us without any actual motive for her reconstituting her experience in this way, 'seven years' after the event, only the more insinuates our sense of her doing so like any other novelist; as a means of interpreting and coming to terms with not only one phase of it but all her experience. But she does not appear to do so with any success that can satisfy us, which has left her (this is to say) a more competent personality at the end of the tale.

Placed as she is *by* her tone and posture, in contradistinction to Dickens's, her full significance emerges, I believe, only with the last eight chapters (lx–lxvii), not least in their character of anticlimax. The elaborately plotted story of Lady Dedlock's downfall, her exposure and the long chase after her, has come to an end. The narratives that follow are some of them summary (lxiii, for instance, on the later fates of Sir Leicester, Mrs Rouncewell and Sergeant George, the Dedlock estate and cousins); the others deal with people about whom – for reasons I have already aired – our interest is less fully stirred than with the quickened tempo and detective story stimulus of what has gone immediately before. We are also given intimations of the inadequacy of the new industrial order in the ironmaster's world; our doubts about the sufficiency of his virtues in opposition to the Dedlock ones are filled out, and that is important enough. But both chapters lxiii and lxvi are more significant as short tracts in which the impersonal narrator is retreating from the action and as it were out of the novel. Chapter lxvi has no dialogue, but is a summary with a continuously falling, valedictory rhythm. Everyone characterised there is shown to have fallen upon very different days from those we have seen earlier; the intimation is complex: boredom, peace, inertia, tranquillity. The momentum has left the book as a story, and Rick Carstone's decline and death, Esther's apotheosis in her marriage at the new 'Bleak House' have been pretty amply expected without having been tragic or comic enough, in the Aristotelian sense, to have been utterly gripping. Nothing is so much at issue in these chapters 'Esther' pens (lx–lxii, lxiv–lxv, lxvii) as the 'narrator's' own status in such a world as this, where the frustrations and cramps, the positive mutilations which have shaped and environed so many lives are such that the life of the seer himself, or the artist—diagnostician, is also inescapably tainted — tainted with the situation of comfort and repletion amidst the enormous dearth, with the impotence of the man awake amidst a society of somnambulists, with the difficulty of finding a value and a meaning in his artistic impulses and their fulfilment which radically engages with the prevailing miseries. Esther's charities are far from valueless (as Charley would amply testify) but her attempts at making reading and writing themselves meaningful to Charley are significantly baffled, are shown to be irrelevant to everything that is most gracious and creative in Charley's living (cf. the opening of xxi). And the rather irritated sense we all have of Esther's complacently roaming round Bleak House jangling her keys is born, surely, of our registering what Dickens has fully accounted for in the novel, directly and de-liberately: the fact that like the other dwellers there she has settled for a shrunken reality (the reality in which all the diminutive terms of her language are appropriate) with the hard world locked out effectually by nothing so much as her good fortune. To say this is not to derogate from the real worth of her real kindness to Jo or to the brickmakers' wives or her mother or anybody else. But these intimations, taken in conjunction with what now appears for a more exclusive share of our attention (in the story's wake as it were), are deeply disturbing. What appears has always been implicit in her position and her character: its metaphoric relations to Dickens's own. Nothing in the book is sterner or more unflinching than the way he sustains her manner of discourse in these last pages. Her closing words, after all, are not felicitous, but even before them she has directed the readers' attention firmly and fixedly towards herself most of the time (as in her account of her suitors in lxiv, considered above). If we only come to the realisation with the closing paragraph, we cannot miss its implicit self-gratulation and we conceive with a shock that she has written her part of the book in considerable measure to enjoy an image of herself that only she can provide. Not only is she the 'Dame Durden' (allegedly, this is to say, an elderly figure of sexual impotence) who deprecates as ugliness the looks and as insufficient the personality of which she greatly appreciates other people's actual enjoyment. She has a double pleasure in writing her report: it ministers to the anxieties of her self-oriented insecurity, the wish to reassure herself of her friends' suffrages, amity and confidence; and it gratifies her with an image of herself that is beautiful expressed as in a literary mirror. Heaven knows she has her reasons, poor girl, but the evidence is inescapable in the closing lines that her part in the narration of *Bleak House* has been considerably narcissistic.

The ethics of passivity 'pure' and 'simple' have been found as little satisfying as those of simple protest, and the difficulty for the individual such as Dickens who *is* awake in 'these bad days'[32] well beyond the measure of a Jo or an Esther Summerson is that, even in registering all these truths and dangers, his enterprise itself as a novelist verges — or so much is intimated in the through-running metaphor he has found for *it* — on the self-affirming. The writer who most radically challenges the norms of days so bad may in certain respects be the victim of which the general failure, 'the family curse', the preponderating paralysis (if it may be momentarily personified) might most have cause to be proud. For his enterprise as artist may go furthest of all in a direction this novel has generally opposed: towards a diminished and self-endorsing kind of response to the general 'bleakness'.

Yet 'paralysis' is the last word we would use of the novel; how can we, where the mystery and difficulty of these problems are concretised with (what have defined themselves as) so much breadth, energy and generosity of vision? The measure of *Bleak House*'s sanity is that we don't put it down simply catching our breath. Nor evidently did its author: he returned again to the question, as Mrs Leavis puts it, of 'the possibilities of goodness in such an environment' with a focus of concern and application creatively narrowed, twice during the next four years (1853–7). I believe that in *Little Dorrit* he brings his deepest intuitions to their most luminous and liberating expression of all.

3 *Little Dorrit*: The Triumph of Reality

In *Bleak House*, then, we encounter a world which is tragic in that its human relations are seen to have the logic of a cause in Chancery. But even there what Dickens sees, or his way of looking at the world, is pregnant with generosities which leave the reader, like the novelist, nowise merely paralysed with a view of things which 'quietly declaims the cursings of itself'.

A price has been paid, however – deliberately and creatively, I hope to have shown – for an account of the social predicament which so veils many of its characters' motives and attitudes. The novel is appropriately named after a residence, a building, not one of its *dramatis personae*, because its centre of gravity remains essentially a social image. In *Bleak House* we are to behold a populous diorama and the unacknowledged connections between man and man there which lead to its deep human frustrations; we do not penetrate the innermost workings as such of the human heart.

Such a process is radically the issue in *Little Dorrit* (which by contrast takes its title from its heroine). Here it is the essential proclivities of the human imagination which are themselves ana-tomised. The delinquencies of the encompassing social system are no less than before offered to our just indignation; but what we are also shown is that they are born 'in the foul rag-and-bone shop of the heart'. Amy Dorrit herself and Arthur Clennam, far from being wholly good or even supremely decent, carry within themselves those tendencies which in different spheres and finding other expressions have made their society the dark negating organism it is.

Yet the book does not make gloomy reading, for Dickens also identifies a permanent, independent resource within the psyche which, if it does not always contain the destructive pretensions of the individual, is powerfully resistant to them. This resistance, where its agency is successfully denied, extracts a fearful penalty; but where it is not wholly extirpated it militates continuously for a renewal of the self upon terms that are life-enhancing.

I

However exhilarating *Little Dorrit* may be as to what it discovers in our human nature, Dickens at this stage in his career (1855–7) can hardly be accused of developing any fondly unrealistic views of the social process around him. As J. C. Reid has remarked in his study of the novel, it abounds with bad parents and poor family life. Even the Plornishes, the only relatively happy family, have to accept that Old Nandy must spend most of his time in the workhouse, such is their poverty; and they 'lack the vitality and glow of the Peggottys'.[1] William Dorrit is a neglectful father and a destructive influence upon his children; Miss Wade's 'grandmother' and Arthur Clennam's 'mother' are cruel to their young charges. Casby holds his daughter Flora in emotional thrall (but yet theirs is more a non-relationship than any kind of intercourse. Some of Mrs Finching's endless loquacity and fantasising is doubtless the consequence of her inhabiting so solitary a private world in the home she shares with him). Mrs Gowan brings up her son to be an unhappy parasite. The Meagleses' treatment of poor Tattycoram is the more stifling – she herself feels it to be so – for proceeding from people of good will whose imagination is acutely limited. The eccentricities of their home in Twickenham or their travelling customs do not strike us as endearing but rather as being irritatingly 'twee', self-endorsing at their best and at the worst openly and unadmirably Philistine. Their inability to be settled in any place for long, travelling to alleviate a serious restiveness, to obscure a basic aimlessness in their bored lives, their obtuseness in dealing with sensitive areas of relationship: such things must bode ill for the health of their society as much as in their personal affairs, for we take the Meagleses as representative of a whole class and the most genial members of the class at that. 'Pet's' marriage follows logically from all this on one level just as the triumphs of Lord Decimus on another. When the wheel has come full circle and 'Tattycoram' is trapped again with her suffocating foster-parents and her dreadful name (the girl's outburst against it is unanswerable) what Mr Meagles says to her about 'duty' as they watch the figure of Little Dorrit cross the Marshalsea yard below is singularly irrelevant moralising in exactly the representative fashion of that class. We have seen that it is not 'duty' which has 'given [Amy's] eyes their expression' (II, xxx, 812–13) it is love and goodness – *and*, for the matter is complex, until lately a morbid psychic masochism. The

novel has shown us how 'duty' alone, both in Arthur Clennam's case
and in that of the woman he marries, is not enough to rescue the
individual life from self-imprisonment – morally, psychologically.

The one exception to the generally poor parenthood in the world
of this novel is that of Amy for Maggy, which exists between two
people who are practically of an age and unrelated by blood. Amy is
probably not least rewarded for her generosity here in that such
womanhood as has developed within her over the years must have
been nourished by Maggy's dependence upon her as an arrested child,
drawing out of her and into considerable play – as we behold in the
scene of their being locked out of the Marshalsea by night (I, xiv) –
her rich maternal instincts.

As Reid says, there is an 'almost clinical examination of the English
class system' in this work, 'and its accompanying patronage and
snobbery. . . . [Dickens] anatomises the . . . vice of snobbery on all
levels of society. . . .[2] Powerfully protected by their social status and
buttressed by the myth that Government is a mysterious ritual
conducted by a priesthood, appointed by apostolic succession' – a
myth that is at once continually woven and renewed by such
conversations as those at Hampton Court at which Clennam (I, xxvi)
is obliged to attend – 'the Barnacles patronise everybody.' With his
'wonderful air of benignity and patronage and his belief that he is
conferring great favours on those who pay for his comforts . . .
William Dorrit is a parody of Lord Decimus Tite Barnacle. And as
the self-importance of the Barnacles takes its toll in bad government
and human misery, so Old Dorrit's takes its toll in its effects on his
children.'[3] There is Fanny's 'contempt for the others "who are all on
their own level, Common,"' and Tip [Dorrit] accepts as due to his
"station" Clennam's obtaining his release with the same air as
Stiltstalking and Mrs Gowan despise "the mob"'.[4] The irony always
remains of course that to a detached eye coolly observing the scene,
the Stiltstalkings, Barnacles, *et al.* are so many free-booting 'Gipsies'
(see I, xxvi, 311); not in the sense of being real Romany, but mere
poachers and parasites operating on a socially grand scale. Mrs
General, in exploiting the whole patronage system to her own
advantage, 'poses', in Reid's words, 'as a superior arbiter of manners
and taste'.[5] For her, observing the 'correct' human behaviour is a
negative code, another version of 'How not to do it.'

'The Whole Duty of Man', which at the end of Ecclesiastes' dry
and drained contemplation sprang up fresh, that he should 'fear God,
and keep his commandments' (xii, verse 13, in the Authorised

Version) has been corrupted in this hypocritically Sabbatarian organism to become hard-bargain-driving, ruthless commercialism (as is compactly expressed in the conversation between Pancks and Clennam on man's being made for nothing else but 'business' (I, xiii, 160)). So much are society's values money-oriented that the great sin here is the failure to pay one's debts (financial debts; other kinds of debt don't matter), and the punishment for it is the exclusion of the debtor not only from the community as a whole, but also from the very freedom to make good his defaulted obligations; that is, what the Marshalsea has to offer, figuratively and literally, is not only imprisonment but also a species of damnation.

On the one side there is the sheer banal tedium of life in working London, as in Bleeding Heart Yard with its serious rent – unemployment problem and only 'one little golden grain of poetry' (I, xii, 136) in it; a life so tedious and limited that, as Plornish the plasterer says, people who objected to the poor taking one day off in the year – 'with his wife and children going to Hampton Court [of all ironical destinations!] in a Wan' – 'seemed to want to make a man mollancholy mad' (I, xii, 143). (I am sure there is a deliberate point here in Dickens's showing us the Plornishes' predilection, on their rare holidays, for going to gaze at this mansion of the socially great, the representative circumlocutionary parasites.) And on the other there is the routine of leisure among the rich of Park Lane and its attendant mewses, where life on a Sunday is equally, as Mrs Sparkler observes, 'like lying in a well' (II, xxiv, 693). Words there are used to form lips, not to create meanings between people, to promote real intercourse. But the marriage-market flourishes under a variety of subterfuges throughout society. Edmund Sparkler and 'Pet'Gowan, and also Affery the giddy skivvy well past her salad days, are actual sacrifices to the principles of convenience or ambition on the part of their parents or others. People are dehumanised by being the victims of relentless domination, practised as supports to others' pride or offered by themselves as a release from full human consciousness amidst their slavery. The thrall in poor Affery's case stretches right across the spectrum from materially serflike dependence upon 'the two clever ones' (Mrs Clennam and Jeremiah Flintwinch) to her victimisation at the hands of their gratuitous personal tyrannies, and the terror of the ghostly, the unseen supernatural (in the Clennam house with its dust 'dropping . . . so softly', its 'walls with long crooked touches' – II, xxx, 785).

The book ends with the Barnacles *et hoc genus omne* as much ensconced in all the offices of state as they have always been and the 'Bleeding Hearts' as little delivered out of their wretchedness. Fanny and Tip still weave the wind with their social pretensions — now at some extra human cost to Fanny's family of unwanted children and Amy's resources as a mother; and the prison that Arthur Clennam quits with his new bride is yet fully occupied with hapless debtors who are not allowed out to work off their debts. Even the belated dignity of Mrs Clennam's confession, while it rescues her from part of the lie she has lived so long and from a literal death (she leaves her old house to admit all that she has perpetrated over the years, just before it collapses), does not save her from a new and now irreversible paralysis; there is a grim irony in such an escape. In the way of life to which her son came back at the story's opening there was 'Nothing to change the brooding mind, or raise it up.' In a 'coffee-house on Ludgate Hill' he was surrounded by

> Ten thousand responsible houses . . . frowning heavily on the streets they composed . . . [and] Fifty thousand lairs . . . where people lived so unwholesomely, that fair water put into their crowded rooms on Saturday night, would be corrupt on Sunday morning; albeit my lord, their county member, was amazed that they failed to sleep in company with their butcher's meat. (I, iii, 28)

In short this world in its human character is grim; so grim that it is the prostitute whom Little Dorrit and Maggy meet (I, xiv) — a woman who, in despair at her poverty, is effectually committed by her profession to subverting the essential cohesive matrices of society itself (marriage, family-life) — who seems the most instinct with the human compassion which is so much lacking through the rest of the social scene.

As the tale winds to its close, Ferdinand, the 'sprightly young Barnacle' goes out of his way to assure Clennam that nothing of all this will or can change (II, xxviii); and we entirely believe him. But his assessment of the national stagnation is so convincing exactly because over the whole course of the work we have been made to see the truth of his central assertion that 'our place is not a wicked Giant to be charged at full tilt; but, only a windmill showing you, as it grinds immense quantities of chaff, which way the country wind blows' (ibid. 738).

With the Meagleses in question Dickens openly designates the origin of the national malady:

> Clennam could not help speculating, as he seated himself in his
> room by the fire, whether there might be in the breast of this
> honest, affectionate, and cordial Mr. Meagles, any microscopic
> portion of the mustard-seed that had sprung up into the great tree
> of the Circumlocution Office. His curious sense of a general
> superiority to Daniel Doyce, which seemed to be founded, not so
> much on anything in Doyce's personal character, as on the mere
> fact of his being an originator and a man out of the beaten track of
> other men, suggested the idea.   (I, xvi, 194)

The retired banker is no lazy parasitic aristocrat: rather, he has an
agreeable professional rectitude and sees the arrogant fleas of the
governing caste for what they are; he hates their treatment of his
friend Daniel Doyce and is articulate about this being a typical abuse
on the part of the government (I, x, 119–22.) But his honesty does
not reach out to any ruthless self-knowledge and he dearly loves a
lord:

> 'Aye, aye?' said Meagles. 'A Barnacle is he? *We* know something of
> that family, eh, Dan? By George, they are at the top of the tree,
> though! Let me see. . . . Nephew – to – Lord – Decimus,' Mr.
> Meagles luxuriously repeated with his eyes shut, that he might
> have nothing to distract him from the full flavour of the
> genealogical tree.   (I, xvii, 203–4)

If really thorough, creative – and peaceful – change is to come about
it is Meagles and his ilk in this community who alone have the means
to encompass it (they are the well educated, are not anarchic
revolutionaries; they have the votes after all and the money to run for
Parliament). But, as John Butt points out with reference to an article
(called 'The Toady Tree') published in *Household Words* on 26 May of
the same year (1855) as this number of *Little Dorrit*, Dickens has
already satirised the divided attitudes of Meagles's social group:

> In it Dickens enquires why it is that society does not accept the
> obvious conclusion about administrative reform which the
> Northcote–Trevelyan Report of 1853 advocated more than
> twelve months before the Crimean War revealed the extent of the
> civil administrative confusion. Why is it that Englishmen do not all

immediately recognise that 'No privileged class should have an inheritance in the administration of the public affairs'? The only reason can be that they are snobs and toadies; they all love to sit under the shade of the great Toady Tree, 'the tree of many branches, which grows to an immense height in England, and which overshadows all the land'.[6]

Meagles's behaviour toward the Barnacle—Gowan faction answers only too well to Blandois—Rigaud's repellent deductions about human society:

> 'Here I am! See me! Shaken out of destiny's dice-box into the company of a mere smuggler; — shut up with a poor little contraband trader . . . and he instinctively recognises my position, even by this light and in this place. It's well done! By Heaven! I win, however the game goes.'   (I, i, 9)

Human society, on the view of this murderer, is divisible into two kinds: *hoi polloi*, those who are intrinsically servile; and the Few, the natural aristocrats, who can enjoy all the privileges of their arrogant nature merely with a minimum dexterity in eliciting that servility.

Yet in case Blandois's superficially cultivated airs of 'a gentleman' should mislead us, it is important to insist how the book shows that this view is not just an upper- or middle-class vice. Plornish the plasterer is capable of deliberately censuring the governing classes who 'do nothing for him' and his life (the end of I, xii). But in his relations with his own personal Barnacle or Stiltstalking he is another Mr Meagles:

> 'Ah! And there's manners! There's polish! There's a gentleman to have run to seed in the Marshalsea Jail! Why, perhaps you are not aware,' said Plornish, lowering his voice, and speaking with a perverse admiration of what he ought to have pitied or despised, 'not aware that Miss Dorrit and her sister dursn't let him know that they work for a living. No!' said Plornish, looking with a ridiculous triumph first at his wife, and then all round the room. 'Dursn't let him know it, they dursn't!'   (I, xii, 139)

He has actually supported William Dorrit with 'tribute in copper' of his own (I, vi, 66), while his wife has been so proud of the acquaintance that 'she had awakened some bitterness of spirit in the

Yard, by magnifying to an enormous amount the sum for which Miss Dorrit's father had become insolvent. The Bleeding Hearts resented her claiming to know people of such distinction.'

This matter is more complex than our response to any of the Barnacles' impostures can be. If William Dorrit languishes in prison unable to earn his own bread under an absurd and cruel dispensation, and if he has any right to live at all, then that life must be supported by the efforts or charity of other people. Yet we notice how he treats Plornish's authentic, honest deference with the same high mien as the insincere obeisances of most of the rest of the 'Collegians': namely, as his due, his proper desert in life for doing nothing but living in as much style as may be procured at other people's cost. Nor is this all:

> It was uphill work for a foreigner, lame or sound, to make his way with the Bleeding Hearts. In the first place, they were vaguely persuaded that every foreigner had a knife about him; in the second, they held it to be a sound constitutional national axiom that he ought to go home to his own country. They never thought of inquiring how many of their own countrymen would be returned upon their hands from divers parts of the world, if the principle were generally recognised. . . . Against these obstacles, the lame foreigner with the stick had to make head as well as he could; not absolutely single-handed, because Mr. Arthur Clennam had recommended him to the Plornishes . . . but still at heavy odds. However, . . . when they saw the little fellow . . . doing no harm . . . they began to think that although he could never hope to be an Englishman, still it would be hard to visit that affliction on his head. They began . . . treating him like a baby, . . . laughing immoderately at his lively gestures and his childish English — more, because he didn't mind it, and laughed too. They spoke to him in very loud voices as if he were stone deaf. They constructed sentences, by way of teaching him the language in its purity, such as were addressed by the savages to Captain Cook, or by Friday to Robinson Crusoe. Mrs. Plornish was particularly ingenious in this art; and attained so much celebrity for saying 'Me ope you leg well soon,' that it was considered in the Yard but a very short remove indeed from speaking Italian.   (I, xxv, 302–3)

This is funny, of course; and the fact that Mrs Plornish's attempts to patronise her lodger (significantly he calls her 'la padrona') are so artless is also part of Dickens's meaning. Yet it is something else too.

'Mr. Baptist's' emotional needs may be of so rudimentary an order that in his own particular case consideration about the hurtfulness of the Bleeding Hearts' attitudes looks fairly priggish; yet their easy ability to diminish a human being in this way to the status of a child's toy or house pet, their delight in performing before him as a superior order of beings, we can only relate to what Dickens has pointed out with the immediately preceding paragraph: their fellow Britons' being 'escorted to the poll in droves by Lord Decimus Tite Barnacle', or themselves being 'as ill off . . . as they could desire to be' and getting 'their own skulls promptly fractured if they showed any ill-humour' (ibid.).

The theme is never forsaken. Much later in the tale we have this:

> They [Clennam and Rugg] walked through the Yard to the other end. The Bleeding Hearts were more interested in Arthur since his reverses than formerly: now regarding him as one who was true to the place and had taken up his freedom. Many of them came out to look after him, and to observe to one another, *with great unctuousness*, that he was 'pulled down by it'.   (II, xxvi, 717–18, emphasis added)

Already they have shown themselves able to purchase any number of goods from Mrs Plornish, after she has set up her shop, without actually paying for them (II, xiii, 575); and the whimsy with which the author appears to speak of this custom does not minimise its potential significance (for Mrs Plornish and her kindred if she is reduced to bankruptcy by so large and unremunerative a 'connection') in a world where the degradation of character through imprisonment for debt has been very much present to us as other than amusing. There are the 'cyphering measles' (II, xxxii, 796) which break out in the Yard even when Merdle has collapsed, much in the spirit of the eulogia his enterprises were accorded during the days of his prosperity (II, xiii, 571–2). And even Mrs Plornish's regard for her father, while it amiably supports his vulnerable self-respect, is instinct with satisfactions so mindless, so undiscriminative, that Dickens finds it appropriate to draw its connection in likeness with the kinds of veneration characteristic of higher society:

> If he had come from Court on these occasions, nay, if he had been the noble Refrigerator come home triumphantly from a foreign court to be presented and promoted on his last tremendous failure,

Mrs. Plornish could not have handed him with greater elevation about Bleeding Heart Yard.   (I, xxxi, 365)

Only 'a few bilious Britons' object at all to Edmund Sparkler's appointment as a senior civil servant (for which, as for anything else, he is totally unqualified). 'But their objection was purely theoretical.' They do not hold themselves but rather other people — 'some other Britons somewhere, unknown, or nowhere' — responsible for making an efficient complaint or instituting serious change in these matters (II, xiv, 586). 'The bosom moving in Society . . . attracted *general* admiration', we are to notice (I, xxi, 247, emphasis added), and from chapter to chapter we are given one quiet indication after another which marries with the sentiments expressed in a letter Dickens wrote on 4 October 1855 to his friend the actor Macready, at the beginning of *Little Dorrit*'s serialisation:

> what with flunkyism, toadyism, letting the most contemptible lords come in for all manner of places, reading *The Court Circular* for the New Testament, I do reluctantly believe that the English people are habitually consenting parties to the miserable imbecility into which we have fallen, and never will help themselves out of it . . . at present we are on the down-hill road . . . and the people WILL be content to hear it, sing 'Rule Britannia', and WILL NOT be saved.

What we cannot fail to observe is that the particular thrust of Dickens's various animadversions and ironies (in the text of the novel) is to the point in a world where such representatively destructive figures as Merdle, the Gowans, William Dorrit, the Chief Butler, Casby and indeed the pretensions of 'Society', of circumlocutionary government as a whole, rest upon nothing other than a certain mastery of manner, a thin plausibility which yet the largest part of mankind is only too ready to endorse. Indeed we come to see that Daniel Doyce is almost alone amongst the people to be met in this story in being genuinely committed to the ideal of a world in which all walk six feet tall. Worship of the kind which surrounds Mr Merdle or William Dorrit, Blandois or Lord Decimus, will be endemic in a community where few desire neither to dominate their fellow-beings nor, 'bowing down, [to] feel exalted'.[7]

For there are different modes of self-abasement — all within the one spectrum of unhealthy, covert self-justification; and some of the most subtle are characteristic of the novel's hero and heroine.

> That child had no doubts, asked herself no questions, for she was but too content to see him with a lustre round his head. Poor dear, good dear, truest, kindest, dearest, were the only words she had for him, as she hushed him to rest.   (I, xix, 231)

> There was a classical daughter once — perhaps — who ministered to her father in his prison as her mother had ministered to her. Little Dorrit, though of the unheroic modern stock, and mere English, did much more, in comforting her father's wasted heart upon her innocent breast, and turning to it a fountain of love and fidelity that never ran dry or waned through all the years of his famine.   (Ibid., 229)

> One comfort that she had under the Ordeal by General was more sustaining to her, and made her more grateful than to a less devoted and affectionate spirit, not habituated to her struggles and sacrifices, might appear quite reasonable . . . .   (II, vii, 503)

Dickens recurrently shows us Amy Dorrit's great responsiveness to human need; as in her care of poor Maggy, for example, or the way she is concerned delicately to efface the impressions of slight or insult which old Mr Nandy may have received from the other members of her family (in I, xxxi), or her nursing the evidently homesick and already disillusioned 'Pet' Meagles in the St Bernard Convent with quiet and gentle attentions (II, i). It is no matter of irreconcilable opposites, her being truly warm-hearted and responsible in some connections and woefully faulty in others. Yet it remains a testimony all its own of the expectations the world has brought to such an author, that in 120 years so little has been made of the fully critical fashion in which its heroine is presented.

The reference (above) to the classical legend of Euphrasia of Syracuse feeding her father (King Evander) in prison with her own breasts' milk is hardly a pleasant one, doubly reversing as the story does the natural order of things. In the original fable it was at least an emergency, and like Lady Godiva's sacrifice or many other humiliations in history or legend, signified a commitment to love which could even transcend the claims of high laws and dignities — almost essential human dignities — for the sake of values yet higher. But in the case of this twenty-two-years-long relationship where the father has come to no new insights, has not grown as a personality — except to be but the more inured in his neglectful self-aggrandisement — it perfectly images the kind of dependence each has upon the other, the very unhealthy (though not incestuous) way in which Amy is only too glad to allow her parasite—parent to feed vampire-like upon her adult womanhood, her capacities for motherhood and wifeliness. The Amy—William Dorrit relationship is something in this respect very different from—indeed rather a perversion or parody of—its momentous Jungian archetype (as with Antigone and Oedipus, or Cordelia with Lear): the old man and his youngest daughter together braving life interdependently, in physical weakness and moral strength. It is degradation here, not mutuality, it betokens a moral debility in both, rather than renewal from profound and mysterious sources.

Sheer compassion, sensitivity, as in the instances I named before, *is* the leading characteristic of the girl; and to it, to the ineffable cause of her developing a different response to her environment from that which distinguishes her siblings, Dickens pays deliberate tribute in his first introduction of her:

> It is enough that she was inspired to be something which was not what the rest were. . . . Inspired? Yes. Shall we speak of the inspiration of a poet or a priest, and not of the heart impelled by love and self-devotion to the lowliest work in the lowliest way of life! (I, vii, 71)

But this characterisation of the young woman is a complete one. And we are fully shown how the way she cares for her family panders to some of their worst traits. This is of the very essence of the book. Perhaps William Dorrit is beyond reformation, but her avid desperate contriving to assist her father in his pretence that she does not go out to menial work for him by the day, and indeed half-starves herself to make up his suppers, neither earns her his gratitude in any way which would be some recompense for her denials nor assists him towards any open and nutritive acknowledgement of the truth of their situation. Her failure likewise to protest boldly and vociferously at her siblings' fantastic snobberies serves only to fortify their 'miserably ragged old fiction of the family gentility' (I, xviii, 213), which is thrown out at people — like poor Nandy — who are at least as defenceless and vulnerable as they to imputations of shame and disgrace. We bear in mind of course the status of the youngest child, especially the youngest daughter, in the Victorian family and the greater hurdles she would have to surmount in coming forward in that epoch with open criticism of her elders (and 'betters') than in our own day. But Dickens has William's younger brother Frederick make just such a protest against 'the family credit' (II, v, 485–6) – with a realism, a psychological fidelity no less convincing – and we do not feel that the episode in any way discredits *him*; that the author has been concerned to show this normally decrepit uncle offending against valid canons of rank or precedence.

Her meek servility towards them all and to equally offensive people outside the family circle confronts us with too many failures either in discrimination or in moral courage to let us suppose that what Little Dorrit is and does is a satisfactory response to the lies around her. Indeed so much is this the case that we may even read as ambivalent the description of her love for her father; its having 'alone . . . saved him to be even what he was' (I, xix, 231). Her concern not to offend her relations, while we can sympathise with her wish for peace beside the familial hearth, involves her regularly in feints made effectually on behalf of their pretensions. And in the kind of world that deceits for such purposes are seen to have made, in this novel, that should worry us.

> Little Dorrit was not ashamed of her poor shoes. He knew her story, and it was not that. Little Dorrit had a misgiving that he might blame her father, if he saw them; that he might think, 'why did he dine to-day, and leave this little creature to the mercy of the cold stones!' She had no belief that it would have been a just reflection; she simply knew, by experience, that such delusions did sometimes present themselves to people. It was part of her father's misfortunes that they did.   (I, xiv, 167)

If *she* had 'no belief' that these ideas of her father's conduct 'would have been a just reflection', how is it she can so closely imitate the very trick of other people's thought in the matter? And, if the world at large has any tendency to take such a view of her ill-shod condition, why has she so long been incapable of entertaining the reflection and more deliberately evaluating for herself its intrinsic merit or injustice? It is impossible to escape the impression that the author, who could have cast the foregoing paragraph to quite different effect, is deliberately affording us – deliberately, that is to say, at the level of his creative insights – the very cast of Amy's thought and with a closeness which makes us attentive to how (as with the essential coyness of the two quickly repeated 'Little Dorrit's) she is thus sustaining a less than wholly fine persona which is important to her inward sense equally of her own identity and of its public role. The same thing is present in the letters she sends to Clennam from Italy (II, iv and xi). They are likewise instinct with her abiding desire to diminish her full selfhood, which here expresses itself in protestations (too long, too many) of personal insignificance, humility and frail judgement. She writes, for instance, of sending 'another little letter' (II, xi, 550) after having posted Clennam some 1200 words the first time (II, iv) and in both cases all too fragilely alleges these missives' unimportance — when even on her own view at the time she must suppose that their containing information about Minnie Gowan will make them meat and drink to their recipient.

She is of age (in fact twenty-two years old) and the most intelligent member of her family, as to her intrinsic capacity for moral sensitiveness; yet she accepts life — for herself and for others — almost entirely on her father's terms, when in several episodes she is shown to have a much finer sense of what is decent than he: as, most notably, on the occasion when he tries to get her to 'lead on' John Chivery without actually intending to marry the fellow (I, xi); or when she urges Fanny not to make a loveless marriage for position and the rainbow's end of a successful duel with Mrs Merdle in the lists of 'Society' (II, xiv). She repudiates the suggestion put to her in the first case, she attempts to put her insights to creative use in the second. But the more frequent opacities of her outlook, her regular acceptance of her family's delinquencies, betoken a subservience of her moral sense to an emotional need which conditions *a priori* her response to such things as Mrs General's instructions, Fanny's insults or her father's total disregard of any but the most worthless objectives, except on those occasions where an open outrage is asked of her.

These less wholesome features of her personality are not mysterious or inexplicable when we consider how she has been 'drinking from infancy of a well whose waters had their own peculiar stain, their own unwholesome and unnatural taste' (I, vii, 71). Like Fanny Price in *Mansfield Park*, she has been the Cinderella of her family group, despised or ignored while in perpetual use as a convenience, physical, emotional, moral, starved of real affection and denied her individuality. So replete has been her experience with denials — worst of all the emotional inanition — that it is hardly surprising to find her clutching at the relief of a deliberately simplified part (albeit 'deliberately' at a level of response which is not wholly conscious or articulate) in a world where her experience has only taught her to expect further misery from any full recognition of the moral problems with which her family presents her. Her inward life has been forced into perverse channels by the great absence of all health-giving recognitions on the part of those round whom most of her living has centred; so that in a diminished role lie the only satisfactions for the emotional life which she has been able to discover. She has made a pleasure out of her suffering – it is the only spiritual material to hand in her actual experience – and she feeds upon deprivation. Yet though the matter makes illegitimate considerations of judge-ment and blame, such a tendency cannot be seen as one of psychic health or fertilising goodness, mysterious, complete, Beatrice-like; of the kind for instance that R. D. McMaster in his article on *Little Dorrit* believes she embodies.[8] It is rather the case that in being a real, because really flawed, human being, in having developed a role which serves as a kind of comfort in her spiritual desert (and which has seriously cramping concomitants as well), Amy has a status – a significance – that she could not otherwise possess in the dialectic of the novel at large.

That she habitually converts suffering into a kind of secret morbid pleasure, that she is partly indeed sustained by the sense of martyrdom itself and therefore almost desires to invite suffering, is interestingly borne out by a medical expert's diagnosis.

In '*Little Dorrit* and Dickens's Intuitive Knowledge of Psychic Masochism', *American Imago*, XII (1955), Edmund Bergler M.D. speaks of how closely, on his view as a clinical practitioner, Dickens has portrayed variants of the psychological illness named in his essay's title in several of the book's main characters. (This doctor actually views the ailment in question as nothing less than itself the very 'scourge of humanity'.) The disease's rationale is that,

> since everybody lives on the basis of the pleasure principle, the question arises; what pleasure can be extracted from constant punishment, moral reproach, guilt? Obviously none, except that derived from sugar-coating the ominous triad . . . – the making out of displeasure a pleasure . . . .

'The condemnation of, and irony against, the Circumlocution Office, Marshalsea Prison, misuse of wealth' he sees as objectively existing and vindicated assessments on Dickens's part; 'But – and this is decisive — *beneath the superficial layer* Dickens depicts (involuntarily and unwittingly) . . . the victim's own contribution to his tragic fate.' In the case of Miss Wade for instance, what she has, says Bergler, is the unconscious wish to be *unloved*. 'The palimpsest of wanting to be loved is but the inner alibi'; she has the classic desire of the psychic masochist: 'a kick in the jaw, provided it is unconsciously self-provoked'. (And I do think we register in such a chapter as II, xxi ['The History of a Self-Tormentor'], the relish with which she speaks of the rejections she has suffered in her life. Hence, as Bergler points out, that chapter title — the heading of the apologia she hands to Clennam — being what it is, not 'The History of a Victim'.)

'How little external circumstances account for the psychic masochist's inner structure', Bergler continues, 'can be seen in Little Dorrit herself.' She is 'a real type: the "nice masochist" who "specializes on" libidinized suffering' of which 'her constant readiness to take the blame for anything, her dreams of misery, refuting the favourable external situation', her refusal 'to accept the high financial position to which her family is elevated after her father gets his fortune', and her appearance to Clennam when he is himself in the Marshalsea, 'in the shabby dress she had always worn in the bad, old times', are characteristic.

Yet all these considerations dawn upon us as the story unfolds; they are not boldly advertised (though fully available) from the first. There is authentic mystery in her responding to her situation in a manner so different from her siblings' — ultimately unfathomable mystery; but it is in the essential nature of the book's artistic method that our first reading of her as a Cinderella-figure is made to show for both an accurate and mistaken estimate as we progress through the narrative. As we grow to appreciate the destructive elements in her charitable self-effacements, considerations about the responsibility of the social matrix for the individual spirit's fettering (as in Lionel Trilling's famous essay)[9] become otiose. If even the Cinderellas of this world are not only flawed, but flawed with the very tendencies which generally make of it a Marshalsea prison, the novel's leading intimation about the nature of the human imagination becomes clear. The *imaginative* consequence of Dickens's *procédé* — his demonstration of this same behavioural theme in 'good' and 'bad' alike — is to suggest the pattern of an essential capacity to be servile, or will to dominate, in the human breast as such; a fundamental (though not its only fundamental) impulse to diminish its own life in one fashion or the other, a powerful tendency in most individuals either to bully or to crouch down before their experience — at its most radical, a fear of life which issues in the paralyses this novel gives us to see, these conformisms and these restraints.

What is Little Dorrit's attachment to the Marshalsea but — primarily — an emblem of this? It has been, of course, her home; which makes for another poisonous complexity. Her hankering after it, on her Italian travels, its overpowering — for her — the reality of the Grand Tour scenes, is a positive as well as a pathetic response. Beside the desiccated vision served up by Mrs General (or Mr Eustace), Amy's experience of *her* 'first world' is necessarily the touchstone of certain truths, avouched immediacies, which are markedly absent from the hired companion's precepts or the lifestyle of all the other members of the travelling party (except her uncle). Yet the family were not less pretentious or dishonest in the prison than abroad; and one can only endorse with a hearty 'Yes!' Dr Leavis's note on the claims of the Marshalsea to offer 'freedom': 'Actually what Dickens's evocation registers is . . . final human defeat . . . a subsidence into a callous living deadness of abject acquiescence.'[10] There are manifold decencies in the world within its walls, decencies (like Bob the Turnkey's kindnesses to his god-daughter, or those of the 'Collegians' generally, towards one another) which may be noticeably less prevalent in the 'froward' macrocosm outside (cf. the last paragraph of the whole tale). But that is the point. Like the mother's womb it offers limited satisfactions which are hard to forsake for the random, uncertain world beyond. Those of its debtors, like Dr Haggage, who have come to embrace and welcome its shelter have effectually contracted with existence on terms of abdication; in return for being no longer assaulted by the anarchy of life — which is creative as well as oppressive — they have settled for a torpid adulthood, a sort of warm agreeable living death. Not for nothing is the central shabby communal resort of the jail called 'The Snuggery' (which again exemplifies the ambiguous value and meaning of the place).

It must be supererogatory to itemise at length all those parts of the novel in which we are shown Arthur Clennam himself making a similar compromise. Again, as with Amy Dorrit, we must see him doing it in response to the kind of hurts he has suffered; the denial of maternal affection and horrible mockery of his childhood, the long exile in a country remote even from such a home as he could call (with whatever shudderings) his own, the dark Calvinist tradition in which he has grown up, the dreary London environment which his early discipline has looked out upon and to which he returns after two decades' loneliness abroad. He purports to begin life on new terms when, on coming back, he severs his connection with Clennam and Co. in a business capacity (I, v). Yet that it is withdrawal, retreat, a fear of exposure to life – in every sense – which is still the issue, we are shown in his reactions to Pet Meagles.

Professor Garis[11] has found Dickens unfairly, indeed painfully, ironic at Clennam's expense in this matter:

> The rain fell heavily, drearily. It was a night of tears.
> If Clennam had not decided against falling in love with Pet; if he had had the weakness to do it; if he had, little by little, persuaded himself to set all the earnestness of his nature, all the might of his hope, and all the wealth of his matured character, on that cast; if he had done this and found that all was lost; he would have been, that night, unutterably miserable. As it was –
> As it was, the rain fell heavily, drearily. (I, xvii, 209–10)

But this passage, like its whole larger context in the chapters treating of 'Nobody's Weakness' and 'Nobody's Rival' (I, xvi and xvii), achieves effects far more complex – in the sense Garis misses, far more 'balanced' – than can be appropriated under the simple heading of 'irony'. It has an ironic undertow but it equally offers itself to us as the plain fact, the literal truth. Dickens brilliantly affords us, as he affords Clennam, a situation in which that returning exile has a free and open choice, where the outcome is inscrutable. Whether or not Arthur would or should have won this girl rather than Amy Dorrit is here a meaningless question, remains locked up

> Down the passage which we did not take . . .
> Into the rose-garden.

It would have been not only possible – this we can observe from the evidence so far accreted – but also perfectly valid for him to have wooed Pet; that he would have been happy with her in no mean or trivial way, we know to the very end of the book and beyond. The novelist makes it clear that her few slender Meagles weaknesses of outlook would have evanesced within a few months of marriage to so devoted and (in the best sense) serious a man. The delicacy is fine, the conviction whole, with which Dickens suggests a girl whose only fault is the inexperience of her youth – itself the very bloom upon her beauty; so that, in default of any *active* interest on Clennam's part, she falls to Henry Gowan (the same inexperience naturally makes her take from her parents, at this epoch, her tone of friendly and loving but superior relationship with Tattycoram). Pet is not essentially a spoiled, i.e. an egocentric, beauty; the final proof of which lies in her natural delicacy and courage later at work in the scenes of her wretched marriage (see II, i, 444; her insistence that Clennam is to know that she is 'very well and very happy'). Like Amy in her Marshalsea days she makes the best of a hard lot and proves herself to be a woman of mettle. But we ought to have observed these qualities already, in her delicate attentions to Arthur on the eve of her marriage (I, xxviii): no really spoiled beauty would have failed to improve the occasion's possibilities for coquetry. Instead she quietly laments his pain, having already (ibid., 333–4) attempted to palliate it by expressing a special confidence in him.

Of course, if Clennam had prosecuted his suit with Minnie and 'found that all was lost', if he *had* in the event been rejected, he would indeed have been 'unutterably miserable' that night. Who in such a situation would not? It would have seemed, what is more, yet another 'failure' in a life marked by unsuccessful human relations; and he could not have missed feeling it the more deeply as a great hurt. Yet the willingness (though of course not the wish) to be scarred in such a way is an integral part of really living, of letting oneself be committed (and therefore vulnerable) to life's creative possibilities at all. To think it better, as he does (see I, xvi, 200) 'to flow away monotonously like the river, and to compound for its insensibility to happiness with its insensibility to pain', is to have given up altogether one's claims to existence on human terms. What is more, it means to get things actually wrong, to be responsible for real disasters, to play life's game into the hands of its predators and cheats – as with this case of Minnie's not being wooed by him at a time when she could very valuably be rescued from Henry Gowan. In short it means abdicating his possible role of a medium for life's regenerative tendencies, equally in his own personal case and in the larger social world. The novelist's emphasis is directed not towards (here irrelevant) questions about the ultimate rightness of such a match, but upon the tragic introversion and defection of will which characterises Clennam's crablike living at this period in his story; which is certainly and permanently tragic – if not for him (since he is ultimately given a second chance of a good marriage), for all three Meagleses. This is why Dickens traces the Gowan wedlock through the rest of the book;

in this important aspect it is a cruel needless consequence of Clennam's abdications, and we are not allowed to overlook or forget the pain which thus arises from (in part) what *he* has done or failed to do.

His attitude to 'Pet' is reproduced in his relations with Amy Dorrit and the frustration there is compounded by *her* withdrawal from life. It is wholly in the nature of their inhibitions that he should give her a child—woman role and a name to match, or that she should rejoice in a title of which Flora Finching remarks with felicitous artless wisdom, 'and of all the strangest names I ever heard the strangest, like a place down in the country with a turnpike, or a favourite pony or a puppy or a bird or something from a seed-shop to be put in a garden or a flower-pot and come up speckled' (1, xxiii, 270). Amy's new name (1, xiv) has just this value for Clennam; it puts her in the light of some such hobby *as* 'a place down in the country' or 'a favourite pony or a puppy or a bird', a nice diminutive interest to visit or tend but with no dangerous, i.e. fully human, possibilities. She on her side is but too ready to think herself unworthy of him — and to add the plight of unrequited love to the stock-in-trade of that preconceived image of herself as one of life's predeterminately and ineluctably defeated people, which is the only self-consciousness from which she knows how to draw strength; a crippled strength and (a necessarily tainted) satisfaction. It is tragic that they should thus frustrate their own most hopeful courses and fulfilments, and ironic that they do it just at the time in their lives when both are most easily able to be united, as far as the outward circumstances are concerned. At this point in their story, Clennam is free to propose marriage to Amy, and William Dorrit in no position to think it anything but a hopeful advantageous match. The scenes in which Clennam repeatedly speaks to this woman who loves him in the accents of 'one who was turning old', 'dwelling upon the difference in their respective ages' (II, xxvii, 730) are truly painful; likewise Amy's story about the princess and the poor woman (I, xxiv, 292– 5) where she is (semi-unconsciously) part imaging, part creating by such means the distancing and derealising of her actual possibilities within the proscenium of a tale as it were out of fatalistic folklore or ballad. But we would be more likely to see in these things a local tragedy if we did not reflect (which at some level or other of our response the text binds us to do) that Mrs Clennam's horrible morality is supported upon a blinkered set of comparably willed assumptions, or that in turn her almost total success in establishing for herself a life-model largely free of humanity and the play of affection has at least something in common with the Patriarchal Casby's untroubled blankness towards his tenants' hardship. Both set themselves up as models of rectitude; both encompass exploitation and deceitful contrivance of a pretty ruthless order; both are wholly (or largely) persuaded by their own rhetoric, their own cruel pretences.

'Blinkered' as a term on its own needs qualification fully to account for these two or for the degradations of the Merdle-worshipping world at large. Scant excuse is forthcoming for the 'multitude' who 'prostrated themselves before him [Merdle] . . . always distinctly knowing why' (II, xii, 556). *Little Dorrit* is not a specifically Christian novel. But the quotations out of Christian Scripture which run through nearly every page of this text almost like recurrent subordinate motifs in a design[12] remind us in a manner imitative of the very process itself that these people of England inhabit a society where a standard, by common consent divinely sanctioned, is continuously upheld before high and low, rich and poor alike, which is radically opposed to the values implicit in the tributes offered during his life to the defaulting financier. The eschatological conclusion of the first chapter — 'and so deep a hush was on the sea, that it scarcely whispered of the time when it shall give up its dead' (I, i, 14) — thus winding up a very intense evocation of man's natural environment at its more uncompromising, only begins a series of references out of the New Testament or analogies to it which continually serve the purpose of contrasting the averred ideals of this community with its real aspirations.

Professor Garis's general complaint against *Little Dorrit* is that what he there takes to be 'Dickens's newly dark and complex view of his world remains an unassimilated malaise; it is not transmuted into a successful work of art.' This, as he deems it, is principally owing to

the fact that the new awareness of complexity has not bred appropriately new methods of operation in the Dickens theatre . . . it is . . . dispiriting to see new insights 'processed' in the old way. . . . Again and again Dickens notifies us of his intention to render complex and ambiguous psychological states; we are repeatedly advised to suspend judgement, to go slowly in ascribing blame and praise in this dark and disordered world. But the theatrical artist cannot take his own advice . . . the studied ambiguity of certain elements in the world of *Little Dorrit* is interrupted, to our embarrassment and confusion, by single-minded denunciations in the old style.[13]

Such a criticism will most probably bring to mind the closing paragraph of II, xxv, which forms the epitaph for the dead Merdle. This at first blush could be seen to justify Garis's view; the more especially in that it is so important an instance. Here is that paragraph and the sentence which immediately precedes it:

So, the talk, lashed louder and higher by confirmation on confirmation, and by edition after edition of the evening papers, swelled into such a roar when night came, as might have brought one to believe that a solitary watcher on the gallery above the Dome of St. Paul's would have perceived the night air to be laden with a heavy muttering of the name of Merdle, coupled with every form of execration.

For, by that time it was known that the late Mr. Merdle's complaint had been, simply, Forgery and Robbery. He, the uncouth object of such widespread adulation, the sitter at great men's feasts, the roc's egg of great ladies' assemblies, the subduer of exclusiveness, the leveller of pride, the patron of patrons, the bargain-driver with a Minister for Lordships of the Circumlocution Office, the recipient of more acknowledgement within some ten or fifteen years, at most, than had been bestowed in England upon all peaceful public benefactors, and upon all the leaders of all the Arts and Sciences, with all their works to testify for them, during two centuries at least – he, the shining wonder, the new constellation to be followed by the wise men bringing gifts, until it stopped over a certain carrion at the bottom of a bath and disappeared – was simply the greatest Forger and the greatest Thief that had ever cheated the gallows.   (II, xxv, 710)

This is the climax of the (deliberately shocking) Scriptural parodies which Dickens has developed through the novel for the purposes I have expressed. The genuine 'leaders of the Arts and Sciences' in England 'during two centuries', 'the peaceful public benefactors' are cast by the narrator almost in the role of the prophets of Old Jewry; neglected in their day like their prototypes by the nation they have honoured with their works, but in this case for a being whose adulation in a Christian country is particularly grotesque. Merdle has honours paid to him as if he were necessary to life itself – and by the leaders of the Church (see, for example, II, xii, 566). He has become generally accounted a Messiah merely in consequence of his accumulated wealth, his financial credit. And in one clear sense, of course,

'Mr. Merdle's Complaint' *has* been 'simply Forgery and Robbery'. If the man is ever to have had his opportunity of possessing a human value (i.e. individuality) at all, then he has engaged in a life of fraud — and fraud not only financial — on his own responsibility. It was ultimately his choice to co-operate with the general wish for a worthless public idol, to become a personification of the rapacious materialism that here supports the empty and destructive idea of 'Society' — which in its turn means a deliberate denial of the very principle of mutuality. But with the whole long close of such a chapter focusing the public reaction to Merdle's death rather than its consequences to them or any final inward account of the defaulter's 'complaint', the novelist directs attention principally towards the quality of *their* presented thought and rhetoric.

Thus with the animus of the passage. It is there but is surely much more directed at society at large — which is to say at its here-indicated individual members — than at the defunct swindler for whom Dickens has shown equal pity and contempt. 'Lashed' and 'roar' imply a likeness between the London crowd and a maddened beast. The telling image of the 'solitary watcher on the gallery above the Dome of St. Paul's' suggests that it is an irreligious public who are raging in the streets below after the Merdle crash. 'Solitary' gives the impression of London's largest temple being (habitually?) left empty in a national crisis and for reliefs (themselves fatuous and self-defeating) the very reverse of those incident to sacred prayer: 'a heavy muttering of the name of Merdle, coupled with every form of execration'. We can hardly fail to be carried back to the ironies of an earlier reference to this cathedral:

> Then said Mr. Merdle, 'Allow me, sir. Take my arm!' Then, leaning on Mr. Merdle's arm, did Mr. Dorrit descend the staircase, seeing the worshippers on the steps, and feeling that the light of Mr. Merdle shone by reflection in himself. Then the carriage and the ride into the City; and the people who looked at them; and the hats that flew off grey heads; and the general bowing and crouching before this wonderful mortal, the like of which prostration of spirit was not to be seen — no, by high Heaven, no! It may be worth thinking of by Fawners of all denominations — in Westminster Abbey and Saint Paul's Cathedral put together, on any Sunday in the year. (II, xvi, 618)

The evidently null and void quality of his character and appearance has all along had part of its meaning in this, that Merdle was an idol of their — the ordinary folk's — making and without their connivance would never have been in a position to ruin so many (see II, xii, first paragraph). The 'multitude' (ibid.) may have 'worshipped on trust' (though Dickens stipulates they do so 'distinctly knowing why'), but, for all that they have been taken in not only by the Merdle-figure itself but also by his credit with High Society, they have in one literal respect received their deserts; those, this is to say, who have invested in his 'enterprises'. (This does not mean that Dickens, or any reader, is untroubled by their tragic and frightening ruin — see, for example, the first paragraph of the succeeding chapter, II, xiii.) What is instinct at its best but intelligence less than wholly articulate? Doyce is not just exercising his tongue or expressing — with whatever hesitation of modesty — an unsearched and meaningless bias when we are shown this:

> 'If I have a prejudice connected with money and money figures,' continued Doyce, laying that plastic workman's thumb of his on the lappel of his partner's coat, 'it is against speculating. I don't think I have any other. I dare say I entertain that prejudice, only because I have never given my mind fully to the subject.'   (II, xxii, 673)

But he does not need to have done so, still less to receive at this point Clennam's agreement that his view is 'the soundest sense' (ibid.). The 'plastic workman's thumb' is quite telling enough for us as the essential hint. The real ultimate argument against speculation — with savings however small and from a walk of life however constrained — is its development of a social ethic in which there is no longer a rational connection between what a man does and what he receives in payment for it. Dickens has already argued the responsibility of government so to order the commonwealth as to give all citizens an honourable task and a decent livelihood (as in Plornish's and Clennam's discussion at the end of I, xii); but the 'numbers of men in every profession and trade' who 'would be blighted by [Merdle's] insolvency' (II, xxv, 710) were after all wanting something for nothing. If the upper classes who partook of 'his magnificent feasts . . . would have done better to worship the Devil point blank' (ibid.), what did the 'multitude' want with *their* investments in him — imaginative and moral as well as financial — but equally to be partakers thereof?

Dickens is not easily contemptuous or vindictive towards the ordinary man in this novel. The comic tone with which he can render with equal propriety some of the earlier reactions to the Merdle collapse embodies the complexity of his feelings for *l'homme moyen sensuel*, his alert sense of that being's sympathetic qualities and positive moral resources as well as his failings. Yet even in a comic mode we are always being reminded that the notion of Mr Decent Everyman, while it may well be a creative myth, is yet a 'myth':

> Pressure was so entirely satisfactory to the public mind, and seemed to make everybody so comfortable, that it might have lasted all day but for Bar's having taken the real state of the case into Court at half-past nine. This led to its beginning to be currently whispered all over London by about one, that Mr. Merdle had killed himself. Pressure, however, so far from being overthrown by the discovery, became a greater favourite than ever. There was a general moralising upon Pressure, in every street. All the people who had tried to make money and had not been able to do it, said, There you were! You no sooner began to devote yourself to the pursuit of wealth, than you got Pressure. The idle people improved the occasion in a similar manner. . . . This consideration was very potent in many quarters, but nowhere more so than among the young clerks and partners who had never been in the slightest danger of overdoing it.   (Ibid., 709)

All the four last paragraphs which close this chapter are concerned with the public's attitude in the wake of Merdle's death, and all but the last of them mediate it to us with an ample series of sentences in the 'free indirect style' of reporting. We know that the element of hysterical exaggeration in (for example) 'every servile worshipper of riches who had helped to set him on his pedestal, would have done better to worship the Devil point-blank' (ibid., 710) is not Dickens's; the more certainly because it immediately follows and is qualified by the author's intimation in the same mode, of the 'whispers' with which the growing anxiety of the public has first expressed itself: 'He had sprung from nothing, by no natural growth or process that any one could account for; he had been, after all, a low, ignorant fellow' (ibid., 709–10). All this develops an excoriating view of the community as even more culpable for being willing now to locate in the figure of the dead defaulter, and with him to bury entirely and dismissively, its own measure of guilt in the whole affair, which is the

Little Dorrit: the Triumph of Reality 147

principal one.

It is only in the last paragraph that we become uncertain whether the denunciation offered there (in its last fourteen words) is the author's or the majority view. 'Simply the greatest Forger and the greatest Thief that ever cheated the gallows' is ambiguous as to the provenance of its intonation owing to the nature of the imagery which immediately precedes it. Such metaphors as 'the uncouth object of such widespread adulation, . . . the roc's egg of great ladies' assemblies, . . . the bargain-driver with a Minister for Lordships' obviously reflect the narrator's more detached and more satiric position. Yet in the wake of all the rhetoric as of the ordinary man in the foregoing paragraphs, there is no syntactic or other sign that Dickens is not still intimating the inadequacy of the crowd's view. So that this concluding denunciation (which is of exactly a kind that it has been shown the public is very ill placed to make) challenges us to define just where we are in the spectrum of almost universally guilty attitudes. If we find ourselves enjoying it, then we have half convicted ourselves of free participation in the general hypocrisy which has made this world the imprisoning place it is.

The essential point of all this, as with the change in their mood from unctuous patronage about 'Pressure' to a feral rage which ruins Arthur Clennam when he steps forward courageously to take his small share of the unrestricted responsibility in the affair (II, xxvi), is to show us the disparity between the apparent commitment to traditional religion and morality which most people in this society lay claim to and invoke – it is their view of Merdle now, we remember, that 'every servile worshipper of riches who had helped to set him on his pedestal would have done better to worship the Devil point-blank' – and their actual disregard of the same. And, if there is little or no excuse for such apostasy in a community which regularly reads or hears about 'the sick brought out and laid in the track of the Apostle – who had *not* got into the good society, and had *not* made the money' (II, xvi, 614), we may feel disposed rather to ponder the question, 'After such knowledge, what forgiveness?' What is of value here; are any of the members of this society *worth* 'saving' from the misery of their general condition?

II

The foregoing questions are open ones, and we have to answer them dismissively in the case of many of the personages brought before us during the course of the novel. If 'Society' is triumphant first and last, success in it is no enviable achievement. Dickens shows us the lives which are characteristic of it as thin and empty. There is nothing tremendous about the egotism of a Lord Decimus Tite Barnacle trotting, with the complacency of an idiotic elephant, among howling labyrinths of sentences' (I, xxxiv, 408). The 'Great Patriotic Conference' is a dinner-party without one second's interest, and we surely find ourselves thinking 'So what?' of 'Bar' being made Attorney-General in the years to come (II, xii, 562) if that means his permanent immersion in a 'Society' which is in fact so non-, even so anti-, social, in an ambit so asphyxiatingly sterile. Who could be jealous of Mr Tite Barnacle? To have 'only one idea in one's head and that . . . a wrong one' (ibid., 561) seems a heavy price to pay for failing to be driven distracted by the tedium of such a lifestyle. Poverty makes Mrs Plornish 'somewhat slatternly', we are told upon our first introduction to her (I, xii, 137), and Clennam, who also has serious defects of character, is likewise not to be described as happy during the greater part of the tale. But her want or his boredom and loneliness (which are made scarcely less present to us) are experiences with a different value from those of Fanny Sparkler (*née* Dorrit) when she is thrown back upon her own resources and has no glittering assemblies at which to twit her rival (II, xxiv).

All the 'Society' scenes are airless in that way, whether in London, Venice, or Rome. Dickens makes them tolerable by his company, his fine sustained comic treatment, but he gives us the full force of the stagnant pointlessness of it all. Of course most of the Society figures do not appreciate this or question their way of life. But it is just in this respect that Shaw's famous observation '*Little Dorrit* is a more seditious book than *Das Kapital*'[14] was well made. For Marx, on his analysis, showed the governing castes of contemporary Europe for themselves as much the products as the beneficiaries of an inexorable impersonal historical process. But Dickens exhibits a class of which the commitments to their egotisms have literally dehumanised them. We cannot feel that killing Lord Decimus, for instance, would be an act of murder, because there is no aspect of his consciousness which deserves the respect we normally pay to life, mere life, in any member of our species. Hence the comically degraded animal imagery with which he is continually associated and his figuring as having at best a merely scenic function; the 'idiotic elephant' idea or the bovine quality of his outlook:

> When he had achieved this rush of vivacity and condescension, his
> Lordship composed himself into the picture after Cuyp, and made
> a third cow in the group.   (II, xii, 562)

This is funny but it is also part of a whole serious issue. Philosophers
will always reason that there is more to the life even of a Barnacle of
the worst kidney than this; critics will point to the complexities of
thought, the shifting uncertainties and scruples which Trollope
memorialises in the case of his *Palliser* figures; and both will dispute
the essential equity of Dickens's characterisations in the High-Society
sphere here in this novel. But, quite aside from the fact that the
protagonists of Trollope's political fictions belong (in part) to a new
political age, while Dickens is here still dealing with the old Whig
aristocracy and the Civil Service in its unreformed days, *Little
Dorrit*'s most challenging intimation – not easily to be dismissed – is
to ask us where *radically* in the individual lives of the British
Establishment there is even a latent and potential value?

We begin by assuming that such accounts of their political and
social rituals as we find in I, x ('Containing the Whole Science of
Government') or I, xxvi (the visit to the 'old ladies of both sexes' at
Hampton Court) are deliberately on the author's part written with
the hyperbole of burlesque and the reductiveness (including the
limited faithfulness) of satire. But, though Dickens is patently after
effects of that kind, what we come to recognise playing over these
scenes is a kind of bleak full daylight of literal truth. We look beyond
an apparently metaphoric account of these people's behaviour only to
find that the metaphors alone express the visible truth, they only can
render the essential commitments and the literal banality of the
consciousness and contribution of these beings. It is not only the case
that rituals which were originally undertaken to achieve egoistic
ends – for the individual, for his social group – have become
autonomous, have taken over the entire life-process of these now
merely humanoid mechanisms. To be sure, Mrs Merdle or the
Dowager Mrs Gowan, like the Circumlocution Office, have an end
in view behind all their social fencing, their clever dishonesties and
sustained pretences: power, wealth, status, privilege. But Dickens can
refer to Mrs Merdle as 'the Bosom' with ultimately a more than
locally comic pointedness because the end of all her rigmarole can

only be the reduction of her life to an inorganic model; all she has become, on the very deepest view, *is* a stand 'to hang jewels upon' (I, xxi, 247), just as her arms, at the best, have developed into nothing more than 'the very thing for bracelets' (I, xxxiii, 392). There *is* no other kind of meaning to Lord Lancaster Stiltstalking's social rituals, to his existence, than his appearing at diplomatic feasts to 'shade the dinner, cool the wines, chill the gravy, and blight the vegetables' (I, xxvi, 313). And the most that can be said for Lord Decimus, the most charitable because in one sense innoxious account of him, is that he goes to dinner-parties to form such images as that of a cow in a Cuyp group. This is the appropriate way for Dickens to talk about him because anything we could call human personality is in him so fugitive, recondite and evanescent that he can hardly be held responsible for doing no more with his life than that — or the other performances through which he is ponderously led by the 'coach or crammer from the Circumlocution Office' (I, x, 106) who may happen to attend upon him at any given time. He and his ilk have entirely lost their status as human beings.

The vision, at its darkest, of nullity as both the heart and the ultimate — if in one sense 'unwitting' and involuntary — end of such procedures and commitments as characterise the Gowan—Barnacle — Stiltstalking way of life, is presented to us in the persons of Mr Merdle and Mrs General. In Rome,

> it seemed to Little Dorrit that a change came over the Marshalsea spirit of their society, and that Prunes and Prism got the upper hand. Everybody was walking about St. Peter's and the Vatican on somebody else's cork legs, and straining every visible object through somebody else's sieve. Nobody said what anything was, but everybody said what the Mrs. Generals, Mr. Eustace, or somebody else said it was. The whole body of travellers seemed to be a collection of voluntary human sacrifices, bound hand and foot, and delivered over to Mr. Eustace and his attendants, to have the entrails of their intellects arranged according to the taste of that sacred priesthood.   (II, vii, 512)

This takes up the abiding religious metaphor in a new way, the theme of the repulsive idolatry of men prostrating themselves before wealth and status which in the constant references to the false gods of society at large is sustained through the book. Among the suggestions operative here is the idea that the zealots of such principles will come in time not to see anything through their own eyes, even when simply engaged in travelling for pleasure; more malign still, that if one fully devotes oneself to such things as position, 'spirit' in the Dorrit sense, social status, one will come not to have a whole mind with which to make choices and commitments at all. Being 'bound hand and foot, and delivered over to Mr. Eustace and his attendants', though this is comic, is not only humorous. It suggests that what remains of the individual's essential principle of individuation, his ability to think, know, elect, opine, at the very simplest level, for himself, will be taken over by external agencies committed to unrealities. The whole paragraph is a strong clue as to how Mr Merdle and Mrs General have become the nullities *they* are. In some respects the matter is preternatural in its suggestion of human shells with only a kind of psychic deposit, sediment, or 'entrails' remaining inside. So that a new commitment for such people (of the kind which Merdle himself is perhaps trying to make in appealing to Fanny – II, xxiv – for the means of his own suicide; it is as if his strange visit is a final attempt in these ultimate straits at a last – or rather first – human contact) is now out of the question, is a possibility irreversibly closed.

I am not just tacking a Thomist interpretation onto one slight though graphic metaphor:

> Up, then, would come Mrs. General; taking all the colour out of everything . . . scratching up the driest little bones of antiquity, and bolting them whole without any human visitings – like a Ghoule in gloves.   (II, xv, 612)

It is developed more largely, as in the macabre comedy of Mr Dorrit's short-lived courtship of the varnisher:

> with great solemnity [he] conducted her to the room door, where he raised her knuckles to his lips. Having parted from her with what may be conjectured to have been a rather bony kiss of a cosmetic flavour, he gave his daughter his blessing, graciously.   (II, xix, 646)

The suggestion is that Mrs General has become really a kind of skeleton with merely a veneer of flesh and social forms; that she is at once a nothing, there is nothing there, and that she 'speaks for' or out of a kind of negation powerfully 'active' in human affairs. One is reminded of George Herbert's lines,

> Sinne is flat opposite to th' Almighty, seeing
> It wants the good of *vertue* and of *being*.[15]

The fact that Dickens portrays for us two people—things whose lives
are essentially as trivial as they are destructive and against whom — or
at least against Merdle — one can feel very little animus, points to the
depth of the insights Dickens here clothes in the imagery of religion.
On this view they have not yet descended into complete a-humanity,
but of such a final metamorphosis we are given proleptic images in
that strange, telling 'Ghoule in gloves' passage and in Fanny
Sparkler's last glimpse of the man who goes off with her tortoiseshell
penknife:

> Thoroughly convinced, as he went out of the room, that it was the
> longest day that ever did come to an end at last, and that there never
> was a woman, not wholly devoid of personal attractions, so worn
> out by idiotic and lumpish people, Fanny passed into the balcony
> for a breath of air. Waters of vexation filled her eyes; and they had
> the effect of making the famous Mr. Merdle, in going down the
> street, appear to leap, and waltz, and gyrate, as if he were possessed
> of several Devils.   (II, xxiv, 701)

The same could be said of Miss Wade's vision — one can hardly call it
less — of Henry Gowan, of which she gives an account in her *apologia*
as being

> like the dressed-up Death in the Dutch series; whatever figure he
> took upon his arm, whether it was youth or age, beauty or ugliness,
> whether he danced with it, sang with it, played with it, or prayed
> with it, he made it ghastly.   (II, xxi, 669)

These people, then, are seen to have eliminated all that made them
once living, humanly choosing entities, or to be fast proceeding
towards that condition. They have become committed — even when
against what remains of their own will — to no less a principle than
Death. And as with the devils on the religious view, there is no
possibility of their being recalled back into humanity as such, let alone
any higher residence of values.

Merdle is, emphatically, a portrait of the Victorian capitalist but
not only that. He embodies the spirit itself at the heart of the rage for
money. Out of the major defaulting swindlers of his age Dickens has

put together a creature of extraordinary wealth and predominance. John Sadleir[16] and the rest are transmogrified into a new Mammon-image, a tremendous embodiment of all that this society worships, whose ruin practically fires the country; and the warning will not have been lost upon contemporary readers that such are the ever-possible consequences to a society which invests its interest and initiative in this kind of trade. In a rentier world, the collapse of one can mean the ruin of too many. Yet, as Professor Reid says in his study, Merdle in himself 'seems less an active agent of evil than a passive instrument of the corrupt will of Society'.[17] And this is what makes his situation more frightening than any menaced by Blandois. He seems to have become half mechanism with not enough selfhood left to change course, a puppet of the forces abroad committed to the eradication of the essentially human. His puppet nature pathetically expresses its detachment from what he is involved in doing, in such ripostes as this to one of Mrs Merdle's remonstrances:

> 'A carpenter!' repeated Mr. Merdle, checking something like a groan. 'I shouldn't so much mind being a carpenter, Mrs. Merdle.'   (I, xxxiii, 397)

There are depths and recognitions in this man which we seek in vain among the other 'Society' figures; but he has become incapable of converting his insights into any action which is not destructive (of others, as of himself). His suicide strikes us not so much as a desperate measure in the face of a run on his credit (we are not in fact informed that any such reckoning has come about), as an act of ultimate despair at his spiritual possession and ineluctable self-defeat; and, like all he stands for, it spells ruin for thousands of others.

This process of dehumanisation is shown to have one further, final stage:

> Mr. F's Aunt holding out like a grim fortress, and Flora becoming in need of refreshment, a messenger was despatched to the hotel for the tumbler already glanced at, which was afterwards replenished. With the aid of its contents, a newspaper, and some skimming of the cream of the pie-stock, Flora got through the remainder of the day in perfect good humour; though occasionally embarrassed by the consequences of an idle rumour which circulated among the credulous infants of the neighbourhood, to the effect that an old lady had sold herself to the pie-shop to be made up, and was then

sitting in the pie-shop parlour, declining to complete her contract. (II, xxxiv, 821)

This, in a comic mode, hints at the essential truth about Mr F's aunt, a
truth which is allied to the point of the 'entrails' passage and which in
the manner of their understandings the juveniles of the district ('out of
the mouth of babes and sucklings') have perceived. Alan Wilde has
seen her 'as the medium for the dark powers which infect the world of
Little Dorrit . . . making of it one huge pest-house, for victims and
victimizers alike'.[18] But in a sense this dignifies her role when she
tyrannises others, beyond its deserts. She is ridiculous, her behaviour
being so contingent, disconnected, a-rational and clearly outside of
her own control because (as one necessarily presumes) the original self
which could have ordered and structured it has lapsed. She deserves
the author's repeated mockeries, as in this instance:

bending over a steaming vessel of tea, and looking through the
steam, and breathing forth the steam, like a malignant Chinese
enchantress engaged in the performance of unholy rites.   (II, ix,
534)

For what Dickens essentially portrays in her is an image of how
humanity can be reduced to a frightening – and ludicrous –
sediment of itself when some egotism has taken over the entire
personality. She has evidently farmed herself out upon her nephew
and his relict, having convinced them, in the manner of Blandois or
Mr Dorrit or the Chief Butler or the Lords of the Circumlocution
Office and their families, of her possessing some special claim upon
the world's respect or admiration, for which there is absolutely no
evidence. The consequence of her success in imposing this solipsistic
view upon her immediate environment we see in what she *is*.
Ferocious self-centredness has made of her a wild thing in which the
discreative forces can freely rage, and part of the terror she inspires in
poor Clennam is that of a creature who constitutes a dire metaphys-
ical warning. Humanity reduced to a doll-like existence (I, xiii, 157),
she offers us a picture of what, near the 'end of the line', a too great
disregard for 'the Other', an insistence of our own wilful arbitrary
egos upon the world at large, will make of us.

All the same, a solution to this intellectual and spiritual darkness as
it finds expression in political terms cannot be found in revolutionary
action or by any other means. The vices of the Establishment world

are but those of 'the rest' writ large; the root cause of this terrible failure lies in the human breast. I say 'terrible' because it ought to be a moot point whether any human member of this world is redeemable from such vain imaginations. Mrs Clennam having once adopted, or constructed, her cruel world-view, is it not simply rational in her, if also covertly self-gratifying, to adhere to the frigidity which characterises her painful relations with her 'son'? Hers is a self-consistent as well as brutal philosophy. And what can rescue Arthur or Amy Dorrit from debility so inspissated as theirs, when through all of Part I we see both shrink from every liberating possibility like nocturnal creatures agonised by the light of day?

Yet, against the novel's full dark account of a negative bias in the social and personal life and, with this, its abiding imagery of imprisonment, there is posed Dickens's equally powerful intuition of the truth — which is to say, the reality that we observe going dishonoured in all these cases — as itself entrenched in central positions, deep-lodged redoubts in the human mind, from which it presses for acknowledgement. Indeed its power as a kind of environing force seeking any orifice through which to pour its besieging tides upon the pretences humanity makes is testified in the very subtlety and sophistication of the methods by which the denizens of 'Society' and all other offenders against it seek to suppress its ineradicable appeals. Each distortion, each suppression, has to be vindicated or dignified.

The marriage-market debate between Mrs Merdle and the dowager Mrs Gowan in I, xxxiii is as close an observation of the relationship between actual will and acknowledged motive as any in Jane Austen or Henry James; and it shares their qualities of wry humour, realising for us in a sensitive manner how the rascals of this world deliberately shake off the demands of right against wrong between the onion-skin-like layers of their complicated deceits. But such is an art which emphasises the self-existence in objectivity inviolable and ineradicable of these same demands; it shows right and wrong to be something of which human nature is so conscious, through whatever processes of self-delusion and public mendacity, that it has to resort to extremely complex subterfuges in order to accommodate this awareness to its monstrous egotisms and parasitisms.

Mrs Merdle and Mrs Gowan are both so successful (socially) because both are very skilled adepts at the sort of trickery with which they advance the specious claims of, the one, her devotion to the simple life of Rousseauistic ideals (see, for example, I, xx, 239, 242–3), and, the other, her regard for her son's 'innocence' and welfare (I, xxxiii). But the need, the call for such skills is what effectually we are given to remark. There is little question of their imposing these frauds upon an innocent and credulous social sphere. Dickens's account runs specifically to the contrary:

> In answer to this direct appeal, Mrs. Merdle assured Mrs. Gowan (speaking as a Priestess of Society) that she was highly to be commended, that she was much to be sympathised with, that she had taken the highest of parts, and had come out of the furnace refined. And Mrs. Gowan, who of course saw through her own threadbare blind perfectly, and who knew that Mrs. Merdle saw through it perfectly, and who knew that Society would see through it perfectly, came out of this form, notwithstanding, as she had gone into it, with immense complacency and gravity.   (Ibid., 393–4)

The reality of all these people's lives has to be overlaid with a veil of pretension – not to meet any threatening social opposition, but for their *own* comfort. And we attend upon Mrs Merdle or Mrs Gowan as on past mistresses of a high art, of skills which do not come so very easily; the Lords of the Circumlocution Office have to be coached in the forms of *their* ritualised charades to pass muster in Parliament. A jobbed majority awaits anything they say, but the form is necessary to the effective dishonouring of the inwardly acknowledged realities:

> Then would he be there to tell the honourable gentleman that it would have been more to his honour . . . if he had left the Circumlocution Office alone, and never approached this matter. Then would he keep one eye upon a coach or crammer from the Circumlocution Office sitting below the bar, and smash the honourable gentleman with the Circumlocution Office account of this matter. And although one of two things always happened; namely, either that the Circumlocution Office had nothing to say and said it, or that it had something to say of which the noble lord, or right honourable gentleman, blundered one half and forgot the other; the Circumlocution Office was always voted immaculate, by an accommodating majoirity.   (I, x, 106)

These, however, are people and institutions ruthlessly committed to obscuring wholly the truths — as to where the positive values lie against which they sin. And in one very limited sense such severe remorselessness is a valuable advantage, for the morally more complex or sensitive consciousnesses are greatly harassed by the promptings they fail entirely to suppress.

Frederick Dorrit's outburst against Fanny's treatment of her sister (II, v), or Amy's own remonstrance concerning Miss Dorrit's will to marry Edmund 'Sparkler', plainly awaken echoes in Fanny's own judgement:

> When he was gone, she said, 'O Fanny, Fanny!' and turned to her sister in the bright window, and fell upon her bosom and cried there. Fanny laughed at first; but soon laid her face against her sister's and cried too — a little. It was the last time Fanny ever showed that there was any hidden, suppressed, or conquered feeling in her on the matter. (II, xiv, 596)

We are shown a young woman of spirit, intelligence and wit who has to perfect a role — the role *of* the impetuous self-willed young matron and society beauty — before she can finally tread 'the way she had chosen . . . with her own imperious, self-willed step' (ibid.).

When Dickens tells us of Mrs Clennam that

> More than forty years had passed over the grey head of this determined woman, since the time she recalled. More than forty years of strife and struggle with the whisper that, by whatever names she called her vindictive pride and rage, nothing through all eternity could change their nature (II, xxx, 775)

we may feel his commentary to be unlawful authorial intrusion; advice about what to think of Mrs Clennam's state of mind, rather than any 'dramatisation' of it, any natural realisation of her consciousness by fully fictional means. Yet the truth of this observation has been present to us all along. As Lionel Trilling argues in his Introduction to the Oxford Illustrated edition, Arthur

> conjectures that her imprisoning illness is the price she pays for the guilty gratification of keeping William Dorrit in his prison. In order to have the right to injure another, she must injure herself in an equivalent way. 'A swift thought shot into [Arthur Clennam's] mind. In that long imprisonment here [i.e. Mr. Dorrit's] and in

her long confinement to her room, did his mother find a balance to be struck? I admit that I was accessory to that man's captivity. I have suffered it in kind. He has decayed in his prison; I in mine. I have paid the penalty.'[19]

She has sinned, however, not only against William Dorrit and his daughter (whose legacy she has suppressed). What the revelations of II, xxx make plain to us is a horrifying tale of the torment inflicted by her and Arthur's great-uncle Gilbert Clennam, upon his father and real mother: the weak man for whom Gilbert had already arranged a loveless marriage, and the 'graceless orphan trained to be a singing-girl' who has 'carried it against' this 'hard woman'. While the uncle proved a foolish domestic tyrant (on his death-bed he repents what he has done), Mrs Clennam has pushed ahead in her galled pride with his matrimonial scheme. She has wedded herself to Arthur's father — who she knows has already married the 'graceless orphan' by a secret ceremony (so much for her respect for the ordinances of Holy Writ when these do not facilitate the passages of her jealous wrath). Then she has set about very successfully breaking her rival's heart:

> I ask, what was the penitence, in works, that was demanded of her? 'You have a child; I have none. You love that child. Give him to me. He shall believe himself to be my son, and he shall be believed by every one to be my son. To save you from exposure, his father shall swear never to see or communicate with you more; equally to save him from being stripped by his uncle, and to save your child from being a beggar, you shall swear never to see or to communicate with either of them more. . . .' That was all. She had to sacrifice her sinful and shameful affections; no more. She was then free to bear her load of guilt in secret, and to break her heart in secret; and through such present misery (light enough for her, I think!) to purchase her redemption from endless misery, if she could.   (Ibid., 776–7)

By her self-immurement in the gloomy Clennam house, Arthur's putative mother has been able to 'pay for' these barbarities without having to acknowledge them, to herself and to the world, as such. Yet what else does all this self-punishment mean (for Dr Bergler accounts her also one of the principal psychic masochists in his reading of the tale)[20] but the recognition of guilt, deep and heavy guilt, at the heart of her being?

Critics have complained that the narrative compressed into this chapter is complicated, confusing and appears too late in the work to modify our experience of what has come before in any fashion comparable to the quantity of information now so tardily retailed; in short that it is an apology for, not a successful prosecution of, performance on the part of its artist. And they can lean for support upon Dickens's number-plan for the double-issue in which this episode appears;[21] which shows him to have left the details of these, his story's antecedents, to a very late term in its composition before thus fully defining and collating them. Yet, though I disagree with this view, I would rather bypass than confute it. For to argue out the matter thus is to miss the essential point. We had to be informed sooner or later what exactly Mrs Clennam's crimes have been. But, with her dreadful rituals of harsh frigidity and 'expiation' before us all along, we have never supposed that she is not, has not been, morally if not legally a criminal. What matters is that everything which is ultimately revealed does match our expectations. But it could have been omitted, all this retrospect, without seriously wounding the book, because throughout we have known that cruelties and suppressions of an injurious kind are the reality behind the mask and the dreary rituals of this 'hard woman', whose loveless condition also does not fail to stir our pity. The essential ethical drama has been clear to us from the first; in Mrs Clennam's relations with her son, in her attitude to her Bible, to Flintwinch or to Affery. The offences there revealed against the truth with which Dickens has been principally concerned, against truth as a morally positive force, creative and indivisible in all varying human relations, are what count. Revelations about the specific origin or motive of Mrs Clennam's mysterious incarceration can wait, when her outlook on life, antedating even the days of her brutality towards Arthur's real mother, is the phenomenon at issue; and this in its truth-denying nature.

It is in William Dorrit, however, that we are given the novel's fullest account of the human mind's capacity to suppress the truth of its situation, considered in a moral point of view, for the sake of self-endorsement which is cramping and destructive; and yet its simultaneous inability — ultimately, fundamentally — to credit its own lies. Dorrit is the tragic victim of a cruel values-system, the ethos of his society as a whole, the society which here finds a representative expression, in Dickens's thought, in its having until recently made debt an offence punishable by law with imprisonment. But we are all debtors, the very term has an ample resonance. At every moment we

owe to Nature — to our environment, our heredity — and to each
other a multitude of necessaries we can never repay. And we are all
captives in 'the prison of this lower world' (II, xxx, 763). So that the
most serious and ugly error a human being can make — that which
inter alia originates in the social macrocosm such a practice as
imprisonment for debt — consists in responding to this total dependence in any fashion which attempts to obscure or repudiate the
obligation and our common nature, in his unique case.

Towards some pretensions the novelist shows himself capable of a
warm or unhysterical human latitude; this being Middle Earth as well
as a revolving jail. If our sages have to scream at us for every offence,
to save the world's chance of integrity, then the service becomes
greater than the god, we hold our existence in its hopeful creative
aspects on terms too fraught to make the gift worth the trouble. Such
pretensions as Captain Maroon's in I, xii, where Clennam and
Plornish go to settle Tip Dorrit's debts, or Flora's performances as a
'statue bride' and 'moral mermaid' — deceits which animate
a dull round or encourage a dreary existence without being able
truly to impose upon others — Dickens patently gives us to enjoy.
Although by showing its universal ramification, they do extend
the theme of the endemic dishonesty of most people's social roles,
yet there is that vital distinction that they do not impose upon
others. Even the not-brilliant Plornish well knows what the Captain will really take in settlement of *his* debt and Flora is always
discrediting her own fantasies with outbursts of robust commonsense
or self-exposure. But William Dorrit's pretences concerning the
character of his role in the Marshalsea rely upon his denying the equal
human importance with himself of the people around him. Far from
so bringing up his children as to work their release from the kind of
life forced upon him — and their establishment later in wealthy
Society is the most random stroke of luck in this aspect of the case —
his obsession with status has turned both the elder siblings into
insensitive ne'er-do-wells while lowering the burden of his own
maintenance entirely upon his youngest daughter. So that Tip will
always be a debtor (in the wrong sense, that of the man who does not
meet life responsibly), and Fanny will, like her father, choose to step
from one kind of prison to another, whatever cards fate itself may
deal them. In 'Poverty' and 'Riches' alike (the titles of the two books
into which the novel is divided), all sustain at all costs 'the miserably
ragged old fiction of the family gentility' (I, xviii, 213) and they are
tragic as well as unlikable for doing so in that this leaves them no time,

space, occasion, air for ever truly living. Each is incapable of
happiness.

That the Father of the Marshalsea has developed little interest in
real honour — so long as his social dignity is secured — we are shown
in the painful episode of I, xix, where he suggests to Amy that she
should 'lead on' John Chivery, a suitor whose interest she can only in
honesty immediately reject (as she has already done: I, xviii). The
scheme is instantly still-born in face of her silent deprecation; but the
grief with which he meets this bafflement, while complex in the
response it demands from us and deeply moving as the agony of a
man also much sinned against, is yet characteristic in the theme to
which it continually reverts — his superiority over his fellow-
creatures:

> 'Amy,' he went on in a suppressed voice, trembling violently, and
> looking at her as wildly as if he had gone mad. 'I tell you, if you
> could see me as your mother saw me, you wouldn't believe it to be
> the creature you have only looked at through the bars of this cage.
> I was young, I was accomplished, I was good-looking, I was
> independent — by God I was, child! — and people sought me out,
> and envied me. Envied me! . . . And yet I have some respect here. I
> have made some stand against it. I am not quite trodden down. Go
> out and ask who is the chief person in the place. . . . '
>
> He burst into tears of maudlin pity for himself, and at length
> suffering her to embrace him . . . let his grey head rest against her
> cheek, and bewail his wretchedness. Presently he changed the
> subject of his lamentations, and clasping his hands about her as she
> embraced him, cried, O Amy, his mother-less, forlorn child!
> O the days that he had seen her careful and laborious for him! Then
> he reverted to himself, and weakly told her how much better she
> would have loved him if she had known him in his vanished
> character, and how he would have married her to a gentleman who
> should have been proud of her as his daughter, and how (at which
> he cried again) she should first have ridden at his fatherly side on her
> own horse, and how the crowd (by which he meant in effect the
> people who had given him the twelve shillings he then had in his
> pocket) should have trudged the dusty roads respectfully.   (I, xix,
> 227–8)

It is this bias in his outlook which can lead him, in a condition of actual
prosperity even greater than the substance of these recollections, to

have still less regard for the feelings of the girl who has been his family's 'affectionate invaluable friend . . . devoted guardian . . . more than mother' (II, v, 485) than in the days of his long captivity. His attempt to suppress the past by altering his relations with Amy (in II, ii–xviii, he rarely sees her *tête-à-tête* as in the old days) and by altering *her* (for which he hires Mrs General in the first place) can only very limitedly be a proper object of our sympathy. With the past he wishes to cancel not only all sense of his former degradation but also his dependence, like any human being, on the ministrations of others. When he remonstrates with her, ' "I say, sweep it [i.e. their history] off the face of the earth and begin afresh. Is that much? I ask, is *that* much?" '   (II, v, 479), our response is modified by the knowledge of just what kind of alternative life he seeks in this new era of wealth; an existence very much like that of his Marshalsea days, charged with the 'setting up of superiorities' (about which his brother protests in his outburst at the breakfast table – ibid.) not only against Amy but against all the world. The family which could be so freely and easily cruel to Mr Nandy (I, xxxi) now take a high line with such people as Tinkler (the valet) or any other members of human society whom they can patronise with impunity.

It is equally the case of course that he has to find a role which offers him some kind of self-respect during the long age he is pitilessly kept in prison; and we may well consider ourselves ruthless if we demand, on our side of the bars, alternatives to the fantasies and pretensions he develops there. Dickens elicits, with this large finely-nerved portrait, no glib or peremptorily dismissive judgement. Our various considerations as we read amount to a fully empathising and compassionate sense of complexity, rather; but judgement nevertheless does enter the case. It has to, if all human autonomy (and therefore value) is not to be sacrificed. The fullness of the characterisation – the deep rich sense Dickens gives us of everything that can have made Dorrit like this and which in that sense excuses his tragic performance – is of the essence of the matter. But we have to notice how 'the Father of the Marshalsea' responds to the prison environment differently from his brother or his younger daughter. They are effectually no less its victims; but they do not make his sort of impositions.

So that I think the novel's emphasis falls in the last analysis upon the sheer process of watching Dorrit waver in his commitments. Dickens's habit of getting us to observe the development in him of a moral choice, wrestling with himself as between this and that course of action, this role and that reality, enhances the sense we cannot help but take away from the text; that his egotistic and hurtful deceits are not the result only of what society has done to him, or of ineluctable, if always unique, structures in the super-personal macrocosm surrounding the individual life, but come ultimately from a personal — an aboriginally and mysteriously personal — centre in the will; the choices of which are finally, on Dickens's view, the responsibility of the 'I' which suffers, desires and acts. The consequence with us, however, is not a verdict of simple praise or blame. We can sympathise and even identify with him too much, for that; we can understand too well the process by which he has come deliberately to obscure or ignore the 'connections' that do not feed his vanity.

But the self-defeating character of his impostures has been no less powerfully suggested from the beginning. The array of pretensions by which he has sought to deny the value of other people, to sustain his ego in the wrong way, has been very grudgingly maintained deep within. His stammer (the 'ha's and 'hum's which so punctuate William Dorrit's discourse) is itself a token of this and noticeably deteriorates or diminishes according to the degree of the given falsehood he is foisting upon his interlocutors — and himself — at any given time. And the practised years of such deceits are shown to have nowise abated their cumulative toll. When he is violent with John Chivery for having visited him upon his return to affluent London, and having waited upon him in all amity and reasonableness at his hotel, we are shown a man whose health itself is afflicted by the denial with which he meets reality; which is to say, the real friendships and respect he has been offered, the psychically nourishing connections:

'What else did you come for, sir?'

'Nothing else in the world, sir. Oh dear me! Only to say, sir, that I hoped you was well, and only to ask if Miss Amy was well?'

'What's that to you, sir?' retorted Mr. Dorrit. [This from the father who once solicited Amy's 'leading' Chivery 'on', when his respect in the Marshalsea might depend upon the good favour of Chivery senior.]

'It's nothing to me, sir, by rights. I never thought of lessening the distance betwixt us, I am sure. I know it's a liberty, sir, but I never thought you'd have taken it ill. Upon my word and honour, sir,' said Young John, with emotion, 'in my poor way, I am too proud to have come, I assure you, if I had thought so.'

Mr. Dorrit was ashamed. He went back to the window, and leaned his forehead against the glass for some time. When he turned, he had his handkerchief in his hand, and he had been wiping his eyes with it, and he looked tired and ill.   (II, xviii, 632)

These symptoms do not augur any change of heart, however. The pride and hypocrisy, the attempt to use other people for a measure merely of his own elevated status, which as a general principle has made this whole society so grim, quickly return in the nasty postlude to the interview:

Mr. Dorrit was not too proud and honourable to listen at the door, that he might ascertain for himself whether John really went straight out, or lingered to have any talk with any one. There was no doubt that he went direct out at the door, and away down the street with a quick step. After remaining alone for an hour, Mr. Dorrit rang for the Courier, who found him with his chair on the hearth-rug, sitting with his back towards him and his face to the fire. 'You can take that bundle of cigars to smoke on the journey, if you like,' said Mr. Dorrit, with a careless wave of the hand. 'Ha — brought by — hum — little offering from — ha — son of old tenant of mine.'   (Ibid., 634)

Yet the inner voice, or claim, or instinct, still exacts its toll. We have been no less adverted by this interview with John Chivery than in all the dialogues with his daughter that part of Mr. Dorrit is torturingly resistant to all his pretensions and cheats; and his loftiest fancies of 'building castles in the air' are accompanied by a final disintegration, the breakdown of his health on the journey back to Rome (II, xix). When Frederick Dorrit protests against his family's concern for its 'credit', Dickens is doubtless writing figuratively in telling us that, 'As his hand went up above his head and came down on the table, it might have been a blacksmith's' (II, v, 485), but the impulse of inward psychic health here externalized as physical power is wholly credible. The truth about the relation between spiritual and physical health thus imaged has already been made real to us throughout the portrayal of both the brothers. Frederick, for all that his nature is by and large debilitated through a kind of vacant resignation in the face of his reverses, is not in rebellion against himself, with one part of his being at war against the rest of it. He has no pretensions, no continuous and fatiguing labour of self-conviction to keep in constant repair, as to his dignity and status; whereas Mr Dorrit's inward life, like 'kingdom'd Achilles' in Shakespeare's play, is at the deepest level (and albeit largely inarticulately) that of a man who 'in commotion rages, and batters down himself'.

His public-faced consciousness finally disintegrates, at the banquet given by 'the Bosom' in Rome (II, xix, 1), only for all his impositions and supressions to fly into view, freed from their tight moorings at the heart of his being, and show themselves for what they have been. The human debts he has refused creatively to acknowledge, the payment of which *is* their mere acknowledgement, what he owes to his daughter, all the essential obligations of his life rush to exposure with his rehearsal of the little testimonial-soliciting welcome he once traditionally gave to newcomers to the Marshalsea. Once the self-assertive appetitive ego loses control, he instantly becomes the very opposite of all he ever sought to be. He stands there a witness to truth; the truths of his own past career, and of the kind of 'connections' — between them and the poor, them and a social system which imprisons for debt, between man and man simply — which the guests at the dinner-party are in all their living only too happy to disavow. There is ironic felicity in the likeness (already noted: II, vii, 511) between the worlds of the Marshalsea and Mrs Merdle's hospitality being thus peremptorily unconsciously enforced; both equally deserve the preposterous, moving testimony of degradation with which Dorrit once introduced only the redoubt he inhabited in London. But this climacteric is the book's most powerful single instance, among many, of the truth-enforcing tendency within the human mind; the tendency, this is to say, which in all cases of life where there *is* yet *life*, where there is still something to be redeemed, something remotely worth being concerned for, surfaces and exposes itself to view. Or, to put it conversely, the fact that he can break down like this is a proof of William Dorrit's yet abiding humanity, his — for all his ruses and subterfuges of a lifetime — having still a human value (as Lord Decimus or Mrs General do not) which has not been eliminated.

Once we note this central theme — and it is thematic in both the sense of its being a major part of the author's creating idea-emotion at the heart of the work and its being continuously, naturally, effortlessly shown in human behaviour on all sides, under his hand, like a musical motif — we find its tokens everywhere. They have exhilarated us almost without our recognising them. On a detached view we might well consider implausible Miss Wade's drawing up an *apologia pro vita sua* on the unlikely chance of her being able to deliver

it to the stranger Arthur Clennam, whom anyway she dislikes (II, xx).
With what else however is Miss Wade preoccupied, first and last, but
her need to justify what she cannot instinctually endorse in her
attitude to life? As Dr Leavis has remarked, 'she *has* been
wronged . . . irremediably . . . [but] . . . she *needs* to be wronged
in order to keep up the intensity of her resentment, the passion which
for her is life'.[22] Miss Wade's vaunted contempt of ordinary human
beings (as weak, hypocritical, sentimental) and her avowed retirement are blinds, however much they may serve to impose upon
herself. Far from withdrawing into a thin indifference to the ways of a
merely despicable world (her alleged view), she lives by defining
herself in terms of her injuries, real and imagined, at its hands and her
opposition to it. It is the suffocating tumult of her obsession, indeed,
with what other people think of her, her need to challenge them and
outrage them at every turn, which is of the essence of her
characterisation at its most convincing (but it is all convincing). So
that this woman's interest in justifying herself to those with whom she
is in most actively hostile *and* distant relation, is of the very nature of
her tragic perversity and self-defeat. Few of us, doubtless, would
draw up a *curriculum vitae*, few would go to her lengths generally. To
many intents and purposes she is mentally deranged. But it is wholly
of a piece with her particular insanity — the extreme form in her,
among the representative personages of this novel, of the attempt to
live as oneself alone, independent of all other human supports,
obligations and responsibilities — that it should express itself in this
particular way. And that it does so makes her behaviour, like William
Dorrit's petulance on many occasions, testify to a deep-hidden but
active sense of her own mistaken folly. If you are blandly and
fatuously confident of the rightness of your course through life — like
Lord Decimus or Mr Tite Barnacle — you do not draw up an apology
for it.

In the same way, while Henry Gowan is a completely destructive
parasite, yet his parasitisms find their inculcation and excuse by
continual reference to their opposing virtues. An indolent
and cynical man, he purports all the same — with every manner of
infidelity to it — to belong to the strenuous, selfless life of the artist,
with its vision of a world of absolute values. His wit is an instrument
of discomposure and universal depreciation, yet it can find a place for
itself only by maintaining the thin pretence that it is the function of a
genuine intelligence, of authentic brilliant epigrammatic insight.
These considerations show him, as our reflections upon her show Miss

Wade, for the more rather than less depraved. But they also demonstrate something the medieval scholastics would have found themselves entirely at home with, though in this case on terms entirely self-probatory, empirical and untheological: the parasite relation of mischief to good. Much of Dickens's vision is a fully engaged view of how darkly and comprehensively the Barnacles and Barnacle-worshipping principles in the human heart lay the world waste; in almost all respects it is a novel of scanty consolations, of fully sustained dark vision. But we are equally shown how the bad tendencies can wreak their will only by conspiring with difficulty against the grain, the inward-abiding felt realities which continually press for utterance or acknowledgement in human affairs, which achieve *some* acknowledgement — if not open, wholesome and creative, then perverse but recognisable — as a tribute to the authentic nature of human and social relations in the morally beleaguered world.

The tendency ramifies in all directions; some, as in Mrs Merdle's and Mrs Gowan's discussion of the marriage-market in 'Society', we have already noted. There is Ferdinand Barnacle's need to pay his respects to the truths he professionally thwarts, in his visit to Clennam in the Marshalsea (II, xxviii). John Chivery with his day-dreaming contributes an unwitting satire upon the habit of pre-empting one's experience with the kind of premature despair which particularly signalises Clennam's response to life and which must be among the acutest dangers for the sensitive, reflective and responsible spirit in society. The successive epitaphs he composes for his own imagined grave near the Marshalsea are 'send-ups' of Clennam's retreat from open and responsive living, all the more informative for being — like Flora Finching's discourses — unconscious comedy.

Equally amusing, in its semi-macabre way, is the career of Jeremiah Flintwinch's twin, Ephraim. The Clennam servant embodies the very quintessence of the Calvinist-commercial world figured in his mistress's home and in the London, generally a human affront, to which Arthur returns at the beginning of the story. A very pattern of the cramping rites, the bloodless emotionless cash-nexus morality, of its twisted forms of religious endorsement and its denials of humanity even in the most intimate relations (as with his wife), this is how he greets the son of the house after that dutiful scion has returned from an absence of twenty years:

He had a candle in his hand, and he held it up for a moment to assist his keen eyes. 'Ah, Mr. Arthur?' he said, without any emotion, 'you are come at last? Step in.' Mr. Arthur stepped in and shut the door.

'Your figure is filled out, and set,' said the old man, turning to look at him with the light raised again, and shaking his head; 'but you don't come up to your father in my opinion. Nor yet your mother.'

'How is my mother?'

'She is as she always is now. Keeps her room when not actually bedridden, and hasn't been out of it fifteen times in as many years, Arthur.' They had walked into a spare, meagre dining-room. The old man had put the candlestick upon the table, and, supporting his right elbow with his left hand, was smoothing his leathern jaws while he looked at the visitor. The visitor offered his hand. The old man took it coldly enough, and seemed to prefer his jaws; to which he returned, as soon as he could.

'I doubt if your mother will approve of your coming home on the Sabbath, Arthur,' he said, shaking his head warily.

'You wouldn't have me go away again?'

'Oh! I? I? I am not the master. It's not what *I* would have. I have stood between your father and mother for a number of years. I don't pretend to stand between your mother and you.'   (I, iii, 31–2)

For all his endorsement of Mrs Clennam's variety of righteousness, it does not come as total shock to us to learn that he has not been averse to the possibility of a spot of blackmail, when, in the *dénouement*, all is revealed by Blandois's final demands in the Clennam home and Mrs Clennam's own frenetic attempt at self-justification. It transpires that, having entrusted his partner's guilty document – the will that lady suppressed – to his foreign-dwelling brother, some years back, he has been outwitted by the no less scheming Frenchman in its recovery from this same twin, who has since died (II, xxx, 780–4). It has been alleged of the plot of *Little Dorrit* (and of *Great Expectations*) that it is 'not only weak through inherent melodrama but doubly weak by revolving around wicked deeds of violence performed long before the action of the book begins'.[23] His is only one of the mischiefs so performed in this case; yet no more astonishing and spontaneously convincing paradigm has been afforded us of a major part of the intuition from which the whole novel derives than this bifurcation of Jeremiah into two people and these ensuing reported events. That we learn much of his story *by* report and in the closing phases of the tale is of the essence of the episode's ability exactly to mirror that part of the life of the self which 'steals a march' on and betrays the irresponsible, repressive, will-enforcing ego. At this point Jeremiah is as surprised, in his own fashion, as we are. We find ourselves recognising an authentic account of the sort of price which will always and inevitably be paid for such a rule of conduct as the Clennam House's factotum has assumed through so many years. Flintwinch has divided himself against himself. What else could he do with all this effectual disowning of his own humanity? So that the appearance of an identical twin who lives a life which is an apparent antithesis of his brother's — though, all significantly, it is by no means a wholesome creative alternative itself, but rather that of a sleepy, loose-tongued drunkard tippling his way about the Flemish ports (II, xxx, 78) — would surely unite all the different schools of modern psychology in applause at its perfection as a model of the response which inescapably results where repression (in the clinical sense) is at issue. Where the individual for whatever reason disavows and disorients the springs of his own humanity — his ability at fellowship, his capacity for openness and mirth, his human mutuality (in sum) — then the deep inner needs and powers revenge themselves. And they do so more often than not after a goodly interval when they have been supposed long benumbed and buried. We have one symbolic hint of the two brothers having thematically this suggestive function towards one another in Jeremiah's automatically taking over the part of Ephraim, as an open reprobate with a taste for drink on the Dutch wharves and quays, as soon as he hears of Ephraim's death. Another is offered in the scene of Affery's nightmare near the beginning of the book.

The inside of the Clennam house at night is one of the places where we seem to come upon the preternatural in the inner 'as distinct from' the outer world, in this novel. We have an encounter with the preternatural in the latter medium when Little Dorrit and Maggy meet with the young prostitute by London Bridge on the night of 'Little Dorrit's Party' (I, xiv, 174–6) — she speaks and gestures like one of the souls in the *Inferno* out of a Dantean, heightened reality, showing the empirical for all-symbolic and *vice versa*. The value of both these episodes in the general tendency of the novel is to confront us with potent aspects of the life of the mind and spirit, which the foolish suppose can be ignored without inevitably derived consequences. The scene is non-'realistic' in its artistic method and, with its utterly inward psychology, wholly convincing. (' "You can't do it," said the woman [to Amy]. "You are kind and innocent; but you can't look at me out of a child's eyes. I never should have touched you, but I thought that you were a child." And with a strange, wild cry, she went away.') Affery in her 'dreaming' appears to encounter spiritual phenomena in the corridors of the unconscious — not only *her* unconscious, but also that of her tormentor and husband. (They are, we remember, according to their — however horribly per-functory — marriage in a Christian church, 'one flesh'.) No 'expla-nation' can reduce this scene in which Jeremiah talks to his double (I, iv) either to the status of inept mechanical symbolism on Dickens's part or to that of the merely empirical. It is too vividly realised for that, even down to the details of the giddy slavey's innermost terrors as we cannot but feel they would express themselves in this rare, strange situation ('She expected to see Jeremiah fast asleep or in a fit' — ibid., 42); imagistically it sorts too well with what men have always intuited of the process of dreaming, and what so much modern theory argues the phenomenon to be doing — tearing a hole in the boundaries of the conscious and subconscious life for information from the one to enter the other by indirect means. ('In one corner of the hall, behind the house-door, there was a little waiting-room, *like a well-shaft*, with a long narrow window in it as if it had been ripped up. In this room, *which was never used*, a light was burning' [ibid., emphasis added]. Again the suggestion of an unexplored part of the self being opened — or, rather, 'ripped up'.) Of course this is not the only suggestion with which this episode is pregnant, though it is a striking instance of the alter ego made visible and palpable, and is heightened in its turn perhaps by the suggestiveness of Affery's descending to the little cell-like office, as to some small secret area of the mind, down a staircase. (Many volumes have been written by psychologists in exegesis of this image's meaning as a pattern of descent into the depths of the subconscious.) Jeremiah's progress upstairs thereafter is in part so terrifying because it realises what must surely be one of the deepest fears of the human mind: that, having gone to sleep, having begun to dream, we should discover our dream *is* inescapable, has become reality (as poor Affery does — ibid., 43−4), that one should not be able to establish any sense of difference or containment between the dream world and the one which (we hope, on account of its greater clarity and more manageable coherence) encloses it. But this is all part of Dickens's total richness, his unflinching registration of so many of the myriad different features of what it is to be conscious.

What is finally disturbing in the case of Jeremiah (as in Jonsonian comedy) is that the wretched creature gets off scot-free. The treatment of his failure to appear beneath 'the London geological formation' despite the hopes of earnest diggers (II, xxxi, 794— 5) is deliberately comic and genuinely amusing. But the fact is, our last intelligence of this old man who was erstwhile at least an incarnation of the tyrannical greeds and hypocrisies which so disfigure his whole society, and who is still evidently a cheerful irresponsible egotist, is of his consorting 'with the Dutchmen on the quaint banks of the canals at the Hague, and in the drinking-shops of Amsterdam, under the style and designation of Mynheer von Flyntevynge' (ibid.). This ought to counterbalance any suggestion implicit in the destruction of Blandois (the other blackmailer of the story) that in some sort this world will not tend, in the last analysis, to be the inheritance of the cruel, rapacious and cunning. That it *is* so, that the crafty Flintwinch should have contrived an escape even from the consequences of his malversation to revel it forth in easy cheer while others, who have demonstrated a greater integrity, struggle with complexity and paralysis and defeat at home, is only too convincing. (Which is of course not to say that any truly sane person would wish for a share in Mynheer von Flyntevynge's' sort of consciousness.)

In the story of Jeremiah Flintwinch, however, and that of his twin, the truth which presses in upon all dishonest pretensions, which unremittingly urges its own release and publicity, has made itself manifest in yet another mode. To the first brigand who could bribe him with a bottle, the drunkard brother has handed over the very documents which his sibling most prized of all his possessions, the Clennam will, the guarantee of felt and nursed power over his (Jeremiah's) employer. Ephraim — the unacknowledged Flintwinch — has betrayed Jeremiah for what he really is and has messed things up for him; and we recognise the event as part of a general pattern. Mr Dorrit's alienated self speaks out at the Roman banquet. Mrs Clennam's drives her long-paralysed limbs through several streets, almost against her understanding and her will ('This is not recovery; it is not strength; I don't know what it is' — ibid., 789).

As well as these awesome liberating instances, we are given to see how the same power can find its expression in ways wholly happy and creative. To Dr Leavis's account of Flora's felicities of utterance, or of Pancks in Bleeding Heart Yard cutting off the 'sacred locks' of the 'Patriarch',[24] there is but little to add. Beautiful his analysis of the subversive and restorative role of language under Flora's spell (subversive of all meanness and false pretension, restorative in the sense of prompting a living play of all the essential generosities); her superb anti-snobbery (the much more telling, like everything her discourse highlights, for always being unselfconscious, undeliberated, spontaneous and an apparently tangential feature of her discourse); her robust normative good sense (beneath the façade of the 'full mermaid condition'); her revealing poetic conflation of tropes and truths. All these find expression in, for example, her unwitting exposé of the Dorrit family's concern for 'gentility'.

Their pretensions are effectually 'placed' in half a sentence which also shows those pretensions for the rather pathetically ineffective (because factitious) attempts to dominate their experience which, like all their other self-defeating impostures, they must be:

> 'And now pray tell me something all you know,' said Flora, drawing her chair near to his, 'about the good dear quiet little thing and all the change of her fortunes carriage people now no doubt and horses without number most romantic, a coat of arms of course and wild beasts on their hind legs showing it as if it was a copy they had done with mouths from ear to ear good gracious . . . .'   (II, ix, 535)

If this – in some respects – weak-minded woman can so accurately have translated their outward show into the reality it hides (and they have failed the more in that she does so unconsciously), they are self-evidently a long way from repatterning existence itself on their own terms.

Again and again she betrays by comic hyperbole and hilarious inflation the meretricious tendencies around her.

> 'The withered chaplet my dear,' said Flora, with great enjoyment, 'is then perished the column is crumbled and the pyramid is standing upside down upon its what's-his-name call it not giddiness call it not weakness call it not folly I must now retire into privacy and look upon the ashes of departed joys no more but taking the further liberty of paying for the pastry which has formed the humble pretext of our interview will for ever say Adieu!'   (II, xxxiv, 820)

The absurd epitaph thus delivered by Flora upon her own career near the end of the story is nevertheless a pointed one, with its telling version of the life-thwarting attitudes which Amy — her companion on this occasion — has cherished during the greater part of the novel's action and which at this date she has only recently resolved. We shall fully have sympathised with Little Dorrit's misdirections, as with her father's, given all we have been shown that can have prompted her towards her tragic persona. With its silent acquiescence, however, in the destructive roles of others and its defeat of her own capacities for a fully creative achievement (as in the marriage with Clennam, which only the respective and allied inhibitions of both partners at an earlier stage in their careers prevented them from achieving), it has its happy dismissal here in the beautiful unconscious parody of Mrs Finching's offered pose. Under the bright light of Flora's oblivious and revelatory chatter in this episode, there is another typical indication of that tonically re-educative aspect of living which Amy (like her future husband) has formerly too often and too easily neglected. This is the prompting, towards authenticity in understanding, in behaviour and therefore towards personal fulfilment, which exists in experience being spontaneously lived without presuppositions or preconditions. Flora's 'taking the further liberty of paying for the pastry which has formed the humble pretext of our interview' collapses the bathetic pretensions of her peroration ('Adieu!') into the lived experience of a 'humble' event in an actual pub — into the real fabric of which life is truly fashioned. (To live you have to eat pies, to eat pies you have to pay for them, the human condition is based on 'humbler' supports than those of tremulous romantic self-melodramatisation.) The whole episode becomes a comic paradigm of the truth implicit here and we see again how the comic has so informative a value in connection with Flora, for with Amy's departure (ibid., 821) we go on to the problem of extricating Mr F's aunt from the hostelry 'through the remainder of the day'. The adverted contact with the real into which Flora's 'withered chaplet' speech has beautifully collapsed is thus amplified and substantiated by events which further explode the speech's romantic rhetoric. Far from 'retiring into privacy' to 'look upon the ashes of departed joys no more' as with a sweeping grand exit in the immediate wake of her address, Mrs Finching's curtain line is blocked by brute facts of quite a different order — a manic old lady who will not leave a pot-house. In the same way, Flora's appearing at the wedding later in the chapter with not 'the least signs of seclusion about her, notwithstanding her recent declaration' further completes the intimation which she personally may have missed (at a purely intellectual level) but which the reader delightedly has not.

Not only Flora, but Maggy also (Amy's frequent companion) is a 'wise fool'. Maggy is imperfect too; we see her participating in the endemic moral disorder of the larger world when she reveals in herself a cossetted, fondled role of a comparably self-gratifying and self-diminishing kind:

> As long as eating was a novelty and an amusement, Maggy kept up pretty well. But, that period going by, she became querulous about the cold, and shivered and whimpered. 'It will soon be over, dear,' said Little Dorrit, patiently. 'Oh, it's all very fine for you little mother,' returned Maggy, [as if it possibly *could* be for the young woman beside her, to whose sharper wits this cold damp freezing night out in the London which afflicts her as 'so large, so barren and so wild' (I, xiv, 169—70) has been still more wearisome and harassing] 'but *I'm a poor thing*, only ten years old.' At last, in the dead of the night, when the street was very still indeed, Little Dorrit laid the heavy head upon her bosom, and soothed her to sleep.   (I, xiv, 174, emphasis added)

Nevertheless, like Flora, the mentally-arrested girl has no larger pretension to put upon her experience, no skill or interest in 'setting up superiorities' of a social kind (as is indeed explicit, above, in her account of what does set her apart from her fellow-beings). Amy and Arthur accordingly are adverted early about what needless self-defeats are in process between them, when in this very chapter of their first extended conversation together we come upon the following exchange:

> 'As you just now gave yourself the name they give you at my mother's, and as that is the name by which I always think of you, let me call you Little Dorrit.'
> 'Thank you sir, I should like it better than any name.'
> 'Little Dorrit' [Clennam reaffirms].
> 'Little mother,' Maggy (who had been falling asleep) put in, as a correction.
> 'It's all the same, Maggy,' returned Little Dorrit, 'all the same.'
> 'Is it all the same, mother?'   (I, xiv, 167—8)

And another call upon Clennam to consider Amy, and Amy to

consider herself, no longer in the light of 'a favourite pony or a puppy
or a bird or something from a seed-shop to be put in a garden or a
flower-pot and come up speckled' is proffered by this unconsciously
wise fool in her most astonishing unwitting remonstrance of all.
Maggy has a fixation about the hospital in which, for the first time in
her life, she was cared for during that period of her childhood when
she was so brutally ill treated that her intellects were permanently
retarded (see I, ix, 100–1). When Amy returns from her Continental
sojourn to find Clennam imprisoned and ill in the Marshalsea and he
churlishly refuses her offer of financial help, Maggy's fixation turns to
unknowingly oracular purpose with her sudden, apparently inconsequent outburst.

> Maggy who had fallen into very low spirits, here cried, 'Oh get
> him into a hospital; do get him into a hospital, Mother! He'll never
> look like hisself again, if he an't got into a hospital. And then the
> little woman as was always a spinning at her wheel, she can go to
> the cupboard with the Princess and say, *what do you keep the*
> *Chicking there for?* [Yes, indeed!] and then they can take it out and
> *give it to him, and then all be happy.*'   (II, xxix ['A Plea in the
> Marshalsea'], 761, emphasis added)

Is this not the real 'plea' of the chapter's title? The relation between
eating and emotional need or hunger is here aptly exploited. Amy
should recognise that Arthur is more than merely physically a sick
man and that his only real cure can be found in his being nourished by
the consciousness of being openly and avowedly loved. For, as the
book has shown us, nothing other than emotional starvation has
originated and developed the whole process of Clennam's debility
and his failures of will. To all this Maggy bears witness with her
highly felicitous conflation of her own obsession over the 'Chicking'
she received when in hospital (hardly more trivial in having its own
like symbolic value) and the love ('the Shadow') which Amy has so
far kept hidden in the 'cupboard' of her inner life — as she expressed it
to Maggy in the story about 'the Princess and the poor woman' she
made up about herself. Maggy effectually is adjuring her no longer to
hide the moral nutriment away, unused.

What all these intimations collectively suggest, when we take one
instance and then another and then another again all through the
book, is how truth — the authentic debts and obligations, connections
and relations, ethically considered — shows itself for a personal and

yet also an impersonal force in the individual life. Nobody but
Maggy could utter the statement given above, yet the truth there
active manifests itself as an indwelling fount throughout the human
environment which rushes into expression wherever the least orifice
(such as the weak mind of a 'simple' woman) gives it opportunity (as
it did when Mr Dorrit's controlling ego lost the reins at the Roman
dinner-party).

It may be objected that this is but cold comfort. The real
significance of Flora's and Maggy's remarks tends to be lost, to go
ignored, during the tale; indeed for that matter so do the implications
of Mr Dorrit's final public grandiloquence. 'Society', during his
address in the Marshalsea idiom at Mrs Merdle's dinner-table, just
removes itself in a huff; it does not promptly repent or collapse. But
Dickens shows that he is treating of a force the action of which is
stronger than a flower. For this same truth has revelations less
fugitive, and less able to be bypassed.

Certain kinds of imposture will meet with explosive and indignant
rebuttal of a kind which cannot be evaded. Mr Pancks can writhe
only just so long under his sense of grievance, personal grievance as a
special victim of the 'screwer by deputy, the wringer, and squeezer,
and shaver by substitute' (II, xxxii, 800). His outrage at the
'Patriarch's' whole moral imposture with its cruel social consequences
has to erupt sooner or later in the 'discharge' in Bleeding Heart
Yard – an outburst in which Casby's pretensions are finally ruined
(tomorrow they will be the talk of working-class London) without
the man himself being destroyed ('Society' was not so instinctively
discriminating towards Mr Merdle).

To the critical account by Dr Leavis of this scene,[25] as to his
exegesis of II, i and *its* value, I feel indebted as to a commentary which
identifies once for all the primary significance of both these episodes.
Here is the environment through which the 'Society' travelling-party
(*y compris* the newly-enfranchised Dorrits) are making their way,
when Book II opens:

The air there was charged with the scent of gathered grapes.
Baskets, troughs, and tubs of grapes, stood in the dim village door-
ways, stopped the steep and narrow village streets, and had been
carrying all day along the roads and lanes. Grapes, split and crushed
under foot, lay about everywhere. The child carried in a sling by
the laden peasant woman toiling home, was quieted with picked-
up grapes; the idiot sunning his big goître under the eaves of the

wooden châlet by the way to the waterfall, sat munching grapes; the breath of the cows and goats was redolent of leaves and stalks of grapes; the company in every little cabaret were eating, drinking, talking grapes. A pity that no ripe touch of this generous abundance could be given to the thin, hard, stony wine, which after all was made from the grapes! . . .

Seen from those solitudes, and from the Pass of the Great Saint Bernard, which was one of them, the ascending Night came up the mountain like a rising water. When it at last rose to the walls of the convent of the Great Saint Bernard, it was as if that weather-beaten structure were another Ark, and floated on the shadowy waves.

. . . As the heat of the glowing day, when they had stopped to drink at the streams of melted ice and snow, was changed to the searching cold of the frosty rarefied night air at a great height, so the fresh beauty of the lower journey had yielded to barrenness and desolation. A craggy track, up which the mules in single file, scrambled and turned from block to block, as though they were ascending the broken staircase of a gigantic ruin, was their way now. No trees were to be seen, nor any vegetable growth, save a poor brown scrubby moss, freezing in the chinks of rock. Blackened skeleton arms of wood by the wayside pointed upward to the convent, as if the ghosts of former travellers overwhelmed by the snow haunted the scene of their distress. Icicle-hung caves and cellars built for refuges from sudden storms, were like so many whispers of the perils of the place; never-resting wreaths and mazes of the mist wandered about, hunted by a moaning wind; and snow, the besetting danger of the mountain, against which all its defences were taken, drifted sharply down.

. . . There was no speaking among the string of riders. The sharp cold, the fatigue of the journey, and a new sensation of a catching in the breath, partly as if they had just emerged from very clear crisp water, and partly as if they had been sobbing, kept them silent. . . .

While all this noise and hurry were rife among the living travellers, there, too, silently assembled in a grated house, half-a-dozen paces removed, with the same cloud enfolding them, and the same snow flakes drifting in upon them, were the dead travellers found upon the mountain. The mother, storm-belated many winters ago, still standing in the corner with her baby at her breast; the man who had frozen with his arm raised to his mouth in fear or hunger, still pressing it with his dry lips after years and years. An

awful company, mysteriously come together! A wild destiny for
that mother to have foreseen, 'Surrounded by so many and such
companions upon whom I never looked, and never shall look, I
and my child will dwell together inseparable, on the Great Saint
Bernard, out-lasting generations who will come to see us, and
will never know our name, or one word of our story but the
end.'

The living travellers thought little or nothing of the dead just
then. They thought much more of alighting at the convent door,
and warming themselves at the convent fire.   (II, i, 431–3)

And thus Dr Leavis upon these intimations:

What has awed and subdued them has been almost as present to
us as if we ourselves had been with the caravan. The daunting
Alpine transcendence, the changing light, the known factual
remoteness that is contradicted by appearance, the ethereal that is
known by the evidence of the near at hand to be in fact inimically
rugged, forbidding and massive, the de-realizing effect of the
strange and shifting reality. . . .

We are very soon given them within the convent, reinstalled in
their confident egos, and being absolute Society. But it is impossible
(for the reader, I mean) to have forgotten the potent evocation of
time, eternity, the non-human universe, the de-realizing lights and
vapours, and death. The effect is to bring out with poetic force the
nothingness of the Dorrit–Gowan–Barnacle human world . . . .

Dickens's evocation of death, time and eternity and the non-
human universe certainly plays a part in his critical irony, but he has
no more bent than Blake towards conceiving life or mankind
reductively. His exposure of unrealities is a vindication of human
creativity, and an insistence that such a vindication, real and
achieved, can (as Daniel Doyce is there to testify) have no hubris in
it . . . .

. . . The evocation of the Alps is associated, significantly, with
the vision of the mortuary and its long-frozen dead; and the
effect – not merely in relation to the touring party within the
convent – is one, profoundly characteristic of the great Dickens, of
solemn anti-hubristic realism. It is a realism, one must add, strongly
anti-Gowan, enforcing, as it does, the dependence of the human
world on the collaborative creativity that generates it, and sustains
it continually as a living and authoritative reality.[26]

What could be more pertinently said? — Though for the full value of his commentary I believe we must recall how this chapter is paralleled by a comparably palpable treatment of the 'non-human universe' at the beginning of the book. Indeed it is impossible, reading *Little Dorrit* straight through, not to be aware of both the main phases of the novel's action being thus parenthesised and contained by these powerful encounters with the non-human world. The picture of Marseilles 'broiling in the sun' at the beginning of the work operates like the evocation of the Alpine valleys at the start of Book II, to suggest the form and forces upon which human life depends, which are nevertheless supremely indifferent to it. The scorching glare of the sun over the French city and its harbour, is not anti-human, it is simply a-human. All sorts and conditions of men — 'Hindoos, Russians, Chinese, Spaniards, Portuguese, Englishmen, Frenchmen, Genoese, Neapolitans, Venetians, Greeks, Turks, descendants from all the builders of Babel, come to trade at Marseilles' (I, i, I) — have to '[seek] the shade alike — taking refuge in any hiding-place from a sea too intensely blue to be looked at, and a sky of purple, set with one great flaming jewel of fire' (ibid.), which leaves 'the very dust . . . scorched brown, and something [quivering] in the atmosphere as if the air itself were panting' (ibid., 2). (Dickens's thus representing such a landscape in its beauty and intrinsic *interest* cancels out any idea of the natural environment as purposefully indifferent or meaningfully malevolent; as an ambit in which men can strike up — like the heroes of Norse mythology, say — a nobly stoical, or even more heroically resistant, pose.)

In the warm autumnal Alpine valleys Nature's foison is presented as in Hesperidean fable. But all suggestions of the Edenic are fully contained by the reference to 'the idiot sunning his big goître under the eaves of the wooden châlet by the way to the waterfall' and the taste of 'the thin, hard, stony wine, which after all was made from the grapes!' Higher up, the wintering mountains suggest yet another mode in which Nature presents herself, where, as in the other, men can easily count for nothing (like 'the storm-belated travellers' of the conventual mortuary) if they do not keep their wits about them and recognise their whole situation in Nature to be one requiring deliberate humility and never-failing respect. So Clennam's observation of how

A composed and unobtrusive self-sustainment was noticeable in Daniel Doyce — a calm knowledge that what was true must remain

> true, in spite of all the Barnacles in the family ocean, and would be
> just the truth, and neither more nor less, when even that sea had run
> dry — which had a kind of greatness in it, though not of the official
> quality   (I, xvi, 191)

is fully substantiated in the living experience put before us by the
novelist in his tale, both as a tribute to the inventor and to the
philosophy by which Doyce lives. This is seen — in the Alpine
episode, in the whole general demonstration of man's inability for
life, for happiness, other than in recognition of 'the truth' — to count
for more than the sort of hopeful platitude by which good men might
otherwise presumably have to live. Hopeful platitude we have with
the (pretty hopeless because unsustaining, unfeeding) idea of 'duty',
the bloodless abstraction to which Mr Meagles is still dangerously
directing Tattycoram near the end of the story (II, xxxiii, 812–13).

This story, then, *is* an inquest into Victorian civilisation[27] — and it
looks beyond the English Channel too. For anyone who wishes to
derive from it insights into the essential conditions and relations of
contemporary life as Dickens intuited them, he is given ample
material here of a challenging nature for use and comparison with the
fruits of other kinds of historical study. It can be argued, of course,
that we are evidently not shown a multiplicity of representative
Victorian scenes (we see little of rural England and nothing of the
industrial north, for instance), but the life exhibited in and around the
Marshalsea, the ambience of the idle expatriates in Venice (with its
Austrian military occupation and everywhere throughout peasant
Italy 'misery wrestling with magnificence and throwing it with the
strength of fate — II, iii, 464), the conditions of Bleeding Heart Yard
and all else that we *are* shown, are self-evidently the appropriate and
cardinal means, symbols, representative signs, on Dickens's view, by
which his world was to be typified at this epoch.

Yet the novel is also a study of the human heart (in all seasons); it is
an anatomy of the world in that sense too. And it is the condition of
this book's ultimate greatness that it can hold together *as* one unitary
act of perception an analysis of our human dealings which is at once
fully alert to all that is destructive in them and which at the same time
is equally expressive of its sense of an equal truth; the life-giving
recognitions which it sees always liable to well up in the individual
case and to renew, if not a whole society then at least, potentially, the
individual career.

Little Dorrit is pessimistic in a way which makes most pessimism look like posturing sentimentality. It is also one of the most exhilarating novels ever written. For what on one hand is its incontrovertibly dark view of human nature and its strict adherence to the grimly actual does not inhibit but rather is seen to substantiate the acknowledgements it affords, with no less honesty of what, in the changing process of time itself and in people as human individuals, makes towards renewal, release and health.

III

The personages who are these processes' happiest beneficiaries, in whom the tendencies towards health most flower and fruit, are the couple whom we cannot but identify as the heroine and hero of the novel, Little Dorrit (its namesake) and Arthur Clennam. They distinctively do not contribute (and deliberately, of course) the erotic interest in a New Comedy of social regeneration; their wedding at the end is no triumphant upshot with that kind of significance. Indeed (as we must feel from the way their story does not even explicitly dominate every other chapter of the tale) their meaning is only part of the whole as the great love-stories of the fiction are not. Where their history is important lies in its exemplifying that recreation which Dickens sees possible in the individual case (or cases) with which the reader is most likely to identify for himself. If we have truly been awake to what the novel shows us of the canker in the very hearts of men (as men), its honestly developed account of the invincible corruption and hypocrisy of the social world, its large and powerful presentation of the general darkness, the obtuse greeds and clam-like tyrannies of the environment by which the individually sensitive spirit is inevitably surrounded, then – unless we count ourselves for merrily insensitive or joyfully comatose – we do want to ask what personal meaning can be found, what individually valid contribution we can make, in the 'prison of this lower world' from which none of us escapes. From the first we trace the lineaments of Arthur Clennam's sickness overtly and consciously. But that does not diminish his stature as the embodiment of certain decencies which distinguish him *as* a sensitive, responsible, reflective spirit (that rare being in the William Dorrit – Gowan – Barnacle – Merdle – represented universe, which is also the ambit of Bleeding Heart Yard and the Marshalsea prison). For all his retreat from life, he does deserve a better fate than the emotional starvation and intellectual paralysis to which he appears condemned (partly self-condemned as we have seen) in consequence of his upbringing.

He has certainly had his failures: with Pet Meagles; with Amy herself even till near the very end; in his speculating with Doyce's funds against his partner's advice; in extravagantly embracing the opportunity to immolate himself in the Marshalsea (of all the debtors' jails he could go to – II, xxvi, 715– 17; it is all the same impulse to self-martyrdom as that which distinguished Amy's casting herself earlier in the role of the Poor Woman with a 'Shadow'). But he has also attempted to be honest with other people (as in the soul-searching with which he analysed his motives in disliking Henry Gowan– I, xxvi, 318). He has been courteous and considerate on all occasions (as toward the Plornishes, the Dorrits in their poverty) to all others in weaker social case than himself; and charitable (as when he helps Baptista Cavalletto, then a complete stranger, after his street accident – I, xiii, 161– 5). Even in some of these features – most notably, for example, in his concern to redress some unknown imagined wrong his parents may possibly have perpetrated in the past (I, v) – we may discern mixed motives. Is he not seeking an externalised dissociated redress for an internal and personal wound? But, while Dickens shows how most motives are mixed, nevertheless we are equally given to see and feel that Arthur Clennam embodies an uprightness which is not the uprightness of Lord Decimus or the dowager Mrs Gowan or the (horrific) Chief Butler. If we have any spark of these virtues or tend to reach after them in ourselves, then we do, as Dr Leavis has said,

> tend to *be* Clennam [just as we tend 'implicitly to identify ourselves with Pip and *be* his sentience (in *Great Expectations*) – while remaining, nevertheless, as the reader, another person'] as we obviously don't William Dorrit, Mr Meagles, Daniel Doyce, Henry Gowan, Pancks – or any other character in the book. He is for us . . . *the* decently ordinary person among the *dramatis personae* ('ordinary' here not being used in a placing or pejorative way, but reassuringly), and he has at the same time a special status, unavowed but essential to his importance. . . . Without having suffered his childhood, we accept with ready sympathy the sense of the world represented by this earnest, intelligent and pre-eminently civilized man; we respect him as we respect ourselves.[28]

The situation in which this our representative finds himself at the beginning of the whole novel – nothing less, namely, than England, London, on a typical Sabbath – provokes the total enquiry it is Clennam's artistic function to make and in a sense embody,

> the beginning of an urgently personal criticism of life in Arnold's sense – that entailed in the inescapable and unrelenting questions: 'What shall I do? What *can* I do? What are the possibilities of life – for me, and, more generally, in the very nature of life? What are the conditions of happiness? What is life for?'[29]

The full answer to these questions, which we may equally envisage any friend to Amy Dorrit wishing to propound on her behalf, is provided by, *is* the novel as a whole. But, as to 'the conditions of happiness', it is in this area of the work's exploration that Amy's value for Clennam goes beyond the simpler significances of a traditional 'love-interest'.

We have seen that Clennam has been starved so long of affection that his characteristic spiritual debility has become ingrained. It is idle now to require of him that he should mend under his own steam. Dickens talks of William Dorrit's 'wasted heart' and 'years of famine' to which Amy has turned 'a fountain of love and fidelity that never ran dry or waned' (I, xix, 229), but such refreshment has been turned off in Arthur's case simply too much and too long, and he can no more acquire more will, courage and hope, can no more *not* be a melancholy man in retreat from life, than by taking thought he can add a cubit to his stature.

As the novel progresses, we see his condition deteriorate. After the failure of his final attempt at achieving a special meaning and value for one individual (his battle with the Circumlocution Office and his speculation on Doyce's behalf) he really washes his hands of existence altogether. The debtors' prison, with its bitter-sweet associations of Little Dorrit and her father in the room he is given, is a place where he goes to die. If in the event he is rescued, and by the open declaration of Little Dorrit's 'undying love', Dickens is not thereby signifying a *dea ex machina* which is, all improbably, immanent in every darkest hour. But he is betokening the more than uniquely personal and single blessing which will tend to flow from one individual's realising (in both senses) the truth of his (or her) own human relations. Such a person here is Amy Dorrit, whose progress is in some respects analogous to Cordelia's in Shakespeare's play. We do not see so very much of Amy after her father's departure from the scene. Her development, once she is embarked upon her Continental travels, is more implied than the object of an explicit authorial treatment. Yet when she arrives again towards the end at the place where Clennam is (on his view) 'a broken, bankrupt, sick, dishonoured prisoner' (II, xxix, 757), she is perceptibly, indeed cardinally, different. She comes with the kind of achieved, conscious yet now integrated and spontaneous sanity — and the freely self-expressive warmth of that — which we felt she lacked in the beginning.

Amy's first great advantage is the removal of her family from the prison (I, xxxvi); the other is her father's departure from life itself. Both events give her, necessarily, large disturbance and hurt. But it is only in the troubling of her whole frame of reference (as is figured in the Marshalsea gate and bars themselves)[30] by which she has measured and pegged out her disastrous compensating role, that she is encouraged to abandon it. And in her father's death the last knot is loosed, the great incubus of her life is as it were finally 'drawn'. It will be argued that both events — his opportune demise (though it has come, after all, only at the end of twenty-two years!), still more the descent of a fortune upon the Dorrit and their consequent enlargement into the alien vistas of the Continental scene — are straight out of the heart of convenient fairy-tale; the more so in that the author is evidently unconcerned to afford more than a casual token explanation of the great accession (I, xxxv). But the significance of the 'Riches' (which first metaphorically and then literally the Dorrits convert back to 'Poverty' in Book II) lies in their writing large the changes incident to existence in a time-organised creation. While we experience reality successively, temporally, alteration will befall the apparently most arrested life. It invades Mrs Clennam's deliberate retirement. It affronts William Dorrit with his breakdown and death. The visit to Arthur's 'mother' by a blackmailer from a far-distant shore, who has gained her guilty secret, only intimates a truth which these other events substantiate as both their own reality and as metaphor. Collapse will overtake long-sustained pretensions. The transformations will be major indeed, they will bring changes on a scale appropriate to the size of fates in legend or folktale, when they come to lives fixed in patterns so sterile which those who lived by such patterns hoped immutably to impose upon their experience. All this if (and this is Dickens's great theme) they can come where there is still health to resuscitate, a spark to blow upon, where there has still been a recalcitrant urge towards the creative existence, as well as sickness, in the soul. A Lord Decimus, wholly untroubled in his complete inanition of spirit, will be assailed by no redemptive visitations.

The first sign of an incipient movement towards the reversal of Amy's self-defeating role comes in the conversation between her and Minnie Gowan in the St Bernard Convent:

> 'Perhaps you don't,' said the visitor, hesitating — 'perhaps you don't know my story? Perhaps he never told you my story?'
>
> 'No.'
>
> 'O, no, why should he! I have scarcely the right to tell it myself at present, because I have been entreated not to do so. There is not much in it, but it might account to you for my asking you not to say anything about the letter here. You saw my family with me, perhaps? Some of them — I only say this to you — are a little proud, a little prejudiced.'   (II, i, 444)

Because this statement is a quiet one in a quiet scene we are liable to overlook its revolutionary character. This is the first time that Amy squarely confesses to her family's great fault. It is her first open acknowledgement — as such, dramatic, portentous — of their inadequacy, in terms which are evidently the result of an inward reasoning which has at last begun to distance her from their pretensions and her need to accept life (with misgivings wholly suppressed) on their terms.

Some hint as to how the change can have come about is afforded by the very scene I have just remarked, that through which the travelling party has lately passed. Once they are within the convent, we may indeed be 'very soon given them . . . re-installed in their confident egos, and being absolute Society';[31] but such retreats from the intimations afforded by 'the daunting Alpine transcendence, the changing light, the known factual remoteness that is contradicted by appearance, the ethereal that is known by the evidence of the near at hand to be in fact imically rugged, forbidding and massive', in short and in essence 'the derealizing effect of the strange and shifting reality',[32] are, by virtue of the integrity Amy does possess, a resource inaccessible to her. All that is habitually good, all that is rightly sensitive and authentic in her nature makes quite alien the possibility of her finding refuge in the others' kind of fraudulent roles. So we have to assume that for her the experience — of the Alps, of her new surroundings in general — remains unavoidably challenging. She cannot retreat from it into 'being absolute Society'. And with its tendency to dissolve the realities near at hand in favour of the

apparently remote, the whole episode images in scenic terms the slow
transformation of her entire frame of reference, in a moral and
emotional aspect, by the new physical and social environment of the
Continental tour. With the neatest economy Dickens suggests the
degree to which she feels herself – the degree to which she actually
is – a new person in a new situation, having with difficulty to try and
relate that to her former life, when he introduces this second book of
his novel with a chapter where characters whom we have already met
in the narrative go nameless and are thus partly deprived of their
former identities.

A cumulative process is in question, no sudden conversion, and
Dickens portrays it by implication, not with outright statement. For
upon Amy herself the development creeps up inarticulate and
unawares. But the hints are there for all to note: for example, the
heading of page 463 – 'Little Dorrit's New Part'. The matter below
this affords us, always in the fully serious (though never ponderous)
tone which the author has specially reserved for these intimations,
insight into just this aspect of the girl's enforced development at this
stage of her career:

Sitting opposite her father in the travelling-carriage, and recalling
the old Marshalsea room, her present existence was a dream. All
that she saw was new and wonderful, but it was not real; it seemed
to her as if those visions of mountains and picturesque countries
might melt away at any moment, and the carriage, turning some
abrupt corner, bring up with a jolt at the old Marshalsea gate.

To have no work to do was strange, but not half so strange as
having glided into a corner where she had no one to think for,
nothing to plan and contrive, *no cares of others to load herself with.*
Strange as that was, it was far stranger yet to find a space between
herself and her father, where others occupied themselves in taking
care of him, and where she was never expected to be. . . . But he
had spoken to her alone . . . he laid his parental injunctions upon
her, to remember that she was a lady, who had now to conduct
herself with – hum – a proper pride, and to preserve the rank of a
lady. . . . Thus it had been brought about that she now sat in her
corner of the luxurious carriage with her little patient hands folded
before her, *quite displaced even from the last point of the old standing
ground in life on which her feet had lingered.*

It was from this position that all she saw appeared unreal; the
more surprising the scenes, the more they resembled *the unreality of*

her own inner life as *she went through its vacant places* all day
long . . . only the old mean Marshalsea a reality. Nay, *even the old
mean Marshalsea was shaken to its foundations*, when *she pictured it
without her father* . . . .

Among the day's unrealities would be, roads where the bright
red vines were looped and garlanded together on trees for many
miles . . . .

Through such scenes, the family procession moved on to
Venice. And here it dispersed for a time, as they were to live in
Venice some few months in a palace (itself six times as big as the
whole Marshalsea) on the Grand Canal.

In this crowning unreality, where all the streets were paved with
water, and where the deathlike stillness of the days and nights was
broken by no sound but the softened ringing of church-bells, the
rippling of the current, and the cry of the gondoliers turning the
corners of the flowing streets, Little Dorrit, *quite lost by her task
being done*, sat down to muse.   (II, iii, 463–6, emphasis added)

(Dickens does not send the Dorrits to Italy with no other purpose.
That being the most probable goal of their 'Society' pretensions to the
Grand Tour, Venice – and Florence (see 609–10) – and Rome
evoke Renaissance and Imperial Italy. Western civilisation as a whole
is typified and implicated into what the novel has been saying about
human imprisonment; the more so in that northern Italy is still at that
date (as Dickens reminds his readers here) the victim of Austrian
military occupation and extremes of poverty and wealth (II, iii, 454–
6 and 464, respectively), a country divided and unfree.)

Riches cannot produce real liberty for William Dorrit. Only a
change in his sytem of values could there avail. What they facilitate
can enforce upon Amy, however, and this time in a manner
inescapable (as Maggy's unconscious promptings in Book I, or
Flora's, were not) a dissolution of her masochistic role. At a deep level
she was able to be spell-stopped, she was able to fix herself in her
considerably negative as well as responsible part in the bad old
London days, given the framework of a permanent demand on her
family's side for her services as general provider, contriver, maid of all
work – and, not least, great emotional bank upon which to draw self-
endorsing credits. In the bad new Italian days this role is promptly
made redundant. The new mode in which the family's old disguises
are featured and their capacity to enter 'into Society for ever and a
day' make this only too plain. The old debilitating part she played is

pulled from under her with all the easy essential negligence — as to her inner life, *her* real feelings — which marks all their dealings with her; but she cannot, now, retreat into being useful for them. They leave her nothing to do; and with her father's death her final opportunity to be important to him in a self-denying way (something he and she both avidly grasp on the occasion of his last return to Marshalsea-style dependence) — II, XIX, 648-50 — disappears.

In the next nine chapters Little Dorrit also leaves the reader's view. But we do not require in this period a full evaluative study of her developing consciousness, for we can only expect her to return significantly changed, we cannot but associate the drama through which she has passed — its collapse of the means and supports upon which she has so long been able to erect the performance of her 'psychic masochism' — with the new development Arthur Clennam notices in her when she returns to the Marshalsea (II, xxix) to assist him out of *his* captivity. As the editor of the Penguin edition has remarked, the nosegay by his bed to which he awakes (755—6, pointed further by the running title 'Some Fresh Flowers')

> completes a symbolic presentation of the three women in Arthur Clennam's life (compare Pet's flowers [i.e. the rose-blooms he strews upon the river, in giving her up to Henry Gowan — I,xxviii, 337— 8], and for Flora, the running title on p. 749 ['Flora's Old Flowers' — not available, owing to the different pagination, in the Oxford Illustrated edition]).[33]

We are told that 'she looked something more womanly than when she had gone away', that 'the ripening touch of the Italian sun was visible upon her face' (II, xxix, 757). If 'otherwise she was quite unchanged' (next sentence) that most largely reflects her having retained all that was healthiest from the days of her toiling want; all the sincerity, honesty and good-heartedness which distinguished her, as distinct from the self-attenuating attitudes which compounded her lover's like failures. Both are still imperfect: it is all part of Dickens's truth to the realities he here portrays that Amy comes back in the old worn black dress of her earlier time in the prison, that she still wants to be called 'Little Dorrit' (ibid.) and that Clennam is even more deeply possessed than ever by *his* role of defeat.

Dear Little Dorrit.
Looking back upon his own poor story, she was its vanishing-

point. Everything in its perspective led to her innocent figure. He had travelled thousands of miles towards it; previous unquiet hopes and doubts had worked themselves out before it; it was the centre of the interest of his life; it was the termination of everything that was good and pleasant in it; beyond there was nothing but mere waste and darkened sky.   (II, xxvii, 733)

Again, this *oratio obliqua* enacts for us a self-dramatised martyrdom, there is exaggeration and dishonesty in it. Nevertheless, what is not in question is that Little Dorrit does represent a wholly positive force and nutritive value for Clennam's life, and it should worry us that he can have come to realise this, can have valued her at her worth, yet, even at this late date, *having* done so, cannot acknowledge the rightness of seeking simply to marry her, albeit in his present wretched position. The self-disbelief, the false notions of honour and the Calvinist—commercial morality by which he has been stained (we were explicitly shown this working towards misjudgement earlier, in I, xxxv)[34] assert themselves in the importance he assigns to their relative conditions of wealth and station; as if it did not matter much more that he has heard (from John Chivery) how Amy loves him (II, xxvii, 729), that his own heart and recollection attest the truth and value of Chivery's assertion (730–3) and that her life would be wretched without him on any terms. So that we come to another painful, nearly tragic scene in which the man turns away from a fulfilment which is both utterly right and readily accessible. Amy's offering him her fortune (II, xxix, 759) is really a covert proposal of marriage; not deliberately devised as such but in its own nature so indicative of his importance to her as to require interpretation of that kind. Were it taking place earlier in the tale, the young woman's own capacity for being too quickly deterred by life's rebuttals would have sealed this as their last – and finally lost – opportunity of coming together. Both earlier have turned from the larger, more open possibilities of their experience in pre-emptive attempts to avoid – given their bruised condition – still more denials and hurts. Yet Amy comes back, for the reasons we have observed, renewed in just those parts of her character where such failures have originated. Faced with Arthur's rejection, and no less dogged now in not misinterpreting it, stronger in self-confidence, in deliberate and unbowed maintaining of her standards, she keeps held out to him the healing branch of a frank declaration, she reaffirms boldly the realities she perceives (ibid., 762, sending John Chivery to tell him of 'her undying love'). Maggy, who has just voiced an appeal for this kind of explicit remedial insistence and nourishment (see the discussion of this above at p. 175) is effectually gratified in her wish.

We see the same cardinal difference in her making a stand against Mrs Clennam's self-righteousness. Amy does not rebuke the older woman but she does oppose herself quite deliberately to that lady's 'life and doctrine':

> She tried not to show it [i.e. her revulsion at Mrs Clennam's vindictive apologia], but she recoiled with dread from the state of mind that had burnt so fiercely and lasted so long. It presented itself to her with no sophistry upon it, in its own plain nature.   (II, xxxi, 792)

This fully conscious vision and responsible attitude towards the delinquencies of Arthur's 'mother' is exactly what we missed in her dealings with her own family earlier. She recognises now that that Mecca of her self-abasements, the Marshalsea, has been (as well as her home) a 'poor prison' and that her teaching there *has* been 'very defective' (ibid.); and she explicitly urges an alternative morality, an insistence which rounds up the novel's abiding thematic interest in Christianity as the expression of an ethic endorsed by all the institutions of this culture and deeply at odds with the general tendency of its diseased, self-imprisoning life:

> 'O, Mrs. Clennam, Mrs. Clennam . . . angry feelings and unforgiving deeds are no comfort and no guide to you and me. . . . Be guided only by the healer of the sick, the raiser of the dead, the friend of all who were afflicted and forlorn, the patient Master who shed tears of compassion for our infirmities. We cannot but be right if we put all the rest away, and do everything in remembrance of Him. There is no vengeance and no infliction of suffering in His life, I am sure. There can be no confusion in following Him, and seeking for no other footsteps, I am certain!'   (Ibid.)

In saying this Little Dorrit directly opposes now not only the morality of a sick woman, but a whole society in its gloomy Sabbatarian character, its Calvinist—commercial values, which she never challenged before, though so much of her conduct and instincts had been at odds with its way of life.

Clennam is rescued, therefore, and at the hands of a woman who in

her turn has been saved by the play of those continuously encroaching
forces for regeneration which constantly surround the self – every
self – but which can extricate the individual from his own personal
maze in 'the multiplicity of paths in the labyrinth trodden by the sons
of Adam' only where he (or she) at a personal centre of the will
endorses some kind of active, heroic moral value (however qualified,
however tainted) which can assert itself once made free to the air of
new circumstance, of new and inescapable challenge. The value,
therefore, of making the commitments that Clennam and Amy have
shown themselves from the first to have espoused (for all their faults)
is what their partnership ultimately intimates – as metaphor and
reality. It means not some renewal of their society as a whole, but the
possibility in the individual life of escaping from the maze of delusion
imposed or inculcated by the social matrix, by a fallen culture, by
family life depraved in not only the theological but also possibly the
most literal sense. The delinquency of the earlier home environments,
in both Amy's and Arthur's respective cases, signifies the general
human inheritance. Just as the consistencies of Mrs Clennam's or
William Dorrit's respective positions – or 'Patriarch' Casby's –
cannot be maintained indefinitely without being attended by some
kind of breakdown, whether from within or without, some kind of
dismission of the false pretences; so in the sensitive and would-be
morally responsible life the fetters which inhibit a fully adequate
personal development will equally have working against them forces
which at any time may make of the individual another Daniel Doyce.
He will be earnest, utterly realistic, cherishing no illusory views, and
yet – in the face of so many defeats, so much social and political
darkness, all the environing individual stupidity and negation –
possessed of a 'self-sustainment' which is more (much more joyous
not least) than stoical. Doyce is not a man of whom we may suspect
that his composure derives from continuous contemplation of the
Buddhist verities (though that would doubtless count for much).
What he has and what Amy and Clennam are left with at the end is an
outlook which constantly reaches down to, as it arises out of, a full
recognition and unfettered play of the origins of health – in the self,
in Nature and its resources for the attentive human life (cf. the two
long opening paragraphs of the last chapter of all). These the rest of
the world but kicks against the pricks of their own self-defeats (in the
most important sense) in neglecting or attempting to suppress.
Moreover, those who leave the prison – as bride and groom do here,
at the end – do so with the consciousness of having risen out of the

same mistakes, above the same kinds of delusion and self-bafflement which still characterise the delinquent part of society at large. So that *mere* exasperation at it becomes all the more, temperamentally as ethically, impossible. (' "O, Mrs. Clennam, Mrs. Clennam . . . angry feelings and unforgiving deeds are no comfort and no guide to you and me. . . . " ') That they can go down

> into a modest life of usefulness and happiness, to give a mother's care, in the fulness of time, to Fanny's neglected children no less than to their own, and to leave that lady going into Society for ever and a day. . . .   (II, xxxiv, 826)

without repining and raging, for this reason, is a co-function of their being able to be truly 'inseparable and blessed' (ibid.). Only *this* kind of maturity allows and affords genuine happiness.

IV

The foregoing argument has attempted to show that *Little Dorrit* offers two principal insights. On the one hand Dickens brings before us the maimed and destructive features of his contemporary world, the debased quality of most human relations (then and now, for what comes before us is human nature as such) and the facility with which even the decent individual becomes imprisoned within illusory views of his situation. On the other we are made to observe the independent and vital life of the inexpugnable truth – which is to say what on a more disinterested view are the genuine relations between man and man, the authentic obligations and dependence, recognition of which human pride (or neurosis – it does not really matter how you distinguish it) is always seeking to suppress. Such acknowledgement is seen to be forgone with considerable temporary, but never with total and permanent, success. We remark the conditions of the truth's reassertion (for weal or woe) in the individual life (Amy marries, William Dorrit is deranged and dies); the terms upon which it can devolve a meaning there and a happiness, which is completely inaccessible to the existence of a Barnacle or a Mrs Gowan. These terms are the elements of what we call 'decency', the anterior commitment – however partial, however tainted – within the individual to at least some of the obligations which human folly and sickness are but too ready to disavow. For, as we have seen, there is heroism simply in being decent in such a world, given the education which in its depravity it 'naturally' affords each addition to the human family. There must be some important kind of regenerative principle in the spirit of the man or woman who, having been formed by this heredity and this environment, is not simply a blind egotist. And what the novel on its positive side shows is that for such people a way out of the labyrinth of their own imprisonments and mistaken attitudes is liable to open, owing to the nature of the quasi-impersonal life of this same faculty for recognising 'the truth'. For that is also a feature of the universal psychic inheritance.

But if all this is so central a part of Dickens's case, we may well look to find it embodied not only in his story and characterisation but also in the language of the novel; the very nature of syntax and metaphor in its prose. And our expectation is not defeated.

The Clennam house pregnantly typifies the cramped, imprisoned society around it, the sickness of a whole culture. But when we return to the representative 'Sunday evening, gloomy, close and stale' (I, iii, 28) in which Arthur Clennam has come home, we are not told with the baldest authorial brevity simply that he knocked at its door. Rather, we have this:

> He went up to the door, which had a projecting canopy in carved work, of festooned jack-towels and children's heads with water on the brain, designed after a once-popular monumental pattern; and knocked.   (Ibid., 31)

When Flintwich appears to answer the summons, he is described thus:

> He was a short, bald old man, in a high-shouldered black coat and waistcoat, drab breeches, and long drab gaiters. He might, from his dress, have been either clerk or servant, and in fact had long been both. There was nothing about him in the way of decoration but a watch, which was lowered into the depths of its proper pocket by an old black ribbon, and had a tarnished copper key, moored above it, to show where it was sunk. His head was awry, and he had a one-sided, crab-like way with him, as if his foundations had yielded at about the same time as those of the house, and he ought to have been propped up in a similar manner.   (Ibid., 32)

Both the door and the factotum are fully realised by these tropes; but the very process by which Dickens has individualised them has also subverted the pretensions they embody. Far from being dourly imposing (and thus reflecting the ethos of the inhabitants within), the door is made the object of a detached view of its artistry, and the attitude to life which can express itself in that style of design is shown for an absurd imposition. Flintwinch is evoked as a very pattern of the repressed existence and the imprisoning human–social impulses, but he comes before us so graphically denoted exactly because he is portrayed by a play of intelligence which is the medium of alternative ideas, from within its own resources, ideas which with continuous spontaneity are counterposing themselves to and subverting such claims as he makes, with his appearance, to be a figure of a normative character – in dress, in moral nature. The faint but inescapable suggestions of marine life and endeavour, for instance (his watch as an anchor '*lowered into the depths* of its proper pocket . . . with a *tarnished* copper key *moored* above it', his '*crab-like* way', and so on) constitute not only fresh and vivid metaphor which graphically actualises him, rendering him with the solidity of practically everything imaged in the Dickens world. The freshness and vividness (with their introduction of the larger air of a seashore community, the other horizons of those who toil upon the deep) withholds collaboration from describing him on anything like Flintwinch's own terms.

Jeremiah and his employer, then, are not observed as they see themselves or as they appear to Arthur Clennam, whose real suffering at their hands is nevertheless not sold short ('"How weak am I . . . that I could shed tears at this reception! I, who have never experienced anything else; who have never expected anything else." He not only could, but did' – ibid.).

Examples of this trait throughout the novel could be multiplied indefinitely. It is the very thew and sinew of the Dickensian utterance. There is the description of Mrs Clennam's chamber immediately following, 'the floor of which had gradually so sunk and settled, that the fireplace was in a dell' (I, iii, 33) – where the drab incarceration of the room and her way of life is evoked by means of an ironic hint of Arcady ('dell'). Or there is Mrs General sitting in her apartment in Venice, where Mr Dorrit's valet

> found her on a little square of carpet, so extremely dimunitive in reference to the size of her stone and marble floor, that she looked as if she might have had it spread for the trying on of a ready-made pair of shoes; or as if she had come into possession of the enchanted

piece of carpet, bought for forty purses by one of the three princes in the Arabian Nights, and had that moment been transported on it, at a wish, into a palatial saloon with which it had no connection.   (II, V, 472)

Mrs General has no meaningful social role. There is no valid reason for her to be here in Venice in association with the Dorrit family. Her life is so much a valueless ritual, her commitments are so totally irrelevant to any rational function or the achievement of any personal significance, that, on an objective view, she takes on almost the aspect of a figure in a Surrealist picture; and the vacant inanity, in this kind, of her situation is here irreplaceably suggested by the reference to the world of enchantment and the Arabian Nights — a world in which the coherence of the natural laws is liable at any moment to be interrupted by the inconsequent operations of jinn or magic carpets. Equally, Mrs General *et hoc genus omne* may well seek to extirpate all that major imaginative element in the human inheritance (I mean, what it is to be human) which is in play where the Arabian Nights (for example) are being evoked. But the incongruity of her values and the essential meaninglessness of her social rituals in fact stimulate and feed its operations on the part of the intelligence which is awake, which is liberated; namely, the intelligence of the narrator who is our guide.

This process is allied to the status itself of his idiom. Dickens tends to write long sentences of a compelling authority. The scene is such and such, the reality *was* thus and thus, not interpretably otherwise. For example:

The Chief Butler, the Avenging Spirit of this great man's life, relaxed nothing of his severity. He looked on at these dinners when the bosom was not there, as he looked on at other dinners when the bosom was there; and his eye was a basilisk to Mr. Merdle. He was a hard man, and would never bate an ounce of plate or a bottle of wine. He would not allow a dinner to be given, unless it was up to his mark. He set forth the table for his own dignity. If the guests chose to partake of what was served, he saw no objection; but it was served for the maintenance of his rank. As he stood by the sideboard he seemed to announce, 'I have accepted office to look at this which is now before me, and to look at nothing less than this.' If he missed the presiding bosom, it was as a part of his own state of which he was, from unavoidable circumstances, temporarily deprived. Just as he might have missed a centre-piece, or a choice wine-cooler, which had been sent to the Banker's.   (II, xii, 557)

The 'seemed to' is a friendly sop. We don't for a moment doubt that Dickens's analysis of this man, or his description of his appearance, are other than wholly reliable. Here is no fiction of doubtful hesitant interpretations, in contrast to that suggested no less by the syntax than the psychology of the later Henry James. It does not, like the prose of Conrad's narrators, advertise itself as the necessarily subjective and partial view of one man in a world where absolute reality remains notional. The truth – what all these people and scenes are – Dickens's idiom continually suggests, can be known as absolutely as it ever needs to be (for all that the Dorrit brothers at their deaths are reckoned to have gone 'before their Father; far beyond the twilight judgements of this world; high above its mists and obscurities' – II, xix, 652. The very certainty with which Dickens, at least in his role of social bard, feels able to speak about the life and judgement after death is what we notice there, in any consideration of his characteristic position as narrator).

Being aware of all this knowable truth equally militates towards the possession, as it is a natural function, of a mind freed from the damagingly partial and cramped outlook with which even the unliberated but 'decent' spirit shows itself (over the course of this story) willing to remain. Dickens, we find ourselves noticing, speaks with his semi-oracular authority exactly as a consequence of his not being thus imprisoned and because he offers the tokens of his freedom all the time in this play of metaphor, this tendency of analogy in his prose. Indeed there is a vital 'rude health' in question here, in that prose's capacity to ramify multiplying subordinate clauses of quasi-recondite descriptions, which suggest a mind always capable of freewheeling out of its original direction. Take this hilarious instance:

> The Principal and instrument [i.e. Clennam and Plornish] soon drove off together to a stable-yard in High Holborn [namely, to visit Captain Maroon, Tip Dorrit's creditor], where a remarkably fine gray gelding, worth, at the lowest figure, seventy-five guineas (not taking into account the value of the shot he had been made to swallow, for the improvement of his form), was to be parted with for a twenty-pound note, in consequence of his having run away last week with Mrs. Captain Barbary of Cheltenham, who wasn't up to a horse of his courage, and who, in mere spite, insisted on

selling him for that ridiculous sum: or, in other words, on giving
him away   (I, xii, 141)

or the following; here again is Clennam at his first reunion with the
household of the 'Patriarch':

> Confronting him, in the room in which he sat, was a boy's portrait,
> which anybody seeing him would have identified as Master
> Christopher Casby, aged ten: though disguised with a haymaking
> rake, for which he had had, at any time, as much taste or use as for a
> diving-bell; and sitting (on one of his own legs) upon a bank of
> violets, moved to precocious contemplation by the spire of a
> village church.   (I, xiii, 145)

What we are being given over and over again, with such 'asides' —
'(not taking into account the value of the shot he had been made to
swallow, for the improvement of his form)', 'though disguised with a
haymaking rake, for which he had had, at any time, as much taste or
use as for a diving-bell' — is the natural myriad-mindedness, the
enormous suggestibility, of a spirit who can only just bring his energy
of perception under control; and this not out of irresponsible whimsy,
but out of Dickens's passionate total realisation of the world he is
imaging, out of the condition itself of full mental sanity. This *is*, by
the book's own definition, sanity because it imitates, as it embodies,
the process of upwelling subversive suggestion — suggestion at once
seemingly tangential, apparently originating from alternative centres
of interest to the concern in hand, but in fact richly pointed and apt —
which is an untrammelled operation of the positive faculty we have
seen at work in William Dorrit's case and Mrs Clennam's, in his
youngest daughter's history and, by extension, in that of her husband.

This health expresses itself not only in the given local sentence, but
also on a larger scale. The paragraph, for example, which immediately follows Clennam's sight of Master Christopher Casby's
portrait in I, xiii (and I quoted it in full in the Introduction to this
study) contributes further towards apparently decentring the whole
narrative occasion and moving the discourse away from Arthur's
immediate preoccupation (to see Flora again, the aptly named
goddess of his youth's spring), and the development of the story as a
whole, into an ever more amplified and exhilarating tangent. But by
the same token that the author has the creative impulse to pirouette
off into arabesques of this kind (in this case on the theme of Casby —

his appearance, his nature, the reflections and exclamations he has inspired in others) taking us with him, leaving the thread of his story apparently 'dropped'; so he has the power successfully to bring us back each time to his fable and his theme – within the sentence, within the paragraph. In fact it is all relevant, all of the essence of the work; these divagations only seem to be sidetracks. Quite apart from 'giving' us Casby (or anything else in the *Little Dorrit* universe) in a vivid way, such a procedure enacts the very health the novel has been talking about. Not for nothing is it almost parodied in Flora's utterance:

> 'Romance, however, 'Flora went on, busily arranging Mr. F's Aunt's toast, 'as I openly said to Mr. F when he proposed to me and you will be surprised to hear that he proposed seven times once in a hackney-coach once in a boat once in a pew once on a donkey at Tunbridge Wells and the rest on his knees, Romance was fled with the early days of Arthur Clennam, our parents tore us asunder we became marble and stern reality usurped the throne, Mr. F said very much to his credit that he was perfectly aware of it and even preferred that state of things accordingly the word was spoken the fiat went forth and such is life you see my dear and yet we do not break but bend, pray make a good breakfast while I go in with the tray.'   (I, xxiv, 283)

But not merely parodied. Flora has her failures of responsibility too. Mr F's aunt signifies the ultimate fate of the egotisms typified in Mrs Merdle or Mrs General. She demonstrates what a commitment to such values as theirs lead to in the end; a condition of being, in an intellectual point of view, still more fragmentary than the 'entrails . . . delivered over to Mr Eustace and his attendants . . . [and] arranged according to the taste of that sacred priesthood' (II, vii, 512); a sub-humanity, an incoherence and quasi-infantile regression itself within the purlieus of merely 'thing-like' existence. She is described as having

> a face like a staring wooden doll too cheap for expression, and a stiff yellow wig perched unevenly on the top of her head, as if the child who owned the doll had driven a tack through it anywhere, so that it only got fastened on

and her visage appears 'damaged . . . in two or three places with some blunt instrument in the nature of a spoon' (I, xiii, 157). She is so dehumanised as even to have lost her name (ibid.). Like the figures of high society, like Blandois, like William Dorrit, Mr F's aunt, with no intrinsic claim on other people's respect, nevertheless exacts homage and comfort from those about her whom she finds willing to collaborate with her pretensions and, in that she does so, Flora is wrong to countenance what in fact are horrifying manifestations of the naked malignity, violent and irrational, of this old woman's residual psychic forces.

But this is one of Mrs Finching's few real failures. The more we make acquaintance with her mode of speech — itself a paradigm in little of the book's narrative voice — the more we come to recognise how Flora's utterance expresses not only certain important decencies but also a mode of imagination which is itself supportive after the fashion, and by no means in more limited or trivial degree, of Daniel Doyce's 'quiet self-sustainment'. We cannot help feeling that she carries about with her a resource at least as feeding and satisfying as the most ideal 'Romance' could ever be, in the quality of this inward life of her imagination thus exposed to us. We see it in her relations with Arthur. He is valuable to her as a figure she can idealise and dramatise (she also fully respects his authentic human nature — as when she visits him in prison), but if he actually married her he would soon, surely, become another Mr Finching in her eyes:

> I revere the memory of Mr. F as an estimable man and a most indulgent husband, only necessary to mention Asparagus and it appeared or to hint at any little delicate thing to drink and it came like magic in a pint bottle it was not ecstasy but it was comfort . . . . (I, xxiv, 285)

What more than 'comfort' could Arthur provide? He could scarcely match Flora's aspirations of romantic ardour and cloak-and-dagger mystery half so well as the Mr Finching who, with his seven proposals — 'once on a donkey . . . and the rest on his knees' — his 'adoration' (I, xiii, 154) and his being 'so very unsettled and in such low spirits [i.e. about the possibility of Flora's refusing his suit] that he had distractedly alluded to the river if not oil of something from the chemist's' (I, xxiii, 270) has evidently, right under Flora's nose, been the real thing, the very stuff of her improbable visions in the 'full mermaid condition'. The fact is that Flora's imagination — at once, in its verbal address, so vagrant and so pointed — is the circumambient Hesperides she carries around with her. As Clennam sees early on, 'the relict of the late Mr. F' is 'enjoying herself in the most wonderful manner' with all these 'performances' (I, xiii, 155). The theatric image is itself pointed and apt.

Yet that does not diminish the absolute status or value of an openness such as Flora's to the activity of an imagination unconstrained by the egotisms and pretences endemic in the larger part of human society, especially in a life in which she must resign herself to celibacy, solitude and the affection of two egotists (one of them clinically mad) in a dreary home. (Her overeating, her blowzy drinking, are evidently signs of a real emotional hunger which in such a household is hardly surprising.) For this imagination of hers is not essentially an escapist organism; or, if it is, its kind of escapism feeds back into social health. She is generous, creative, open to magnificent insights at every turn (for example, her view of Mrs Clennam – 'like Fate in a go-cart'; of Flintwinch as 'a rusty screw in gaiters'; of her father's presumptions in his 'smoothly blundering in'). It is Flora who gives Little Dorrit work when she needs it and takes good care of her (I, xxiii–xxiv); it is Flora who visits Arthur in jail despite her father's disapproval. It is she nearly alone, in this society, who has an instinctual natural courage and a complete freedom from the tendency to see all human relations highly coloured by notions of rank. (That courage – unconscious and sublime, like her anti-snobbery – is in play, as Dr Leavis has remarked, when she visits William Dorrit in his London hotel – II, xvi.) With the figure of Mrs Finching, Dickens is not imaging a full answer to the problem of living in this world. But her typical idiom beside what *is* instinctively healthy in her supply us with a hint as to the value of the narrator's own 'performance', *his* characteristic utterance. What both share in common are the multiplying clauses, the attraction towards the apparently tangential. In both cases we appear to enter a language-world where the semi-incongruous and unconstrained, the only partly organised and foreseen intuition is spontaneously rushing in upon the (of course in large degree necessarily) ordered design by which coherent statement is made at all.

Dickens as narrator, in short, speaks a tongue which is redolent of, as it imitates, the very activity by which the individual has been shown to be redeemable from his share in the corporate imprisonment. What the story has revealed is that he is besieged by a whole environment of promptings-towards-truth (namely, that recognition of the genuine reality of his situation and dependences of which his – or her – inward imprisonments contrive to defeat the acknowledgement). The real assails and drenches his resistances at every chink, like the Democritean atoms of the visible world, like Hopkins's

> Wild air, world-mothering air . . .
> That each eyelash or hair
> Girdles; goes home betwixt
> The fleeciest, frailest-flixed
> Snowflake; that's fairly mixed
> With, riddles, and is rife
> In every least thing's life;
> This needful, never spent,
> And nursing element . . . .[35]

He is so engaged, by virtue of a redoubt (not easily namable as 'conscience', which I have accordingly avoided throughout my argument — as I have tried to intimate, the faculty here in question is less articulate, more subrational than the promptings that that term suggests) at the very centre of his being, which finds its correlates and expression in the surrounding world — including the world of Nature — as well as in an inward psychic contest. It expresses itself most characteristically by suggesting other scenes, other modes of life, other moods even, than those from which he has tended to derive his outlook.

In consequence we have a prose-'style' here which is like Shakespeare's verse in being 'myriad-minded'. When Coleridge paid Shakespeare that compliment he referred to the poet's unique capacity for empathetically realising the individual world and idiom of each of his *dramatis personae*; while this play of metaphor in Dickens characteristically suggests a particular vision of life, a special outlook upon it. Yet we can resent its inferences only if at the humblest level of conviction we find Dickens's characterisation unbelievable. Only if we withhold assent from his portrait, say, of the Father of the Marshalsea (with all his self-defensive mechanisms and his final breakdown), or Mrs Clennam and her self-incarceration in nervous paralysis (in her attempt to thwart and stifle *her* inward promptings, inarticulate yet potent as they are); only then can we resist as less than wholly substantiated and justified by what the whole process of the book has exhibited this prose's suggestively exhilarating life. Yet surely the portraits of these two 'cases' are, from beginning to end, of the first order in the novel's strengths — I repeat, at the very simplest level of credibility.

It may be objected that such an idiom distinguishes most of Dickens's writing. But this is just my theme. In this novel we are effectually offered what amounts to a full-dress case for the world-view implicit in or underlying most of his work — *Our Mutual Friend* being in several phases (as I have attempted to show) the important exception. Perhaps only in *Little Dorrit* does it find this total expression as story, symbol (the imprisonment motif), theme. But we can see in retrospect how Dickens can attach, as to the Staggs's Gardens of Paul and Florence's first visit there in *Dombey and Son* (vi, 65–6), a high value to landscape which especially prompts the kind of imaginative activity which characterises his prose — in that case suggesting 'confused treasures of iron, . . . Babel towers of chimneys, . . . a hundred thousand shapes and substances of incompleteness, wildly mingled out of their places. . . . Hot springs and fiery eruptions, the usual attendants upon earthquakes . . . .' Such suggestions tend to subvert the pretensions and constraints of those features of the scene which are humanly imprisoning, even in the case of the individual life of goodwill — by which in its turn it has been the more prompted to feed, tributary-fashion, the general stream of social depravity which at various points on the wheel of this vicious circle has originated the non-Edenic environment in the first place. Enfranchisement of this kind, mere hygiene (cf. the 'healthy public walks' which in *Dombey*, xv, are shown to have superseded the 'frowzy fields . . . and dustheaps, . . . mean houses, and patches of wretched vegetation' of the earlier environment) — though Dickens is grateful for it and welcomes it — cannot wholly supply; and as a consequence we have the complex rhetoric of his treatment of the improvement of Staggs's Gardens during the later visit there, as noted above in Chapter I, section III.

It is for a like reason that a fictional medium is so valuable to Dickens which, while it purports to enjoy that one-for-one correspondence with the empirical nature of contemporary society, the prosaic diurnal reality of his readers' world that is the (at least apparent) modality and the special appeal of the novel itself as a form,[36] can yet lead a double life as 'realism' and *Märchen* simultaneously. Action and character take place so often in Dickens on two interpenetrative dimensions — that of mere brute event in the hither world, and that of a heightened, typal drama in a more figurative landscape. At no single point could a contemporary reader say of *Bleak House* 'This is definitely not of 1851, this is utterly *impossible* in the England I know, the country of the Great Exhibition and daguerrotypes, of Palmerston's rather smug foreign policy and developing tensions with Russia', and so on. Yet Mr Boythorn's garden; Lady Dedlock's melodramatic cries and gestures in their convincing, suggestive aspect — as at the burial ground in Tom-all-Alone's; Esther as 'Dame Durden'; a miraculous unaccountable fortune and fairy-godfatherliness (like John Jarndyce's) seemingly not met by the immediate human problems which inevitably accompany almost any kind of charitable donative; Jo's wholesomeness as it is made articulate by Dickens: these are not wholly of that world. They are its intrinsic nature rendered outwardly as visible (or audible) appearance, action, speech. Dickens writes his kind of 'meta-novel' not to elude the full challenge of life's actual mundane complexity. Rather, we have seen in this very case of *Bleak House* how all the folktale elements (the names that, uninterpretably, somehow express something of the essence of their owners' natures, the evident Cinderella-story, the landscapes 'larger' than life) serve in major part to constitute a new sense of the massive compound difficulty — for the author, for everyone — of achieving a fully honest position in the contemporary world, the impossibility of not being implicated in its delinquencies. But by the same means the actual mystery of this world which the forms of daily life and the scenes of our common acquaintance by their very conventionality displace is thus restored to the reader's imagination, and their power to enforce acceptance of the immediate on staled and second-hand terms (simply because customary) is subverted.

The regenerative energies within the personal and the social life which the Dickens idiom is thus able not only to portray but also to enlist all too evidently constitute, nevertheless, no occasion for a vapid optimism. How could they? At the end of *Little Dorrit* the citadels of the social 'order' remain in the hands of the enemy (which is not only the Barnacle faction and their ilk, but the enemy in every breast). When Amy and Clennam leave the place of their wedding, they go down into 'roaring streets' where 'as they passed along in sunshine and shade, the noisy and the eager, and the arrogant and the froward and the vain, fretted and chafed, and made their usual uproar (I, xxxiv, 826). These words, with the note which Dickens made for his number-plan for this final instalment of the tale[37] — 'They will go out of the Marshalsea to be married — straight to be married — *Very quiet conclusion*'[38] — signify no new emphasis, no new redirection of the imaginative current of the work in its last phase, but chime with the essence of the vision he has presented all along. At its most hopeful there is (circumscribed by the prodigal society on all sides) a limited personal salvation in this world; the general social outlook must remain bleak indeed.

In consequence we have the powerful tension which is the very pulse of the Dickens vision, between all the intimations of a world which on Alan Wilde's view is 'infected' by 'dark powers . . . making of it one huge pest-house, for victims and victimizers alike',[39] and at the same time a narrative idiom which is extremely exhilarating in a comic fashion. But these two intuitions are no merely opposed polarities. Like the terrestrial axis upon which, notionally, the earth's poles lie, in so speaking of them we artificially abstract and hypo-statise their nature. The comic confidence of Dickens's speech is not (*pace* Professor Garis)[40] the function of an endemic tendency, in an essentially incoherent artist, to perform isolated theatrical 'turns', but rather a part of one unitary perception which (as I have tried to show in my analysis of the working of metaphor in the novel), equally with its regenerative properties, gives us a fully sustained sense of a sick world in all its genuine darkness and self-defeat.

We can but come away from recognising this as from the scrutiny of so many of the Dickens features (and I claim only to have looked at one aspect of his achievement here) with a renewed sense of the value of instinct. We were right, we undeflectable disciples, so largely to yield assent to his performances, in spite of the promptings of an alien critical creed. *Little Dorrit* is not totally flawless, nor is any other of the master's endeavours; it has its (minor) faults. But the work as a whole we ultimately must distinguish as the achievement of a major intelligence totally applied. Such a recognition ought to give us pause before we rush in with our qualifications and concessions at the ready about the other parts of the Dickens canon.

Notes

Introduction

1. F. R. and Q. D. Leavis, *Dickens the Novelist* (London, 1970) p. xi.
2. Ibid., p. 2.
3. Ibid., p. 34.
4. Angus Wilson, *The World of Charles Dickens* (London, 1970) p. 234.
5. Cf. John Forster, *Life of Charles Dickens* (1872–4), revised by A. J. Hoppé (London: Everyman's Library, 1966), 2 vols, vol. II, pp. 113–14 (Bk VII, ch. 1).
6. Wilson, *World of Dickens*, p. 234.
7. Ibid.
8. John Carey, *The Violent Effigy* (London, 1973).
9. From John Bayley's contribution to *Dickens and the Twentieth-Century*, ed. J. Gross and G. Pearson (London, 1962).
10. Robert Garis, *The Dickens Theatre* (Oxford, 1965).
11. Ibid., p. 120.
12. In her article 'The Natural History of German Life', *Westminster Review*, LXVI (July 1856) 54–5. Her claim that Dickens, in portraying the lives of the industrial proletariat, 'scarcely ever passes from the humorous and external to the emotional and tragic, without becoming as transcendent in his unreality as he was a moment before in his artistic truthfulness', is less radically challenging. Of course there *are* local, not fatally ruinous, faults where indeed this criticism applies. (The prostitute Martha in *David Copperfield* does not walk off with the rest of the novel and ditch it.) But essentially we see George Eliot stalling at a mode of portraiture alien, though not inferior, to the requirements of her own genius. Yet it is no less significantly inept of her to adduce Mrs Plornish (earlier in the same paragraph) in illustration of her case. For Dickens uses the Plornishes as much as anyone or anything else in his tale not to show 'his . . . artisans' for 'preternaturally virtuous' (next sentence); rather, to exemplify the working classes' free participation in a universal moral failure (see the discussion of *Little Dorrit* in Ch. 3 of this study). Already by the date of George Eliot's article (part 8, incorporating I, xxvi–xxix, had appeared in the same month) the first readers of *Little Dorrit* had been given Plornish's 'speaking [in regard to William Dorrit] with a perverse admiration of what he ought to have pitied or despised' (I, xii), and his wife's (in the context no less darkly meaningful, as well as amusing) patronage of her new Italian neighbour Baptista Cavalletto (I, xxv).
13. William Blake, 'Annotations to Sir Joshua Reynolds' *Discourses*' (written c. 1808), in *Complete Writings*, ed. Geoffrey Keynes (London, 1966) p. 461.

Chapter 1

1. *The Nation*, issue of 21 Dec 1865. The review has been frequently anthologised – as, for example, in the *Penguin Critical Anthology – Charles Dickens*, ed. S. Wall (Harmondsworth, 1970) pp. 164–8.
2. Ibid., p. 168.
3. See his Introduction to *Our Mutual Friend* in the Everyman's Library edition.
4. Garis, *The Dickens Theatre*, p. 187.
5. Ibid.
6. 'Afterword', Signet Classics edition of *Our Mutual Friend* (New York, 1964) p. 901.
7. J. Hillis Miller, *Charles Dickens: The World of His Novels* (Oxford, 1959) ch. 9.
8. Garis, *The Dickens Theatre*, p. 4.
9. Ibid., p. 3.
10. Ibid.
11. See Garis, *The Dickens Theatre*, chs 1–6. (esp. ch. 1).
12. Ibid., chs 7–9, 11.
13. Ibid., p. 228.
14. Ibid., ch. 10.
15. Ibid., p. 228
16. Ross H. Dabney, *Love and Property in the Novels of Charles Dickens* (London, 1967) ch. 6, p. 149.
17. See the references on pages 53–4 and in note 39 below.
18. Bk. I, ch. 2 (in Jowett's translation [Oxford, 1923] p. 29).
19. Dabney, *Love and Property*, p. 167.
20. Ibid., p. 156.
21. See Ian Watt, *The Rise of the Novel* (London, 1957) ch. 5 ('Love and the Novel: *Pamela*') § VI; and R. P. Utter and G. B. Needham, *Pamela's Daughters* (London, 1937) *passim*.
22. *Penguin Critical Anthology – Dickens*, p. 166. (For original, see note 1 above.)
23. Ibid., pp. 165–6.
24. T. S. Eliot, 'Burnt Norton', lines 118–21 (in *Four Quartets*).
25. F. R. and Q. D. Leavis, *Dickens the Novelist*, p. 116.
26. Cf. J. H. Stonehouse, *Catalogue of the Library of Charles Dickens* (London, 1935).
27. F. X. Shea, 'Mr. Venus Observed: the Plot Change in *Our Mutual Friend*', in *Papers on Language and Literature*, IV (1968) 170–81.
28. Ibid., p. 181.
29. Edgar Johnson, *Charles Dickens, his Tragedy and Triumph* (London, 1953) Part IX, ch. 5.
30. Reprinted in *Dickens: The Critical Heritage*, ed. Philip Collins (London, 1971) pp. 464 ff.
31. Ibid., p. 465.
32. Humpry House, *The Dickens World* (Oxford 1941–2) ch. 6, p. 150.
33. See Harry Stone's very good introduction to *Uncollected Writings of Charles Dickens*, ed. Stone (London, 1969) vol. I, esp. pp. 4–5, 58–63.
34. Johnson, *Dickens, his Tragedy and Triumph*, Part IX, ch. 5, p. 1023
35. In *The Letters of Charles Dickens*, ed. W. Dexter (London, 1938) vol. I, p. 66 (to Chapman and Hall).
36. Johnson, *Dickens, his Tragedy and Triumph*, p. 1023.

37. Quoted from Dickens's manuscripts in Forster, *Life of Dickens*, Everyman's Library edition, vol. II, p. 370.
38. Ibid., pp. 371–5.
39. For all these see *Dickens: The Critical Heritage*, ed. Collins, under *Our Mutual Friend*.
40. Ibid., p. 464.
41. Ibid., Appendix I, p. 619.
42. Hillis Miller, *Dickens: The World of His Novels*, ch. 9, p. 305.

Chapter 2

1. A. E. Dyson, *The Inimitable Dickens* (London, 1970) p. 154.
2. Ibid., pp. 167–8, 169.
3. Ibid., p. 168.
4. J. C. Reid, in his study *Little Dorrit* (London, 1967), remarks how 'Sir Russell Brain has drawn attention to Dickens's expert clinical eye in describing the disorders from which his creations suffered, including the paraplegia of Mrs. Clennam, the nacrolepsy of Old Dorrit, the schizophrenia of Mr. F's Aunt and the mental deficiency of Maggy, with the description of her large eyes which "seemed to be very little affected by light and to stand unnaturally still", and which Sir Russell suggests is the first account of "the Argyll Robertson pupil".' (Lord Brain's commentary is to be found under the title 'Dickensian Diagnoses' in the *British Medical Journal* for 1955.) 'In Affery we have, as John Wain says "a mind so deranged that she is inarticulate except when she can call in the aid of movement"; this is another fruit of Dickens's extraordinary knowledge of psychosomatic disorders, which justifies, as it so often does, the physical oddities of his grotesques' (p. 42 of Reid's monograph). Yet Reid seems to me almost to bypass his own best idea here. Dickens's quite outstanding genius resides, surely, not only in this perfection of close scrutiny but in his thus connecting physical with emotional disorder. In our day the observed links between (say) cancer or heart disease, on the one hand, and forms of stress and anxiety, on the other, are too frequent (though not unfailing or ubiquitous) not to suggest the still further meaningfulness of this sort of characterisation.
5. *Dickens the Novelist*, p. 131.
6. See above, Introduction, p. 1 and note 4.
7. See for example, 'The Life [which is offered to us in the reported conversation] of a Coster-Girl', in *London Labour and the London Poor*, original collected edition (London, 1851). Vol. I, Bk I, pp. 45–6.
8. W. H. Auden, *Selected Poems* (London, 1968) p. 127.
9. Balzac, *Cousin Bette*, trans. Marion Ayton Crawford (Harmondsworth: Penguin, 1965) p. 79.
10. Everyman's Library edition of *Middlemarch*, vol. I, pp. 176–7.
11. *Time Regained* (*Le Temps retrouvé*), trans. Andreas Mayor (London, 1970) p.1.
12. *La Comédie humaine*, ed. M. Bouteron (Paris, 1951), 'Avant-Propos', pp. 5–6.
13. Cf. Harry Stone, loc. cit. (see above, Ch. 1, note 33).
14. Watt, *Rise of the Novel*, ch. 1, p. 28.
15. I quote from the translation by R. S. Townsend in Everyman's Library (London, 1912) p. 1.
16. In *Cambridge Quarterly*, VI, no. 1.

17. John Butt and Kathleen Tillotson, *Dickens at Work* (London, 1957), ch. 7. See esp. § II, III and v.
18. Owen Chadwick, *The Victorian Church* (London, 1966) vol. I, pp. 325–6.
19. *English Historical Documents*, vol. XII (1): *1833–74*, ed. G. M. Young and W. D. Handcock (London, 1956) p. 757.
20. See Johnson, *Dickens, his Tragedy and Triumph*, p. 55.
21. See Sir W. S. Holdsworth, *Charles Dickens as Legal Historian* (London, 1927), for a full account of the state of equity law in England in the first half of the nineteenth century. This is a short work and each chapter is relevant.
22. See Johnson, *Dickens, his Tragedy and Triumph*, pp. 492–4, for Dickens's expensive and futile legal battle with the plagiarists of the *Carol*.
23. F. R. and Q. D. Leavis, *Dickens the Novelist*, p. 125.
24. Ibid., p. 132.
25. See Butt and Tillotson, *Dickens at Work*, p. 184; and Forster, *Life of Dickens*, Everyman's Library edition, vol. II, p. 119.
26. In her article 'Change and Changelessness in *Bleak House*' in *The Victorian Newsletter* (New York University), no. 46 (Fall 1974).
27. F. R. and Q. D. Leavis, *Dickens the Novelist*, p. 156.
28. See p. 5 above.
29. Garis, *The Dickens Theatre*, p. 120.
30. In *What Then Must We Do?* trans. Aylmer Maude (London, 1925) pp. 27–9.
31. Garis, *The Dickens Theatre*, p. 90.
32. Matthew Arnold's phrase, from his early sonnet 'To a Friend'.

Chapter 3

1. J. C. Reid, (study of) *Little Dorrit*, p. 29.
2. Ibid., pp. 32–3.
3. Ibid., p. 34.
4. Ibid.
5. Ibid., p. 35.
6. John Butt, 'The Topicality of *Little Dorrit*', *University of Toronto Quarterly*, XXIX (1959).
7. I deliberately choose this gnomic phrase from the credo of a humanist who sees the human experience as tragic and foredoomed (though not having proved itself historically to have been a worthless 'experiment') by exactly this characteristic in the affairs of men, and its concomitant vices – the love of tyranny, the will to violence. See E. M. Forster, 'What I Believe' (1939), collected in *Two Cheers for Democracy* (London, 1951) pp. 81–2.
8. R. D. McMaster, 'Little Dorrit: Experience and Design', *Queens Quarterly*, LXVII (1961).
9. It introduces the Oxford Illustrated edition of the text (London, 1953), from which my quotations are taken.
10. *Dickens the Novelist*, p. 239.
11. Garis, *The Dickens Theatre*, pp. 172–4.
12. For example: 'the labyrinth trodden by the sons of Adam' (II, xii, 556); 'the Barnacles who were born of woman' (II, xxviii, 738); 'perhaps because it was indisputable that if the adherence of the immortal Enemy of Mankind could have been secured by a job, the Barnacles would have jobbed him' (II, xii, 557). Of

Clennam's positive ethical views: 'Duty on earth, restitution on earth, action on earth; these first, as the first steep steps upward. Strait was the gate and narrow was the way; far straiter and narrower than the broad high road paved with vain professions and vain repetitions, motes from other men's eyes and liberal delivery of others to the judgement – all cheap materials costing absolutely nothing' (I, xxvii, 319). Or, treating of the world's view of Mr Merdle's wealth: 'the last new polite reading of the parable of the camel and the needle's eye' (I, xxxiii, 394). There are many other such references. See also Reid, (study of) *Little Dorrit*, pp. 30–2.

13. Garis, *The Dickens Theatre*, pp. 164–5.
14. In his Foreword to the Edinburgh limited edition of *Great Expectations* (1937).
15. 'Sinne (II)', lines 4–5, in *The Works of George Herbert*, F. E. Hutchinson (Oxford, 1941) p. 63.
16. The Irish member of Parliament and confidence trickster, whose default and suicide, on 16 Feb 1856, helped determine Dickens's conception of this character. See Dickens's letter to John Forster, Apr 1856 ('I had a general idea of the . . . business before the Sadleir affair, but I shaped Mr. Merdle out of that precious rascality.')
17. Reid, (study of) *Little Dorrit*, p. 40.
18. Alan Wilde, 'Mr. F's Aunt and the Analogical Structure of *Little Dorrit*', *Nineteenth-Century Fiction*, XIX (1965).
19. Introduction to *Little Dorrit*, Oxford Illustrated edition, p. viii.
20. Article cited above, p. 136.
21. P. D. Herring, 'Dickens's Monthly Number Plans for *Little Dorrit*', *Modern Philology*, LXIV.
22. F. R. and Q. D. Leavis, *Dickens the Novelist*, p. 231.
23. Angus Wilson, *World of Dickens*, ch. 4, p. 145.
24. F. R. and Q. D. Leavis, *Dickens the Novelist*, pp. 240–5.
25. Ibid., pp. 224–6.
26. Ibid., pp. 271–5.
27. Cf. ibid., p. 216.
28. Ibid., pp. 218–9.
29. Ibid., p. 216.
30. See, for example, the paragraph (I, xxiv, 291) which prefaces the episode of her telling Maggy the story of the 'Princess and the Poor Woman':

'There were afternoon times when she was unemployed, when visitors dropped in to play a hand at cards with her father, when she could be spared and was better away. Then she would flit along the yard, climb the scores of stairs that led to her room, and take her seat at the window. Many combinations did those spikes upon the wall assume, many light shapes did the strong iron weave itself into, many golden touches fell upon the rust, while Little Dorrit sat there musing. New zig-zags sprung into the cruel pattern sometimes, when she saw it through a burst of tears; but beautiful or hardened still, always over it and under it and through it, she was fain to look in her solitude, seeing everything with that ineffaceable brand.'

31. F. R. and Q. D. Leavis, *Dickens the Novelist*, p. 272.
32. Ibid., p. 271.

33. *Little Dorrit*, ed. John Holloway (Harmondsworth: Penguin, 1967) p. 912.

34. Here also Dr Leavis is surely right; see *Dickens the Novelist*, pp. 223–4.

35. G. M. Hopkins, 'The Blessed Virgin Compared to the Air We Breathe', lines 1, 3–10.

36. Cf. Ian Watt's analysis of its distinctive features, in *Rise of the Novel*, ch. 1, esp. pp. 13–30 (quoted above, p. 97).

37. The double-issue, Parts XIX–XX, published June 1857.

38. Herring, in *Modern Philology*, LXIV (see note 21 above).

39. As quoted above, p. 154.

40. To whom 'at this latest minute of the hour' I really ought to offer the tribute of my thanks. Had he not so clearly enunciated and argued his view, I should have found it more difficult to define my own position in this attempt to vindicate my suffrages for the Dickens *oeuvre*.

Index

In the following table, characters and scenes in the Dickens novels are listed under the appropriate book title.